POWER AND PREJUDICE

POWER
and Prejudice

WOMEN AND POLITICS

ANNA COOTE
AND POLLY PATTULLO

WEIDENFELD AND NICOLSON
LONDON

Printed and bound in Great Britain by
The Bath Press, Avon

For Eva Pattullo and Ruby Coote

Contents

Acknowledgements

Our warmest thanks to Katie Ferguson who did such excellent and imaginative research, and conducted many of the interviews; to all the women who gave us their time, shared their wisdom and told us about their lives, especially Jan Burrows; and to Rosemary Taylor, Moya Roddy and Juliet Gardiner for their help and encouragement.

PART I

Introduction

CHAPTER 1

Can Any Woman Make It?

In a small room above a corner shop, at the wrong end of a town in middle England, a grocer's wife gave birth to her second daughter on 13 October 1925. The grocer was a poor man, eldest son of a shoemaker, but too near-sighted to follow the family trade. His wife was a former seamstress, daughter of a cloakroom attendant at the local railway station.

As soon as the two girls were old enough, they were put to work at the back of the shop – weighing and measuring flour, sugar, lentils, jam, cheese and lard. Once a week their mother would heave pans of steaming water to a tub in the warehouse and the family would take a bath. There was no indoor lavatory, just a spartan cubicle in the back-yard. Nor were toys or treats a common feature of the grocer's household. The children had no bicycles or party frocks. They walked a mile to school and a mile back, twice each day, rain or shine.

It did not seem a promising start. But Margaret Hilda Thatcher, née Roberts, grocer's daughter from Grantham, grew up to be leader of the Conservative party, and was elected to government in 1979, 1983 and 1987. She was the first woman to lead a political party in Britain, and the first woman prime minister. She has gone on to be the longest-serving British prime minister of the twentieth century and the senior premier of Europe. Her name has become the byword for a political creed that shook the foundations of post-war Britain.

In many people's eyes, Margaret Thatcher stood as a symbol of female achievement. If Maggie could make it, so, perhaps, could any woman with enough ability and determination. Maggie herself appeared to think so. 'Many women have the opportunities but do not use them,' she declared in 1984, 'or they are too easily contented with the job that they are doing and do not necessarily make the effort to climb the tree.'

One of the objects of this book is to understand why so few women exercise real power in mainstream British politics, and why so many are powerless. We want to know what is holding women back and, above all, we want to find out how more women can wield more political power.

Is it true, as Margaret Thatcher suggests, that the way is open, if the will is there, for able women to become powerful in British politics? Do women have only themselves to blame for the fact that so few of them make it? Are they simply not trying hard enough?

Let's go back to the corner shop to look for clues. There is young Margaret, up to her elbows in a sack of porridge oats, which she is neatly parcelling into small paper bags. There is sister Muriel, meticulous with the cheese wire. There is Beatrice, their mother, toiling at the bacon grinder. And there is Alfred, husband and father, his poor eyes bent close to the ledger, reckoning the week's accounts.

It seems to have been a curious household. Not a place known for laughter or singing, or for any dissent in the ranks. One would not expect Margaret or Muriel to dip their fingers in the jam, for instance, or Beatrice to put her feet up after lunch, or contradict her husband's point of view. Nor would Alfred take the family out for a picnic on a Sunday afternoon, or surprise them with presents when the takings were good.

Alfred was not just any shopkeeper, but a man obsessed with the desire to improve himself and his family. He worked gruellingly long hours and expected his wife and children to do the same. He was intensely thrifty, sparing not a penny on non-essential purchases. A devout Methodist and a lay preacher, he reserved Sundays entirely for church-going and religious reflection.

Alfred's habits and convictions were instilled into his family. He told the young Margaret: 'Never do things or want to do things just because other people do them. Make up your mind about what you are going to do and persuade other people to go your way.' He assumed, correctly at the time, that her way and his were as one.

We would not choose to tell a woman's story exclusively through her father in this way. But all accounts suggest that Alfred was the dominant character in the Roberts' household, who set the tone and style of family life. Beatrice appears to have been a quiet, submissive figure who worked unremittingly, without complaint, who was not considered her husband's intellectual equal. Margaret took little interest in her; she was much closer to her father.

Alfred Roberts prospered. He bought a smarter shop up-town. He became a borough councillor, a Justice of the Peace, an alderman and eventually Mayor of Grantham.

He was determined that his daughters should grow up with the advantages he lacked, and have every opportunity to get on in the world. Unusually for a man of his generation, he wanted them to succeed not simply through marriage, but in their own right – particularly Margaret, in whom he recognized some special potential. He did not send them to the local school, but to a superior establishment in a posher part of town. He took them to lectures and concerts. He encouraged them to read and discuss instructive books. He held forth on a range of weighty topics. They followed a strict regime of work, school and homework, with church three times on Sunday. There were no pranks or playmates, no fairy tales or family games. They were told to save their pocket money – not in order to buy something they might want, but in order to have savings.

Both girls won scholarships to Kesteven and Grantham Girls' School – a rare institution (rarer still in those days) that unequivocally encouraged academic attainment in girls. It was a world of blue serge gym-slips, strict discipline, hockey, hymns and at least two hours' homework a night. Margaret proved no genius, but a hard worker who spoke out confidently, especially in the school debating society. She had no close friends. The other girls took her for a goody-goody, a swot. Muriel went off to be a physiotherapist. Margaret succeeded – narrowly – in securing a place at Somerville College, Oxford, to study chemistry. Alfred sent her to elocution lessons before she left home.

Through her father, Margaret was acquainted with the civic leaders of Grantham. She would help out at elections and meet all the visiting political luminaries. At Oxford, she devoted every moment of her spare time to the University Conservative Association, and when she became its first woman president, it was seen as a reward for unremitting hard labour, rather than for any noticeable charisma or flair. By then she had decided on her future. The early discussions with her father, the school debating society and the excitement of electioneering in Grantham had left their mark: she wanted a career in politics.

True to her father's philosophy, she organized her life with fanatical single-mindedness around the pursuit of this goal. She earned her living as a chemist with a plastics firm and studied law in her spare time. In 1948, a year after graduating, she applied to be considered as prospective parliamentary candidate for Dartford in Kent, a constituency held by Labour with a large majority. She was adopted for the seat, became engaged to a wealthy local businessman, and lost the 1951 election with an impressively-increased vote. She married her tycoon, had twins, engaged a nanny, passed her Bar exams and set about finding a more promising seat. She was selected as the Conservative candidate for Finchley in 1959. The rest, as they say, is history.

What do these details suggest? Yes, a woman can become an MP, and even make it to the top in British politics. She needn't be the daughter of an earl, and she needn't be an intellectual giant. She must be clever, hard-working and determined – one would expect no less.

Beyond that, Margaret Thatcher's story offers little to encourage the daughters of ordinary working-class (or even middle-class) folk. For although the Roberts were not unique – they belonged to a tradition of stern, unstinting tradespeople devoted to God and commerce – they were a long way from average. How many other families could match that remarkable mix of single-minded ambition, discipline, social mobility and a capacity to educate daughters as though they were sons?

Would Margaret have moved quite so fast or so far if she had been allowed to play with other children after school? If she had had brothers to preoccupy her father's ambitions? If the family business had failed? Or if, as a young mother, she had been unable to afford what was, in her own words, 'the key to the whole plan': a nanny? She has cheerfully admitted that she could not have combined a career with motherhood if she had been unable to afford a 'first-class nanny–housekeeper', and for that she relied on her husband's substantial income. Suppose she had married not Denis Thatcher, company director, but Nigel Thatcher, struggling schoolmaster, or Basil Thatcher, underrated concert pianist? No nanny then. And no career.

We need not linger over what has been called the 'cock-up' theory of history. Our point is simply that Margaret Thatcher's phenomenal success does not show that any woman (with ability, etc) can become powerful in British politics. It demonstrates only what one particular woman can do in one particular – and by no means typical – set of circumstances.

We might learn more if we leave genteel Grantham and travel north. A young woman sits at her window in a council estate outside Sheffield; it is the early 1980s. She is watching a group of mothers chatting and laughing as they take their children up the road to school. She longs to join them but she is new to the area and hasn't yet dared to approach any of her neighbours. Her own child is still too young for school. She is isolated, poor and powerless. She has no contact at all with the world of politics. She is too busy surviving to fight for anything better.

Jan Burrows was the third of five children born to Fred Hastings, steelworker, and Jean Hastings, betting shop manager. For the first years of her life, the family lived with Jan's grandparents, in severely overcrowded conditions. Jan, her sister and one of her brothers all shared a bed in the bathroom. It was not until she was eight that they got a home of their own. They were one of the first families to move into a brand new council estate – a cause of great delight to them all. Soon afterwards, at the steelworks, Fred was involved in a serious accident which broke both his arms and badly damaged his chest. He won £1,000 compensation, which he spent on new beds for all the family and a Bedford van – the biggest and brightest vehicle on the estate – for taking the family out at weekends. Fred and Jean helped set up a tenants' association and youth club on the estate. Jan was not aware that what her parents were doing was 'political'. She does remember that the girls and boys in the family were generally treated equally, and expected to share household tasks on an equal basis.

When Jan was twelve, her mother died suddenly. Her father had to work twice as hard to keep them all going. He would prepare tea before he went out on his shift. He would wash and mend their clothes, and polish all their shoes, leaving five shining pairs in a neat row each morning. He tried his best, but nothing could fill the terrible gap Jean's death had left in Jan's life. She had always believed that her father favoured her elder sister, not her. She felt lonely and misunderstood. She stopped going to bed because she found it so hard to sleep, and would nap on the sofa instead.

Jan had hated her junior school: she had the same teacher year in, year out, and couldn't get on with her. Secondary school was better. She excelled in sports, loved English and was enthralled to see how a good teacher could bring out the best in a child. She wanted to stay on, but her father said he couldn't afford to support her any longer. She left school at fifteen. Jobs were plentiful then. She started in a fruit shop but since that meant working on Saturdays, she switched to a lower-paid office job, much to her father's disapproval. There was another family crisis when Jan was seventeen. Fred remarried. Jan couldn't fit in with the new domestic arrangements, had a row with her father and left home. She fled to relatives in London, worked for a year as a clerk in a computer firm, fell in love and decided to marry. The man in question, Roy, was an old boyfriend from Sheffield, who had been in and out of borstal. He was back inside before they could wed.

Jan returned to Sheffield determined to drown her sorrows. She got pregnant and married the father, Mick Burrows, while still in her teens. Her son, Mathew, was born in 1975, when she was twenty. Her husband, a fitter on a low wage, was a violent and possessive man. The emotional and physical pressure was too much for Jan and she left him soon after the birth of their child.

That was how she came to be sitting at her window, alone with a small baby, on a council estate where she knew no one, and so far from home that her family could visit only once a month. She would spend her days shopping, cooking and cleaning and looking after Mathew. Her only object in life was to stop her son suffering from the break up of her marriage. The time dragged terribly. She would regularly do the same chore twice, or mindlessly shift furniture from one room to another, just to help the hours go by. She had no prospect of a job, let alone a career. She was often heavily in debt, hiding in the bedroom with the lights off, her hand over Mathew's mouth to keep him quiet, when the debt collectors were doing their rounds.

She was twenty-two, the age at which Margaret Thatcher was poised to make her bid for the Dartford constituency. But to Jan Burrows, the word 'politics' meant men in suits, sitting in television studios saying things she didn't understand. It had nothing to do with her and she didn't want to be bothered with it.

What was it that divided these two women so dramatically by their early twenties – so that one was already trailing blue clouds of glory, while the other was struggling to survive?

Both women came from poor backgrounds; both families were unusual in that the parents did not seem to impose sexual stereotypes on their daughters. There the similarities end. We have considered the peculiar pathology of the Roberts family, with its rigid regime of self-improvement, which marked it out as unusual, even within its own tradition. The Burrows displayed no such peculiarities. Moreover, they belonged to a different tradition – based not on trade and individualism, but on industry and collectivism.

Margaret Thatcher's parents beavered their way into the bourgeoisie; from there, doors to opportunity, however old and heavy and forbidding, could usually be forced open for the aspiring young. Jan Burrows' family never left the working class: doors were not just closed to her, they were absent from the structure of her life.

At fifteen, the daughter of the widower at the steelworks was expected to leave school and earn her keep, while the grocer-mayor's daughter prepared herself for university. The steelworker's daughter went into dead-end office jobs, from which motherhood and marriage were the only escape. The grocer's daughter, meanwhile, planned her brilliant career. The steelworker's daughter made an unhappy match, as many women do in all social classes. The grocer's daughter found herself a rich and supportive husband, as few women do, especially in the working class. Even if the steelworker's daughter had desired to do so, she hardly moved in the right circles to stumble across an eligible and compliant tycoon. The Nanny Question was not asked, let alone answered.

We can see, then, that class is a vital factor in determining whether a young woman has the right start in life to pursue a parliamentary career. But should we be interested in simply getting more women into parliament? The aim of this book is to find out how more women can wield more political power – but is it enough to fill the House of Commons with women like Margaret Thatcher?

To help us answer these questions, we shall return to Jan Burrows. Her story has only just begun.

The first big change came when her son, Mathew, was four and went to nursery school. At last Jan met other mothers on the estate and made friends. She went to a weekly coffee morning at Mathew's school and, from there, joined a group following an Open University course on the Pre-School Child. When the school refused to provide facilities for women with children below nursery age, Jan and half a dozen of her new friends began to meet regularly at her house. At first it was once a week, then three times or more, and before long they were recruiting other mothers and holding open house, every day, for up to thirty women. They drank gallons of coffee, chatted about anything and everything, and generally had a good laugh.

One day, the women decided they wanted to organize some Keep Fit sessions. There wasn't enough room in Jan's house, so they asked the school if they had space. The headmistress said no, but told them of some disused nursery buildings in another local school. The headmaster there sounded doubtful; he would have to 'check with the authorities', but he gave them a key and said they could have a look round. There were three long, low huts with corrugated roofs – cold, bare and structurally unsound. The women weren't put off. They kept the key and took over the huts. Their plans were vague. They had no idea what they were up against, or that their action had any political implications. But they did know they wanted more than just a room to do Keep Fit.

They set about cleaning up one of the huts, and organized a room there for kids. Between them they ran a child-minding rota so that mothers with pre-school children could get involved in what was now their 'centre'. They named it after a local landmark, a bridge with five arches, and it became the Five Arches Community Centre.

The women had no previous experience of organizing anything outside their own homes. Never before had they had any contact with 'the authorities', except when they went to the local Housing Office about rent or repairs. Suddenly, they found themselves writing letters, using the telephone, tackling a great web of red tape. They took advice from two Adult Education workers they had met through the Open University course – the only inhabitants of the 'official' world whom they knew and trusted. They lobbied councillors and council officers. They applied for funds, scrounged equipment and secured the right to occupy the buildings legally. Before long, they were drawing up a constitution, running an office and putting on a programme of classes – Keep Fit, sewing, chat groups, basic English and maths.

Jan emerged as a leader, the one with the nerve to pick up the phone or look a councillor in the eye, whose imagination and energy carried the group from one daunting plan to the next. The centre grew and grew. It took over Jan's life entirely – as it did the lives of many women in the neighbourhood. They installed a washing machine so they could spend more time together – and save on electricity. In winter the centre was often the only place they could keep warm, because they couldn't afford to heat their own homes.

When the centre was about two years old, Jan reached another turning point. Some of the women at Five Arches were bemoaning, as they often did, the shocking state of their debts. Almost all were in hock to the 'loan sharks', who trapped them in spiralling debts by charging astronomical interest rates to those too poor to get credit at a bank. 'Evil Edna', who came to collect each week, was loathed and feared as an ugly and immovable blot on their landscape.

By now, though, a number of official and semi-official agencies had begun to take an interest in the Five Arches Centre. Outreach workers and other well-intentioned experts and white-collar persons were flocking to the place. One of them, a community worker, heard the women's lament. Jan told us what happened next:

> Vicky, the community worker, said, 'They can't do that to you.' We said, 'Yes they can because we've signed.' She said, 'Leave it to me.' And she sent this man up and he said, 'We'll all sit down at this table and do a basic Welfare Rights course.' We said, 'Piss off with your welfare rights, we don't want to know.' He said, 'I bet you want to know this though: if anybody knocks on your door, you just have to give them ten pence and you can't be taken to court.' Well, the loan sharks didn't know what had hit them. Evil Edna knocked on my door and all these women were there and she said, 'Alright, everybody's five pounds.' I said, 'You mean, ten pences.' She said, 'You can't do that.' I said, 'Oh yes we can.'

It was just a beginning. Next, the women learned how to outsmart the gas and electricity boards, and avoid having their supplies cut off. They found they could go to court for an administration order to help clear other debts. They organized a weekly advice session with council officers, where they learned how to cope with problems such as rent arrears. They even persuaded their local councillors to provide a monthly 'surgery' at Five Arches.

Jan and her friends were discovering that they could manipulate and sometimes even beat 'the system' that, until now, had always beaten them. This experience, combined with their success in 'conning' (as they saw it) various departments and agencies into helping them establish their centre, gave them a sense of power they had never had before. They all found their attitudes changing as they developed their own untapped resources; this was partly thanks to the classes they had organized, but mainly just a spin-off from the fun they had had running the centre and the intense warmth and support they got from each other.

As far as they were concerned, none of this had anything to do with politics. They were quite explicit about it: Five Arches was non-political and non-religious. The centre became a talking point in the region and was visited by groups of all kinds. If anyone tried to start an overtly political discussion, the women told them to get lost. They hated politics – in spite, or perhaps because, of the fact that their own families were being badly hit by government policies. Indeed, many would go to the centre to escape from an increasingly tense atmosphere, when their husbands lost their jobs and started getting under their feet at home. Sometimes the women took part in local campaigns – against rate-capping and benefit cuts, for instance, and to save local bus services. But this was not what they saw as 'politics'; it was just helping out in a good cause.

The next big change for Jan was going to college. Increasingly, she had found herself intruding into a world where people spoke a language she didn't understand and had skills she didn't possess. Her first response was to scorn that world; her second response was to want it for herself. She was accepted for a residential course in Social and Community Studies at Northern College, the 'workers' university' at Wentworth Castle, near Barnsley. She was the only member of the group to do so; another woman, Pat, had been on a short course at the college, but had decided not to take it any further.

For someone in Jan's position, there could be no smooth transition from home to college. The contrast was too drastic, the wrench too traumatic. Jan's friends at Five Arches were hurt and angry; they felt she was deserting them. She felt she was being torn away from the very centre of her life. The only way she could handle it was to make a clean break. She gave up her house and got rid of every stick of furniture. She and Mathew went to live at Wentworth Castle for two years.

She might have crossed an ocean, so strange was this new territory. Northern College specialized in courses for working-class people – so it was not as though Jan had arrived at Oxford, to meet a crowd of hoorays squirting champagne at each other. Nevertheless, it had an atmosphere and style that bore no resemblance to Five Arches. People wore different clothes, used different words and concepts, listened to different music, and had different ways of relating to each other. Jan was surprised to find herself increasingly at ease there. She began to put her own experience into a context of ideas. She became interested in issues, and in arguments about feminism, socialism, racism. She found, for the first time, that she could have relaxed conversations with some of the men she met – and have friendships that weren't spiked with sexual role-playing. She changed the way she dressed and the way she did her hair. And she became the first woman to be student president at Northern College.

She tried to keep in touch with the women at Five Arches, but they seemed increasingly wary and resentful. Later, they told her that, as far as they were concerned, she was half way to joining the 'brown rice and sandals' brigade; she was boring, political and 'getting above her station'. Over a period of time, they talked it through and rebuilt some of the bridges, but it was never the same again.

When we met Jan, she was a development worker at the Sheffield Co-ordinating Centre Against Unemployment. She was a sturdily-built, handsome woman with short, dark hair and a forthright, witty manner. Not a grain of rice or a sandal thong could be found about her person, but she wore trousers, a big loose sweater, flat shoes and no make-up – not the dominant style of the northern working-class housewife.

Her job was to make contact with unemployed groups throughout the city and help them set up their own centres and self-help projects. No one like Jan had ever done a job like hers in Sheffield before. She might have changed the way she looked and thought but she had not changed her strong sense of class identity, or her awareness of the great gap in comprehension between most working-class people and the language and conventions of the politicized élite. She was doing the job because she wanted to make the Centre Against Unemployment relevant to the majority of the unemployed, and especially to women.

She told us:

> There's one course being run called 'Is Democracy Working?'
> I said to the other development worker, this bloke who's
> heavily involved in the trade union and labour movement,
> 'Well I won't come on that.' He said, 'Why?' I said, 'What
> are you asking, Is Democracy Working? If you want people
> to come from the unemployed centres to that you're talking
> stupid because they won't come.' And they didn't. So now
> we're actually thinking about how you word the courses –
> I did one called 'Women to Women'. That speaks for itself.
> We got ten to that one.

Jan hadn't yet joined a political party. She said she wasn't ready.
'I want to learn about politics,' she said, 'but I've got a long
way to go.' She was now thirty-two. When Margaret Thatcher
was that age, she was working as a tax barrister and was soon
to be selected for Finchley, her safe parliamentary seat.

It is clear from Jan Burrows' story that political power can
not reside exclusively in parliament and government. The
women at Five Arches were engaged in political activity; they
were finding ways of increasing their power within their community – and using that power to change their own lives.

If we compare Jan's story with Margaret Thatcher's, we can
see that there are collective and individual routes to political
power. Jan's story demonstrates that women from poor backgrounds, whose families are not socially mobile and who themselves are poor and powerless, are likely to remain so while
they are isolated. The women in her group became more powerful as a result of getting together. Individually, they would have
got nowhere, trapped as they were by poverty and parenthood,
by a lack of formal education and, in most cases, by the domestic
requirements of marriage. It's not surprising that the notion of
self-improvement through individual effort was not part of their
culture.

It was, as we have seen, part of Margaret Thatcher's culture.
Accordingly, her route to power was devoid of any sense of
solidarity or making common cause with others. She did her
own thing, by herself, for herself. Yet it is evident that the 'indi-

vidualist' route, too, requires a strong context of support, both material and ideological, from family and class.

Our comparison also sheds light on the accessibility of the political world. From her first contact with formal politics, Margaret Thatcher felt it was a place where she could move naturally. She had no cause to wonder whether she had a right to enter. It was there on her doorstep – user-friendly and familiar.

Jan Burrows had no contact with politics as a child. Her parents' activities in the tenants' association didn't strike her as political – it was just what people did to get by. Formal politics remained a distant and obscure territory. She had no map to it. She made no claim to it. When she ventured into what others called 'community politics', she had no sense of any channels leading from her world to the world of politicians, elections, councils, parliament and government. To learn how to speak the language of political people, she paid a huge price: her home, her friends, her community. All her relationships were severed and those that weren't lost forever were permanently scarred. Even after her leap into political education, Jan continued to see 'politics' as something she would have to work very hard at to get to grips with. She would never feel it belonged to her, or she to it.

We can see from the two stories that, even among women, there are different approaches to politics – and this is linked to the question of accessibility. One is, as it were, 'male', the other 'female'. In effect, Margaret Thatcher cut her political teeth as a middle-class boy might have done. When she was set to work, aged ten, folding election addresses for the local Conservative candidate, Sir Victor Warrender, it was not an apprenticeship in fringe activities, as it might have been for other girls of her class. It was an invitation to a club she could eventually join. This bears witness to Alfred Roberts' unusual 'gender blindness' where his daughter's education was concerned, and it helped make the political world accessible to her. Had she been brought up more conventionally as a girl, she would not so easily have felt that world was hers to possess.

No wonder, then, that she never found her sex a disadvantage. When she entered the political fray, she did it like a man: a chemistry graduate and tax barrister, with a woman at home serving her domestic and child-care needs, and with her sights firmly set on the ladder to success.

By contrast, Jan Burrows' involvement in politics grew directly out of her experience as a woman, and was all about being a woman. Based in the community, and organized around the responsibilities of motherhood, it was fuelled by a sense of sister-hood – by gossip, laughter, forbearance, all based on an under-standing that the women shared a common fate. Thus, the politics of Jan and her friends had a different style and a different purpose from the politics of Margaret Thatcher, and operated on an entirely different plane.

Jan's family upbringing was relatively egalitarian, as we have noted, but that did not lead her to take a 'male' route into politics. If she had, it would have been quite different from that taken by a woman of Margaret Thatcher's class. Not Oxbridge, law and nanny, but a job, a trade union and the political education of the labour movement. It would have offered easier access to formal politics than the woman-centred approach of Five Arches. But it would have been a hard passage to work (we shall hear more about this in a later chapter), and it might not have achieved the same ends.

Our comparison shows that different things drive different kinds of women into political activity. For Jan Burrows the incen-tive was a desperate need to do something about her own immediate environment. She and the other women at Five Arches needed to talk to each other, to find solutions to child-care problems, to educate themselves, to keep warm, to create an identity for their neighbourhood, to cope with debt, to make their lives work better. For Margaret Thatcher the move into politics was an extension of her education and of her family's standing in Grantham. It was interesting and exciting for her. She didn't need it as Jan did, for her life was relatively comfor-table and secure.

If Jan Burrows were eventually to join a political party and play a prominent part in mainstream electoral politics, it would be a development of her need to improve the lives of working-class women like herself – poor and powerless people who were unemployed, who lived on council estates, who were in debt, who were hard-pressed to feed and clothe their children. It would not be – as it was for Margaret Thatcher – a decision to pursue a career in politics because it was a challenging adventure which held out the possibility of making one's mark in the world.

Finally, Jan Burrows' story tells us something about the impact of policy on women's lives. Jan would never dream of joining the same political party as Margaret Thatcher. All her experience led her to believe that Margaret Thatcher's government had done nothing to help people like herself – on the contrary, it had made life ever more difficult and unpleasant for them, with an increasingly gloomy future for their children. The ideas and values that fired the soul of the grocer's daughter – about standing on one's own two feet and pulling oneself up by one's bootstraps, and living by the law of the market – would freeze the blood of the steelworker's daughter, because she had witnessed their impact on the communities of the North of England. She had seen the steel mills close. She had seen families destroyed by unemployment. She knew what it was like to survive on state benefit, to see its value dwindling each year. When bus services were cut, when hospital queues lengthened, Jan and her friends were among those who suffered directly. When the grocer's daughter pulled in the national belt, it was not she, but the steelworker's daughter who felt the pinch.

Let's return to our main objective: to find out how more women can wield more political power. If we were to concentrate simply on getting more women into parliament, how far would that help the majority who remained outside? Too little, if the women at Five Arches are anything to go by – because of the huge distance that they feel exists between themselves and the formal political world. Women need to become more powerful in their communities. But that alone would not be enough. No matter how successful women are at getting together to change things in their own neighbourhoods, their lives will continue to be affected by the decisions of local and national governments. So we are interested in power at all levels.

We want to see women in local councils and at Westminster

who are committed to improving the lives of all women, and to increasing the political power of all women. It seems to us that collective approaches to political power are more likely to benefit the majority than the single furrows ploughed by individualists – although, as we shall see, the House of Commons makes no allowance for the former and positively encourages the latter. We want to see women in all social classes wielding more power than they do at present, and if this is to mean (as it surely must) that others wield less of it, then those others should be white middle-class men, who are currently grossly over-represented.

It is clear, though, that the women who most need political power are those who are now furthest away from it, because their lives need changing most urgently and no one can judge what they need better than themselves. Ultimately, these are the women – poor, working-class women, black and white – who must have access to the political world, who must feel they have a right to enter it and possess it for themselves.

Where does our definition of 'political power' begin and end? We would endorse the maxim of the women's movement that 'the personal is political'. Power is exercised over the cornflakes packet, in the supermarket, in darkened streets, in schoolrooms, between the sheets and through the remote control of the family television set (to name but a few instances). This power is political because it is about the way men and women organize and control their lives and the lives of others. However, we want to find out how women can wield more power beyond the domestic front, in running their communities and in running the country. We are interested in the way power in the private sphere interacts with power in the public sphere. There, power is exercised through diverse means – through industry, business and finance, information technology and the mass media, education and religion – as well as through the formal structures of political organization and government. All these fields deserve close study in terms of the power and powerlessness they can confer on men and women. The main focus of our book, however, is on the latter field – on Politics with a capital 'P'.

What would it be like if working-class women had a voice

in politics which reflected their numbers in the population? If there were more than 300 women in the House of Commons – and they were not just middle-class career women, but working-class women from shops and factories, mothers from council estates? What would it be like if women like this were in government, in equal numbers to men? If they had a truly equal part in running local councils, political parties, trade unions?

It is hard to imagine any such state of affairs – and that is revealing, because it shows what a great distance we are from it. Yet if we do make that leap of imagination and envisage a political system where women and men wield power on a genuinely equal basis, it is hard to escape two conclusions: first, that the system would change under the influence of such a strong contingent of women; and secondly, that it would be fairer and more in tune with the ideals of representative democracy.

In this book we try to find ways of moving closer to our goal. We explore the relationship between women and the political process. We examine how and why women are excluded from power. We look at what happens when women do make inroads into that exclusive world – as they do, at all levels, from the community to the council, from the council to the cabinet. We ask what changes are necessary to make political power more accessible to more women. And we see how women can transform the political process once they begin to wield power in sufficient numbers.

The machinery of British politics is an ancient and cobwebby construction. It has been built haphazardly over centuries, by men with jewelled crowns on their heads, and men with clanking armour on their backs, and men with lace and velvet at their throats, and men with powder on their wigs, and men with pin-stripes on their persons, and (just a few) men with flat caps. There is no user's manual, no manufacturer's guarantee. Trying to make it work in the modern world is difficult enough. Trying to adapt it to women's needs is daunting and often discouraging. But we reckon we must work with what we've got, because it is all we are likely to have in the forseeable future. There are no perfect alternatives, ready to be picked off the shelf, and in any case it seems that the great majority of women these days would consider the price of revolution – scrapping this model and creating a new one – too high to contemplate. So our approach is unashamedly reformist. We shall inspect the moving parts of the machinery, dust off the cobwebs and wig powder, and see what can be done.

By the late 1980s, it was possible to detect a female presence in the machinery. The 1987 British general election returned a record number of women to the House of Commons: forty-one. That was eighteen more than the general election of 1983. The previous record was in 1964, when twenty-nine were returned. Of the forty-one new MPs, twenty-one were Labour, seventeen Conservative, two were from the Liberal/SDP Alliance and one from the Scottish Nationalist Party. In 1987, there was also a record number of female candidates: 327, compared with 267 in 1983 and only ninety in 1964. But these figures must be put into context. In 1987 there were 1,997 male candidates and 594 men elected. The female presence in the Commons represented just over 6 per cent. In the House of Lords, there were 1,186 peers, of whom sixty-seven were women – just over 5 per cent of the total. In local authorities, the female presence was greater: approximately 20 per cent. And women accounted for 18.5 per cent of appointments to public bodies (i.e. people appointed by government departments to serve on boards, commissions, committees, tribunals and so forth).

There was, as we have noted, a female prime minister. When she first came to office in 1979, she was the only woman in her cabinet – and she was still the only woman ten years later, in the middle of her third term. In her government team of 105 ministers, there were seven women, including herself. In Labour's shadow team of eighty-one, there were twelve women, with four in the Cabinet, including a shadow Minister for Women (a post which had no place in Mrs Thatcher's government). In the top three grades of the Civil Service, women represented 3.8 per cent of the total staff; in the next four grades, 5 per cent.

These scores cannot be taken as a scientific measure of the amount of power in the hands of women, but they are a useful indicator. What they show is that, in the pyramid of political power, women wielded only a fraction of the power exercised by men at the bottom of the structure, and almost none at the top, except the prime minister who, in spite of her own unparalleled power, appears to have done little to help other women to become powerful, except, arguably, as a model of female achievement.

This picture of women's absence, or exclusion, from power was not just a national one. It was a problem that had pricked the conscience of the United Nations when, in 1975, it declared a Decade for Women, to encourage its member countries to promote the interests of women through 'Equality, Development and Peace'. In the course of the decade, the UN tried to monitor progress in a number of areas, including education, health, employment and political participation.

A report published at the end of the Decade showed that, in Western European legislatures, women were best represented in Scandinavian countries: 39 per cent in Sweden, 34 per cent in Norway and 30 per cent in Denmark. Next came the Netherlands with 23 per cent, followed by Austria with 14 per cent. West Germany, Luxembourg and Switzerland had 11 per cent; Belgium and Ireland, 9 per cent; Italy and Portugal, 7 per cent. The UK ranked lowest, with France, Spain and Greece.[1]

Elsewhere, countries described in 1965 as 'centrally-planned economies', were said to have 'longer histories of constitutional equality for women'. But change had been slow.

> In the USSR ... though 27 per cent of women are members of the Communist Party, only 8 per cent of the 320-member Central Committee are women, and the Council of Ministers and the powerful Politburo have no women members at all. China admits to a similar, though less extreme pyramid ... 'The situation of our women cadres resembles the shape of a pagoda: the higher the level, the fewer the women.' The shape has begun to change, however, with the percentage of women in the National Congress nearly doubling from 12 to 21 per cent between 1954 and 1978.[2]

Throughout the developing world, the United Nations had found no consistent increase over the Decade in women's participation in politics ... Costa Rica and Venezuela are typical, with women taking less than 6 per cent of places in government. Only 15 out of 200 members of parliament elected in Tanzania in 1980 were women and only 1 of Kenya's 159 MPs elected in 1983. In Malaysia, too, out of 154 MPs, there are just 7 women.[3]

Thus, the level of participation of British women was no higher than that of women in countries such as Costa Rica, Venezuela and Malaysia, all distinguished by their lack of progress towards political equality during the United Nations Decade for Women.

But why does it matter so much that women should participate in politics? Democracy, after all, is about representation. Not everyone can have power. The idea is that some represent others; a few must speak for the many, especially in the upper echelons of government. It has sometimes been argued that women need not necessarily participate, need not exercise power directly, because they have their elected representatives who speak for them in the same way as they do for the millions of men who do not exercise power directly.

This is a fine premise, but it rests on the assumption that representatives – whether at council level or as MPs – can, and do, genuinely represent the people, recognizing their needs, reflecting their experiences and fighting for their interests. No one expects a representative democracy to rest on a perfect harmony of desire between each elector and his or her elected representative. But one can be nearer, or more distant from that goal. We are interested in moving closer to it.

The problem is that in all social and ethnic groups, women and men experience life differently. Most women's lives are centred on their homes, whether or not they have jobs elsewhere. At home, they are responsible for most of the unpaid work which keeps the family going. Men's lives tend to have a different focus – on paid employment (if they have a job) and on other activities which take place outside the house.

Men's freedom from domestic responsibility has enabled them to gain pre-eminence in the labour market, to monopolize better-paid jobs and to designate themselves as family breadwinners. Women have not had the opportunity to compete with men on equal terms, and have been obliged to sell their labour more cheaply. More often than not, they have had to depend on men for economic support.

Because women's lives are organized differently from men's, their needs are different, too. When it comes to allocating public resources, there is often a conflict of interest between women and men – because their needs and experience dictate different orders of priority. For example, women would gain directly from an increase in Child Benefit, or from a programme to increase nursery places for pre-school children, while men would be more likely to gain from certain tax concessions, or from a road-building programme. (The differences in political attitudes are examined more fully in Chapter 2.)

And there is another sense in which their interests conflict. If women are not content to remain economically dependent; if they demand equal opportunities and equal pay for work of equal value (to which they have a legal right), men cannot support that demand and continue to organize their working lives around dependence on women's unpaid labour. Nor can men go on expecting to earn more than women (an obvious enough point, but one which can escape them), or to have more time at their disposal, or to exercise greater economic power within the family. If women are to have more opportunities, more money, more time and more power than they do now, men will inevitably have less in relative terms, and will almost certainly have less in absolute terms as well.

Given these conflicts of interest, it would be both naive and irrational to rely on men to represent women. More than a century ago, the liberal philosopher John Stuart Mill made the same point when he argued in parliament for extending the (then limited) franchise to women, in his amendment to the 1867 Reform Bill:

It is said that women do not need direct power, having so much indirect, through their influence over their male relatives and connections. I should like to carry this argument a little

24

further. Rich people have a great deal of indirect influence. Is this a reason for refusing them votes? ... But at least, it will be said, women do not suffer any practical inconvenience, as women, by not having a vote. The interests of all women are safe in the hands of their husbands and brothers, who have the same interest with them ... Sir, this is exactly what is said of all unrepresented classes. The operatives, for instance: are they not virtually represented by the representation of their employers? ... and generally, have not employers and employed a common interest against all outsiders, just as husband and wife have against all outside the family? And what is more, are not all employers good, kind, benevolent men, who love their work people, and always desire to do what is most for their good? All these assertions are true, and as much to the purpose, as the corresponding assertions respecting men and women. Sir, we do not live in Arcadia ... and workmen need other protection than that of their employers, and women other protection than that of their men.[4]

As it has since proved, women need more than the vote to protect their interests. They need access to political power and they need to wield it on their own behalf, at all levels.

This is not to say that all women, all of the time, share a common set of interests. Women do not constitute a class, or act as one. Our comparison between Margaret Thatcher and Jan Burrows shows that only too clearly. But women do share both general and specific experiences and needs. While these remain hidden, off the political map, while they are neither recognized nor understood by those in power, the lives of all women are impoverished.

As Christobel Pankhurst wrote in a furious attack on the Labour Party in the *Labour Leader* newspaper (edited by Keir Hardie): 'Never in the history of the world have the interests of those without power to defend themselves been properly served by others.'[5]

CHAPTER 2

From Plato to the Primrose League

The city of Sheffield, once fed and fortified by steel but more recently struggling for survival in the wake of industrial collapse, was nothing if not a political place. Known by some as the Socialist Republic of South Yorkshire, it was illuminated by a working-class, trade-union culture, with a radical Labour council running a high-profile political programme. But the women we met with Jan Burrows at the Five Arches Centre in Sheffield were outside all of this. They weren't interested in politics, they said. 'It's now't to do with us. What can we do?'

It was not part of their culture to talk about the political world, even though they had been swept up to the edges of it. And there was nothing in their experience to suggest that they could play a part in it. The Centre came into existence as an escape from home – it gave the women a breathing-space from housework and boredom and, sometimes, from depression and despair. But home, the women reckoned, was where the men thought women should be: 'There's not many men don't think like that.' What men wanted, said the women, was for their wives to look after the kids and have their tea on the table when they came home from work. 'That's all they want you to do and that's all they expect you can do. It's a hard fight for women to get to the top in anything, let alone get involved in politics. That's because men condition so many women into believing that they are second-class citizens.'

All over the country, there were women's voices telling the same story, describing a sense of exclusion from what they regarded as 'politics with a capital P'. It was partly a feeling of being shut out, of not belonging, of not being 'eligible'. But it was also an aversion: no thanks, they didn't want it anyhow.

In Bermondsey, South London, we met a group of young women campaigning to save the docklands for local people. They'd lived there all their lives, but now the developers had moved in to build bijoux residences for settlers from the City. The women were fighting for the right to stay in their community, to have homes with gardens which didn't cost half a million, and access to the river front. They had put together a band, the Touch Cookies, and made a record, 'Give Us Back Our Land', to publicize their cause. One of them, Christine Longbon, a single parent with two children, was working part-time at the Beormund, a local community centre, and was also running a local street-lighting campaign. And yet she told us: 'I'm not involved in politics at all.' She wasn't in any party, she said, but that wasn't the point. Politics to her was something else, somewhere else. 'I might get involved, but I don't understand how any of it works yet. I feel it's all corrupt, it doesn't do any good. But it's nice to see a whole load of women getting together . . .'

The effect of women working together had also made waves in a very different kind of community – in the modestly prosperous grey-stone city of Stirling, in Central Scotland. Here, women had made a successful intervention in local politics. But it hadn't brought them a sense of belonging.

Stirling was the first place in Britain where the council provided a permanent shoppers' crèche. This was the brainchild of Stirling Women's Network – a city-wide organization which also ran a women's centre. Members of the Network were co-opted on to the council's Women's Committee and Child-care Working Group – and it was through these channels that their idea was realized. It remained one of the most popular initiatives taken by Stirling Council. It was the sort of thing women everywhere dreamed of.

For an independent women's organization, it was quite an achievement. It suggested a positive relationship with political institutions and unusually good access to political power (perhaps because Stirling Women's Network was not predominantly working class). But when we met members of the Network, we found that they still saw the political world as foreign territory on which they did not care to tread.

Sue Gutteridge, who used to be the co-ordinator of the Women's Network and went on to become the manager of the shoppers' crèche, summed up the general feeling: 'It's not an arena in which I can operate. It feels so alien.' A graduate in her early forties, with four children, including two daughters under ten, she had joined the Labour Party, but hated going to party meetings: 'I don't know what they're talking about half the time. The whole thing is so incestuous. It has lost involvement with ordinary people and ordinary people's lives. It has become a thing in itself.'

Politics is everywhere – a ragbag of consent and conflict, compromise and challenge, losses and gains that shape the patterns of our lives – but to many of the women we met it was merely something *out there*: an intimidating, uncomfortable place where the language was unintelligible and anyway no one speaks to you, at least not about anything familiar.

Why was this sense of not belonging such a persistent theme? It could be heard not only among the poor and the powerless, although for them it was particularly acute. As we shall see, it also informed the thinking of the most political of women, whether in the House of Commons, the council chamber or the tenants' hall.

There was certainly nothing new about it. Women's experience of being outside politics has a history at least as long as that of the state. Formal powers were first concentrated, as the modern state evolved, in the hands of a small male elite. Women were defined in relation to politics, but they were not part of politics. As Alice Clark wrote in her influential book, *The Working Life of Women in the Seventeenth Century*, the state was only concerned with male individuals. 'Thus it came to pass that every womanly function was considered as the private interest of husbands and fathers, bearing no relation to the life of the state, and therefore demanding from the community as a whole no special care or provision.'[1]

If women's lives were to have no political meaning except as a 'private interest' of men, then it was logical that women were to be excluded from the 'political life' of men – the world of government and diplomacy, armies and bureaucracy.

But how did this come about in the first place? What determined that power should be concentrated in male hands, and that the state should be concerned only with male individuals? If we turn to the political philosophers we shall see that their thoughts on the question 'What are women for?' have had a bearing on women's role in the political process. Susan Moller Okin has argued in her excellent study, *Women and Western Political Thought*, that the modes of thought of the great philosophers 'are still prevalent, in the writings of modern thinkers, and in the ideologies of modern political actors and institutions'.[2]

There was a brief moment – albeit two and a half thousand years ago – when certain women were released from domestic confinements to take their place in equal numbers and with equal power beside men as members of the ruling class. It was, alas, an imaginary society – the ideal state conceived by the Greek philosopher Plato and described in his work *The Republic*.[3]

Plato started from the idea that the objective of the state was a kind of moral harmony in which selfishness and greed ceased to exist. To achieve this he abolished private property and the family (the two were not particularly distinctive in Plato's home town of Athens, since women and children were regarded as property anyhow). And since Plato argued that every person was defined by his or her ideal function, once he freed women from the home and the hearth to live communally (procreation was by 'mating arrangements' at 'mating festivals' and child care was to be socialized), there was no reason why women shouldn't be educated and trained to become Guardians, Plato's ruling class. Here is Plato, summing up in *The Republic* at the end of his section on Women and the Family:

> ... the best arrangement is for our men and women to share a common education, to bring up their children in common and to have a common responsibility, as Guardians, for their fellow-citizens ... women should in fact, so far as possible, take part in all the same occupations as men, in peace and in war, watching and hunting with them like watchdogs, and

... there is nothing unwomanly in this natural partnership of the sexes.[4]

However, this concept of a 'natural partnership' was not to last. In his final book, *Laws*, Plato changed his mind about women. He argued even more forcefully for equal opportunities, declaring it an irrational blunder 'that men and women should not all follow the same pursuits with one accord and with all their might'. But he also reintroduced private property – on the grounds that citizens were not gods and were incapable of holding their property in common. Almost in the same breath, he resurrected marriage and the family. In this property-owning society, women once again became private possessions within the body of the family. 'Despite all his professed intentions ... to emancipate women and make full use of the talents that he was now convinced they had,' commented Okin, 'Plato's reintroduction of the family has the different effect of putting them firmly back into their traditional place.'[5]

And there they remained. While Plato had a valiant go at 'liberating' women, Aristotle sent them back to the kitchen and the nursery. Aristotle was not interested in prescribing an ideal world, but in defining what was in his view 'natural' and, therefore, best.

Aristotle's world was hierarchical and organized according to the functions each element performed best. He didn't think much of women – a sentiment entirely consistent with their chattel-like status in Athenian society. But what they could do was to breed. This was defined as woman's natural function and, according to Aristotle, child-rearing went 'naturally' with child-bearing. Meanwhile, the superior and rational husband went off and did what a man had to do in the public world. In a woman's function was her goodness measured. It was not appropriate for her to have qualities other than those which fitted and reinforced her function. What was good in a woman was not so in a man, and vice versa. If a woman exhibited unwomanly virtues, she became a 'bad' woman.[6]

The tradition held for the English liberal philosophers, Thomas Hobbes and John Locke, as well as for the eighteenth-century

French thinker, Jean-Jacques Rousseau. Both Hobbes and Locke set up the father as head of the family to represent its interests in society, thereby excluding women from political life. As Okin put it: 'Whereas the liberal tradition appears to be talking about individuals, as components of political systems, it is in fact talking about male-headed families.'[7]

Likewise, Rousseau, whose ideas helped to inspire the French Revolution, failed to include women as citizens in a civil society based on the general will. 'In spite of his preoccupation with the male individual and his rights and freedoms, Rousseau continued to apply Aristotelian arguments about the nature and purpose of women,' wrote Okin.

> Her role in the bourgeois family was thereby rationalized: that she should propagate and nurture undisputed heirs to the family property, that she should provide for her husband a pleasant solace from the harsh realities of the competitive world outside, that she should obey him without question, be totally dependent on him and value her chaste reputation as her most prized possession – all these were merely the dictates of nature.[8]

A woman's only political privilege was the possibility of influencing her husband. This was, according to Rousseau, a 'chaste power' in which she should exhort her husband 'to honour and reason' for the glory of the state.

The ideas about a woman's incapacity to serve in public life or, indeed, to be a legal citizen with equal rights, were rooted in a one-dimensional view which saw women only in terms of their reproductive function. That was considered their one true purpose and, as such, their best interests were subsumed under the banner of 'family', proudly carried by the male head of household. It was he who would go forth to reason and rule in the political realm. As Okin pointed out: '. . . what has been alleged to be women's nature has been used throughout history and into the present to justify keeping the female sex in a position of political, social and economic inequality.'[9]

The status of women in ancient Athens was not essentially different from that of women in Rousseau's day. When a woman married in eighteenth-century Britain, her husband controlled all her land and possessions, even her jewellery and clothes. Any money she earned became his. Even if she were living apart from her husband and supporting her children, anything she earned belonged by right to her husband. Her children, too, belonged to her husband and he could whisk them away as and when he wished. In law, a wife was not a person in her own right; she was 'under couverture' to her husband, existing merely to provide him with children, perform what duties he required, both physical and sexual, and, if he were of a certain class, to look decorative and appealing. Mary Wollstonecraft, whose *Vindication of the Rights of Women* was published in 1792, described women as 'the toys of man ... [who] must jingle in his ears whenever, dismissing reason, he chooses to be amused.'[10]

Not all women were content with a life of jingling. There were women in the late eighteenth century who openly resisted attempts by men to exclude them from political power. Those burning ideas about human equality, rights, liberty and the pursuit of happiness which had fuelled both the French and the American Revolutions struck a vibrant chord. As Mary Wollstonecraft argued, if men were to 'contend for their freedom and to be allowed to judge for themselves respecting their own happiness, be it not inconsistent and unjust to subjugate women, even though you firmly believe that you are acting in the manner best calculated to promote their happiness?'[11]

Wollstonecraft attacked not only legal and political inequality but also the idea of femininity, which determined that women should be helpless, decorative, modest, the prisoner of home and husband. The male establishment fought back, as Barbara Taylor has observed, in terms which revealed the close relationship between women's personal and political status.

Viewed through the smoke of the Bastille, Wollstonecraft loomed like a blood-stained Amazon, the high priestess of 'loose-tongued Liberty', whose much-publicised love affairs also helped to convince the public that she wanted to extend libertarian principles into the bedroom as well as into government – a doctrine which 'if received, must overturn the basis of every civilised state.'[12]

Mary Wollstonecraft's dreams of a different social and political reality were, in many ways, Utopian and provided part of the inspiration for early socialists. Among these were the Owenites, whose aspirations were based on the idea of 'perfect equality and perfect freedom' within a classless society. Their visions also included a 'sexual democracy' which, most radically, would abolish the family and 'bourgeois marriage'. Instead, the Owenites favoured wider co-operative units of large groups of men, women and children 'arranged to be as one family'.[13]

Alongside the Owenites, in the great tumult of political and industrial change in the first half of the nineteenth century, were the Chartists with their six-point list of political demands, including universal male suffrage. The notion that ordinary people should have a role in government was an effect both of theory and of practice; the philosophers posed the possibilities of more equal and 'accountable' forms of government, while in the French Revolution the 'people' had triumphed and aristocratic rule had crumbled. For the first time, the vote moved on to the political agenda.

Chartism was a mass movement in which women played a significant part: they demonstrated on the streets, campaigned against the New Poor Law, decorated meeting halls, and organized radical suppers of 'potatoe pie and home-brewed ale' and musical soirées.[14] The question of political equality for women was entertained, but not very seriously. The first draft of the Chartists' six-point plan, the People's Charter, had included a clause about the female franchise. It was withdrawn before the Charter was presented to parliament in 1837, because it was thought that its inclusion would hinder the cause of male suffrage.[15]

It was rare for working women specifically to demand the vote. Dorothy Thompson records one occasion – a letter in the Chartist newspaper, the *Northern Star* (June 1838), addressed to the women of Scotland: 'Fellow Countrywomen – I address you as a plain working woman – a weaver of Glasgow ... It is the right of every woman to have a vote in the legislation of her country, and doubly more so now that we have got a woman at the head of the government. . . .'[16]

In the main, the Chartists preached the virtues of married life and female dependency. Women Chartists tended to express their protest in general terms, providing succour and support to the cause of male, working-class emancipation. 'While we are compelled to share the misery of our fathers, our husbands, our brothers, and our lovers, we are determined to have a share in their struggles to be free, and to cheer them in their onward march for liberty,' declared the women Chartists of Aberdeen.[17]

The ideas of the Chartists and the more radical Owenites waned as changes occurred in the industrial working class. New industries and new methods of employment brought men and women into direct competition for jobs. As trade union organization became more effective – particularly among skilled male workers – strategies focused on a 'breadwinner's wage', which meant a wage with which a man could support his family.[18] In 1875, Henry Broadhurst, Secretary of the Trades Union Congress, was applauded when he stated that the aim of the labour movement was 'to bring about a condition of things, where wives and daughters would be in their proper sphere at home, instead of being dragged into competition for livelihood against the great and strong men of the world.'[19] Women's dependence on the male bread-winner and their work in the family in effect reduced their capacity to organize. It also diminished their political contribution, as the sexual divisions of labour polarized, both inside and outside the home.

Once the radical working-class movements receded, middle-class women who compaigned for sexual and social reform were no longer branded immoral or socialistic by association with radical ideas.[20] At the same time, many well-heeled ladies became involved in philanthropy; helping their less fortunate sisters was a legitimate way of expressing their own grievances. And there were clear improvements in the position of middle-class women, especially in education. All this created conditions for a new wave of female agitation – this time from the middle classes.

The English Woman's Journal, the first newspaper owned and written by women, was launched in 1858, and became the focus of a feminist network which campaigned on women's education, married women's property rights and the vote. Its tone, although dangerously seditious compared to the niceties of Victorian bourgeois convention, was respectable and philanthropic.[21] Its ideas were narrower than the wide-ranging radicalism of earlier social movements, yet out of them 'arose a sustained, pragmatic strategy for the piecemeal reform of women's social and economic condition'.[22] The way was being paved for a reinvigorated attack on the exclusion of women from the political sphere.

The mid-Victorian struggle for reform of legal inequalities was an attempt to establish women as independent human beings. In a number of cases – from the right to vote, to the right to sit as a councillor or be admitted to Edinburgh University medical school – women tried to use the courts to establish their rights. These were known as the 'person cases'. The basic issue was whether or not women should by virtue of their sex alone be debarred from public functions.

The technical issue was whether women could be included as 'persons' which was the word used in the relevant statutes. For six decades (until 1929), the judiciary pondered on this matter and found that women were not 'persons'. 'Without embarrassment or apology, the judges painted a picture of women being too delicate and refined to undertake public functions, and accordingly classified them legally alongside the insane and the insolvent, and even in one case alongside the inanimate.'[23]

The views of their lordships in the person cases are important because they illuminated a prevailing view of women – what Sachs and Wilson called 'the myth of male protectiveness'.[24] Placing women on the proverbial pedestal, it was argued, was doing them a favour by protecting them from the rigours of public life and office which would offend against their innate decorum and gentility. The male establishment, whether in the law courts or in parliament, had a vested interest in maintaining the status quo. Middle-class wives at home, safe in the bosom of the family, were a symbol of their husbands' wealth and prestige. The connection between women's political rights and their social and sexual position was readily acknowledged by the conservative

Saturday Review, which suggested in 1871 that the female suffrage would 'endanger the institution of marriage and the family'.

One advance was gained, however, in 1869, when women were granted the municipal vote. Members of parliament, embroiled in great affairs of state, considered local politics to be a lowly business: women could dabble there if they so desired. This reform backfired on the anti-suffragists: it provided women with valuable political experience and fuelled their commitment to the fight ahead. But parliamentary bills to extend the suffrage to women at national level – a response to some gentle lobbying by suffrage groups – were continually defeated. The Liberal and Conservative establishments inside parliament would not be budged.

What then of the nascent political forces of the Left outside parliament? Two socialist organizations were beginning to challenge the Liberals in their urban strongholds. One was the Social Democratic Federation, the other the Independent Labour Party. Both had difficulties with women's political emancipation.

The SDF, Britain's first Marxist party, held an orthodox view: divisions in society were economic and everything else was peripheral. That included the 'Woman Question'. 'My only objection to the so-called 'Woman Question', argued the SDF's mouthpiece, *Justice,* in 1896, 'was that it threatened a division in our ranks by directing the attention of women from the real enemy, capitalism, to an imaginary enemy, an abstract "brute man".'[25]

It was not that the SDF opposed female suffrage: it paid lip-service to it. For one thing, it needed women in its ranks. But this, too, presented a problem: women were seen as a reactionary force in society, neutralizing the full-blown socialist spirit of their husbands and fathers. The innuendo was that women not only kept men down but also made political cowards of them. Given such premises, the SDF was unsure how to bring women into the party. There were suggestions that women should be lured to socialism with inducements: 'The only opportunity that a Socialist has of getting women to attend a Socialist gathering is to point a glowing picture of a tea fight, of a concert where certain celebrity artists will appear, of a soirée and dance where there will be a possibility of witnessing new fashions,' declared

Justice in 1894.[26] But it was the argument that the franchise was a class issue that made the SDF lukewarm about women. 'Until the electoral register was reformed and the right to vote dissociated from the ownership of property, the enfranchisement of women would merely strengthen the influence of reactionary, propertied women, the enemies of socialism.'[27]

The ILP had a greater commitment to women's suffrage, but it was in two minds about the best tactics and was also divided over whether a limited female suffrage would enfranchise the 'ladies' at the expense of the male working-class masses. Keir Hardie, the first independent working-class MP and leader of the Labour movement, was a staunch supporter of votes for women, but there was a strand within the ILP which believed that women's suffrage was not a socialist demand. Disenchanted with the ambivalence of the ILP, many women supporters deserted, to throw themselves heart and soul behind the suffragette movement. They found a home in the Women's Social and Political Union of Emmeline Pankhurst, who had herself been a member of the ILP.

One such woman was Hannah Mitchell who, in her autobiography, *The Hard Way Up*, captured the political awakening of a working-class woman in Lancashire at the turn of the century. 'If women did not bestir themselves,' she wrote, 'the Socialists would be quite content to accept Manhood Suffrage in spite of all their talk about equality.'[28] She had been an early and impassioned member of the ILP, but as the suffragist movement became a focus for her energies and commitment, she expressed some dismay about men's inability to turn their fine words into action. When she interrupted a Liberal Rally in Manchester with the call 'Will the Liberal Government give the vote to women?', she was arrested and sentenced to three days in prison – only to find that her husband had paid her fine.

> I was not pleased to find my husband outside [Strangeways Prison]. He knew that we did not wish our fines to be paid, and was quite in sympathy with the militant campaign, but men are not so singleminded as women are. . . . Even as Socialists they seldom translate their faith into works, being still

conservatives at heart, especially where women are concerned. Most of us who were married found that 'Votes for Women' were of less interest to our husbands than their own dinners. They simply could not understand why we made such a fuss about it.[29]

Men on the Left were happy to espouse the cause of women in theory, but in practice, according to *Justice* in 1902, they tended to 'ignore and deny it'.[30] Inevitably, this had the effect of making women feel unwelcome in mixed political company – as the female columnist of the popular socialist newspaper, *The Clarion*, pointed out:

> The fault lies somewhat, I fear, with the way in which the ILP and SDF meetings are conducted. Sufficient prominence is not given to the fact that women are not only welcome but WANTED. When the women do venture to these, they often meet with such a cold reception that they are not by any means encouraged to come again.[31]

Nearly a century later, women on the Left would find themselves similarly discouraged. Many would also share Hannah Mitchell's experience of private discord. 'Public disapproval could be faced and borne,' wrote Mitchell, 'but domestic unhappiness, the price many of us paid for our opinions and activities, was a very bitter thing.'[32]

The effect on home life of women's politicking was one reason why the Women's Co-operative Guild was at first reluctant to commit itself to the suffrage movement. (Later it became an enthusiastic supporter.) The Guild had been formed in 1883 as an offshoot of the main co-operative movement and for many years remained the only organization for the advancement of working-class women, providing them with the chance to run meetings, practise public speaking and discuss all manner of issues which offered a window on the outside world. But it was argued within the co-operative movement as a whole that guildswomen should exert a moral, not a political influence. As the *Burnley Co-operative Record* pontificated in 1896: 'We have no sympathy ... with the goggle-eyed human ostrich, the exponent of women's rights who dresses as men [*sic*] and whose bearing so nearly resembles that of a man. Who speaks with a sneer and a high-flown manner that sends a man home with a sneaking gladness in his heart that he was her auditor and not her husband.'[33]

In both Liberal and Conservative parties, meanwhile, the majority of men were staunchly opposed to female suffrage. The women associated with the two parties responded in different ways. Ineligible for party membership, Conservative women had found a home for their political energies in the ranks of the Primrose League. This was the organization founded in 1883 to create an efficient electoral machine and engage the new urban electorate in support for the Conservative Party. And it was the wives and mothers who threw themselves into the political battle with enthusiasm. Lord Randolph Churchill, for example, declared that the League was 'the first political association to recognise the influence which ladies can exercise over all classes of voters'.[34] Meanwhile, his wife, Lady Jennie Churchill, had written the preface for the pamphlet that the League sent out to its new branches and members. She drew attention to the role of the ladies: 'The fact that women have no vote should help largely to contribute to their influence in canvassing, as proving their disinterestedness, and should lend weight to those powers of argument, which they are well known to possess, and in which they can infuse all the persuasive gentleness characteristic of their sex.'[35]

The excursions of the Primrose League women into the rough and tumble of political electioneering was not entirely acceptable to the men. The women defended themselves vigorously, at the same time reassuring the men that they did not wish to run the country but merely to help those who did – and could. Some Tory women were pro-suffrage but the female leaders of the League, the Dames of the Ladies' Grand Council, abstained from support. It was not that they were anti-politics, they were just anti women's politics. The argument was not so much about keeping women away from politics, as about defining their particular role within it. 'The sphere of women's action is moral, whereas that of men is material,' decreed Lord Cromer, one of the organizers of the Anti-Suffrage League.[36]

Liberal women were likewise excluded from the Liberal Party

itself. In 1887 they formed the Women's Liberal Federation. The women were charged with the back-up, workhorse role. The prime minister's wife, Mrs Gladstone, was the Federation's first president. 'It was perhaps the idea that the Federation should be to the party what Mrs Gladstone was to her husband,' wrote the radical Liberal, Rosalind Howarth, Countess of Carlisle.[37] Far greater numbers of Liberal than Conservative women challenged their party leadership and supported the suffrage movement, although at some cost: a majority of women Liberals broke away from the WLF to form the National Women Liberals' Association. The members of the NWLA were not so much anti-suffrage, as unwilling 'to embarrass the party leadership by pressing the issue within the framework of the Liberal Party.'[38]

There were no signs that women would give up their struggle for political power, but the obstacles must have seemed at times immense. As Ann Veronica, the eponymous heroine of H.G.Wells' novel, recited, as she lay in Canongate gaol, imprisoned for her part in a suffragist demonstration: 'For men have reason, women rhyme; A man scores always, all the time.'[39]

The great tidal wave of pressure for the vote in the first two decades of this century was the culmination of all kinds of political agitation – on the meanest streets and in the most magnificent drawing-rooms. The last and the bloodiest battles of the suffrage struggle united women of the middle class and working class, from London salons and northern back-yards, from East End wash-houses and affluent Lancashire suburbs. Their unity was born of the anger of the powerless – different sorts of powerlessness, maybe – but all were insistent on their personhood, their eyes set on a new society in which they could make the laws and select the law-makers.

For all those women who had joined the suffrage movement – the envelope-stickers, the hecklers, the speakers, the ones who had suffered imprisonment and even death – their hopes were pinned on the vote, both as an end in itself and as a means to an end. They would want different reforms, but essentially the vote was the dart to aim at the bullseye, the sovereign parliament. When, in 1918, in the aftermath of the Great War, the vote was finally granted to women over thirty who were householders, or those who were married to householders, Isabella Ford, a Leeds feminist, wrote to a friend in 1918: 'And now, the great tasks that lie before us, Peace, Reform and all the rest, will be so much easier to work at. We shall have a weapon in our hands, and hitherto we have had none.'[40]

But nothing is ever so simple. Two years after the 1918 Representation of the People Act, the feminist political weekly *Time and Tide* was launched (so called because 'time and tide wait for no man'). It was run by women for women and among its contributors were Rebecca West and Vera Brittain. Monitoring the political scene was one of its most important roles, mercilessly lampooning those MPs who failed to support women's rights. *Time and Tide* was painfully aware that the vote had not brought equality for women. By 1926, it had to acknowledge that the 'weapon in our hands' had become 'a frail reed'. The phrase was used to announce a mass demonstration of women along the old route from the Embankment to Hyde Park that the suffragist marchers knew so well: It was a march borne of frustration – against the insult of partial citizenship and minimal legislative reform. 'Rebuffed here, refused there, finding constantly that the vote granted in 1918 was a frail reed, bending whenever used, the women of Britain have awakened the spirit of the years before 1918 and are demonstrating once more as they so often did in those old days, that they mean to get equality.'[41]

The vote was not enough. Nor was it enough after 1928, when it was extended to all women. It was better than no vote, but it did not give women access to political power. The philosophers' assumptions about a woman's place and purpose held fast through revolution, resistance and reform. They were not intrinsically true or just, but were part of a process in which men defined themselves and established the basic relations of power. This allowed them freedom to shape politics in their own image. They could design political building blocks to meet their own needs, control what happened within them, draw up agendas, set the hours, decide the rules of behaviour, orchestrate the rituals – with barely a glance at the women at their sides in the workplace or the home.

So when just one rule changed, the rule which said, yes,

women could now participate formally in voting, it didn't actually make much difference. Men had hijacked politics and the bastions they had built to contain it were hard to breach. Sixty years after the granting of universal franchise, those bastions – as we shall discover – remained largely intact.

Politics is not just about parliamentary power, as we have pointed out in Chapter 1. However, as the focal point of government, the 650 MPs provide us with our image of politicians. As so few women are there, it is hard to place women centre stage when we think of a politician; the sense of exclusion takes hold.

Emma Nicholson, Tory MP for West Devon and Torridge, came from one of those upper-class families whose members have 'served' in politics for generations: her father, grandfather and three great-grandfathers were in politics – 'on my mother's side we go back to 1200.' Politics was in her bones but she was the first woman in her family to 'go into politics'. She believed that the MP was typecast. 'You have a clear idea of what an MP is going to be like – like you have of a vicar or a milkman. The fact that my milkman is a single woman surprises people, but why shouldn't my milkman be a single woman? What's the problem? It's a perception problem of what people see as fitting that particular role.' However many times Mrs Thatcher might be seen on television clearly 'being' a top politician, a prime minister and a woman, her presence is still a shock because the set-pieces of politics which occupy our minds have a different set of players.

'Our picture of an MP,' said Barbara Roche, who stood for Labour in the 1987 election, 'is still a white, middle-class man, who knows everything about party policy, who has an answer to everything, an opinion on everything. It's very off-putting for many people. You feel that's what you've got to turn out like.' The system became self-perpetuating, as one set of clones begot the next.

So we live with a firmly entrenched image of the typical political animal: the stern-jawed white man in early middle-age, foot down on the accelerator of his newish car, as he speeds to Grimsby, Godalming or Glasgow, briefcase in the back, packed with newspapers and party documents and a newly-pressed shirt, mind firmly fixed on the political battlefield ahead.

The stern-jawed politician has left behind him the world most women know – and here is another way in which women have been excluded from power. As Sue Gutteridge in Stirling observed, formal politics has become a 'thing in itself'. To become powerful in politics you have to join the professional stream. It isn't something you can do as a natural extension of an everyday life lived by an ordinary citizen – even though political decision-making is intimately concerned with organizing commonplace lives.

Parliamentary politics is a 'top job' and, like other 'top jobs', hotly competitive. Just as there are fewer women in the most senior jobs in other professions, so there are in politics. Many MPs come from backgrounds in the law, in universities and polytechnics, in trade unions and the media. All these fields are male-dominated, all considered appropriate training grounds for parliament. It is a well-trodden path from the Inns of Court to Westminster; routes from the Senior Common Room, the shop stewards' committee and the newsroom are less heavily trampled, but amply reconnoitred and signposted. If you are trekking in from the typing pool or the hairdressing salon, the kitchen or the One O'Clock Club, you have to cross virgin territory. The effect was not simply to deter women from becoming MPs. A woman who had no such ambitions, but who wanted access to the political process, would have to approach a group of people whose experience and accomplishments bore little or no resemblance to her own, and who appeared to be dauntingly 'in the know' about something she could only guess at.

Another major constraint was time. Eve Hartley, whom we met at the Five Arches Community Centre, had three children and worked as a hospital cleaner. 'I was talking to this bloke and he said, "Would you like to join the Labour Party?"' she told us. 'I said, "When are your meetings?" He said, "Seven-thirty at night, at the Park Hotel." I said, "Well that leaves all us out of it, doesn't it?" He said, "What do you mean?" I said, "What do we do with the kids?"'

Time was a precious commodity for women. They were in

charge of home life and if they didn't put their families first,
who would? Most women also had a paid job. All this left little
time for anything else. It was hard enough to find time for local
party meetings. It was almost impossible to play a full part in
the endless meetings, conferences and engagements which were
expected of a political 'activist'.

Glennys Thornton was the chair of the London Labour Party
when she had her first baby. It was particularly hard for her
to attend six o'clock meetings. 'Six o'clock is when I'm getting
George to bed. I could take him with me, but he'd be very miser-
able.' When we interviewed her, she was still breast-feeding.

> It will be better when he's on the bottle, and I can leave him.
> But I like to be there, just those two hours. Meetings at 7.30
> are easier. Mind you, they won't be when he's older and going
> to school. The men want to meet at six so they can fit in another
> meeting at eight. They see their children at weekends, if
> they're lucky, between conferences. I see it as a major problem
> the way the Labour movement expects people to be out every
> evening and every weekend.

(This was not, by any means, a problem exclusive to Labour.)

Glennys Thornton was secretary of the Royal Arsenal Co-
operative Society and hoped to get into parliament. She said
that, back home in Yorkshire, her female relatives and friends
could think of nothing more horrendous. 'To stand up and make
a speech in a room full of people, especially selling themselves
and saying how wonderful they are, would be an absolute night-
mare, a foreign thing to do.' Becoming powerful in politics was
not just about fitting the image, or having the right qualifications
and enough spare time. It was about knowing how to play the
game. Glennys Thornton learnt it at her father's knee. He was
a plumber who had been expelled from the Labour Party, on
the day Glennys was born, for belonging to the Peace Pledge
Union. As she explained, she grew up in a working-class
environment with middle-class values regarding education (and
there are echoes here of the Roberts' family). 'There were
always books around, we were encouraged to learn, pass
exams, to be confident, make speeches. I used to go away to

public-speaking competitions when I was in my teens. So I grew up quite self-confident.'

It seemed to us that playing the political game did not come easily to women of any class. Emma Nicholson used to be Vice-chairman of the Conservative Party, with responsibility for women. She was deeply involved in getting more Tory women on the party lists and so paving their way to constituency selection. She nursed them through their political apprenticeship – spending time with them, rehashing their cvs, practising their speeches with them, pushing and prodding them, encouraging them when they'd had enough, dropping words in appropriate ears, making sure they were known by the Tory bigwigs. All this was just to get on to a parliamentary shortlist. These were Emma Nicholson's 'high-flyers', the flower of Tory womanhood, yet they needed an intensive course of training and grooming before they could play the game.

For men, the journey into politics meant a new direction for their identities and personalities, their energies and their skills. For women, the journey had an extra dimension: it was an excursion from orthodoxy. Beatrix Campbell discovered that when she talked to women in the north of England for her book *Wigan Pier Revisited*. Campbell's working-class women were a world away from Emma Nicholson's high-flyers but there were similarities in their experience:

> Women live in the shadow of men's seizure of public life, whether in the public bar or public office. Men's participation in public life involves no threat to their masculine identity. Women's femininity, on the other hand, is anchored in private life. For them going into politics is a gesture of defiance, however timid, against their domestication. . . . [42]

Of course, paid employment took women into the public world, away from their 'domestication'. They were needed in the workplace – theirs was vital labour – and their paypackets were needed at home. But to enter the public world of politics was a different experience from working in a factory or an office. Politics took women (and, indeed, men) to new surroundings and unknown environments. It introduced them to new people and new ideas.

It was messy and unpredictable – in politics anything is possible. But for many women, unlike most men, an involvement in politics – that gesture of defiance – carried a heavy cost.

It was rare for women to get involved in political action without encountering some trouble from men in their families and communities. As they became stronger and more confident, with meetings to go to, new friends and interests, they were less inclined to accept unsatisfactory relationships at home. Men often felt threatened or diminished as they watched them change and begin to lead more independent lives. Some refused to let their wives go out, and would beat them if they did. Broken marriages were rife among politically active women. And the fact that there was a high proportion of divorced and separated women in politically active groups made men even more wary – to the point of equating political organizing among women with loose behaviour. 'They think we are going to corrupt their innocent wives,' said Cheryl Brown, one of the women we met at the Five Arches Community Centre. She was thirty-three and divorced, with two children. 'They think we'll drag them into our little circle and take them out, because we have such a wonderful life, us divorced women, and that we are out every night picking up somebody!'

Pat Nelson was a city councillor in Sheffield. When we met her she was forty-five, divorced, with two sons aged sixteen and twenty.

> Women in politics have a difficult time. The men like to think of the wife at home and that a career is a man's world. If a woman wants to make a career out of it, she's a bit alien. Many politicians, even those who speak the most vibrant on women's issues, still like the idea of their own wife at home, to come out of the cupboard at social events and sit at the table.

Pat reckoned she would never have become a councillor if she hadn't been divorced. 'I was married to a man who became successful in the entertainment industry. I don't think it would have been conducive with getting that heavily involved with politics. We moved to a posh area where the neighbours told me not to peg my washing on the line. If I'd stayed married, I'd have probably been a middle-class twerp by now, for want of a better phrase!'

Again and again we heard women describe the way their political involvement had threatened their personal relationships. This was the price they paid for becoming more powerful. Maggie Jones was married at sixteen, had her first baby at seventeen and two more shortly afterwards. At home all day, and doing bar work at night, she began to feel that there had to be more to life than just this. As the children grew up, she became involved in local play schemes and then in a campaign to get environmental improvements on the housing estate where she lived. When we met her, she was employed as a community worker with Rotherhithe Community Planning Centre. As she said:

Going through all this, my own awareness and self-esteem began to grow and as a result, I started to challenge things. My husband and I had always been seen as a couple; now I started to get recognition in my own right, for my own talents. I liked it. What has happened is that I've left my husband behind and gone right in front. He can't cope with my independence and my need to not need him. He's a traditional working-class man – the woman can only be at home looking after the kids, cooking and cleaning. We're going to break up now, but that's a very positive thing for me.

Middle-class women evidently had similar problems, even if the conflict was cushioned by money. Success in politics required positive support at home, not merely tacit acceptance. Emma Nicholson said she couldn't have married someone who wasn't happy with what she was doing. She remembered being driven down to a selection interview by a man friend who had just got divorced. She emerged from the interview – fascinated and animated by the experience: 'I found the young man absolutely desperate. He said, "I don't think we can think of a long-term relationship. I must have a wife who is content to stay at home." We hadn't actually discussed marriage, but it was a very clear statement by a man of what it meant to be with a woman who wants to do things in public life.'

Margaret Joachim, a Liberal candidate in the 1987 election, was one of the few women who could count her blessings.

> I've got a perfectly decent husband who lets me disappear all over the place at the most peculiar hours, with virtually anybody I care to mention. He knew what he was in for when he married me and this is the way we work. But it would drive 98 per cent of men absolutely round the bend. I mean I wouldn't still be married to them. They'd have thrown me out years ago – an absolutely impossible female!

For women who wanted a happy and conventional family life, the right to participate in politics rested on male consent. Men, too, needed the support of their partners, but female consent was easier to come by – in general, because women had different expectations of marriage and family life. All but a lucky few women had to work hard to obtain and keep the consent of their men – a task which added to the burden of their domestic responsibilities. This, in turn, limited their opportunities to participate in politics on an equal footing with men.

Male consent in the private sphere at home was worthless, in any case, without male consent in the public sphere. Legally, of course, women were no longer excluded from politics and power – but the fusty odour of the monopoly once exercised by men still hung in the atmosphere, helping to make the political environment inhospitable to women – and often downright repellant.

Anna Wyatt, chief executive of the London borough of Southwark, used to work as economic adviser to Leeds Council. She lived in Leeds for fourteen years, loving Yorkshire and its people. But, she said, the women there were really up against it. 'That's where you see the most crude outcome of that male-dominated, intensely secretive culture that grows up around power and influence. It seemed that every male was in the Masons or the Rotary Club. It was a closed society where women were not supposed to participate.' She was only the second woman to be appointed at her level of seniority for twenty years. The male councillors were unequivocally hostile.

> They would say things in front of me, like 'my God, how did we come to appoint a woman?' Or 'I'm sorry, here's our economic adviser, she's a woman unfortunately.' The Policy Unit ran a slate on who was going to get me into bed first. It was horrendous in the North. They sold the last woman into marriage in the market place in Barnoldswick, Lancashire, in 1926. Women are regarded as chattels. They are allowed to work, but men are supposed to run society.

This sense that running society is a man's job was not confined to the North. It was nation-wide and it also informed the terms of the political debate. As we have seen, women and men had different needs and experiences, and therefore different political priorities. But because men had traditionally controlled political life, it was they who set the agenda; theirs was the dominant view and it was they who defined what was important and what was not.

Real politics, according to the dominant view, was about the great 'out there' – about Money and Things. It was concerned with matters in the 'public world'. It embraced global problems of economics, technology, defence. It did, of course, play a major part in organizing and controlling the 'private' world of family, home and community. But this was not its primary concern; what happened there was incidental to the main business of the agenda.

Kath Mackey was one of many women who had found that their own priorities bore no resemblance to those discussed at political party meetings. A working-class woman, married with two children, she had started a community play scheme in her local park. 'The council used to run them. They'd just start one Monday after school finished and run it for four weeks and if it rained they sent the kids off home. Nobody in the community felt involved with it. So we challenged the recreation department for a play scheme which we could actually run.' While she was doing this, she joined the Communist Party.

INTRODUCTION

I went to a lot of meetings and listened to the people talking. They weren't talking about what I was even interested in. Because it was Sheffield, it was all industrial. They were talking about the wages struggle all the time, about trade-union issues, and I thought, they never talk about housing issues or what are we going to do with the kids, stuff like that.

In all parties and at all levels, there was a sense that what formed the fabric of women's lives was not a 'proper' concern of politics. No wonder, then, that so many women felt that politics had nothing to do with them.

We have pointed to a number of ways in which women were excluded, or distanced, from political power. But this was not merely a one-way traffic, with women on the receiving end. There was another mechanism at work. As we suggested earlier, women often chose to opt out, to boycott a process they found inhospitable, unpleasant and unconstructive.

At least until the televizing of parliament began in 1989, Radio Four's 'Yesterday in Parliament' provided the most vivid impressions that any member of the public could hope for outside the Strangers' Gallery of the workings of that august chamber. 'You'd think you were at the zoo,' said aspiring Tory parliamentary candidate Doreen Miller of the 300 Group, the organization committed to increasing the female contingent in parliament to 50 per cent. 'The screaming and the booing, the real nonsense of it, you can't tell me that is needed for good government. I think a lot of women would be put off by that. Who would want to go and stand up there and yell to get heard above that lot?'

From ward meetings and council chambers to the House of Commons, we found a strong distaste for the methods of politics. It was not that women didn't want power, but that they were reluctant to participate in a forum where the issues were clouded by posturing and game-playing. Lyn McLean was a co-opted member of Stirling District Council's Women's Committee, representing Stirling Women's Network. A member of the Labour Party, she used to think that she'd like to be a councillor herself.

I can remember a few years ago having a conversation and saying there's no point pissing about on the periphery, trying to get a wee drop of money here, a place there – we were never going to get any money. Women were never going to have any real influence until we were there in equal numbers everywhere, right through the whole system.

She still believed this in principle, but her experience on the council's women's committee had put an end to her own desire to join the political mainstream. 'Stirling is a titchy place, but it's the same machinations, lobbying, backbiting, cheating, losing sight of the objective and concentrating on the method, or, conversely, any means justifying the ends.' Lyn McLean, like many other women, found the world of formal politics un-congenial and unworthy, distorting cherished values. For her, the price of power was not worth paying.

Heather Mayall of the Women's Institute, an important and persuasive forum for women, was clear about her members' views on the political scene:

Members who complain we are getting too political are worried about party politics *per se* and also the way in which they are conducted at a national level – the haranguing, the ill-informed shrieking, the shallowness of understanding dis-played by MPs, the crudeness of expression. The Women's Institute specializes in 'informed opinion', so to hear ill-informed opinion expressed in Parliament is agony to some of our members.

Opinion poll data also suggest a female dislike for this advers-arial, competitive, combative world. Cynthia Cockburn analysed a range of surveys for her pamphlet *Women, Trade Unions and Political Parties*, focusing on the shifts in voting patterns by men and women trade unionists in the 1983 and 1987 elections, and the political attitudes of those groups. In all the surveys she found that women were more likely than men to say they 'neither agree nor disagree', felt 'neither this nor that'; and more women than men were to be found in the 'don't know' and 'no reply' categories. Where respondents were given the possibility of agreeing or disagreeing 'strongly', women more often than men made the more moderate statement. Cockburn commented: 'This – invariably overlooked in statistical analysis – may well be statistically the most significant gender gap of all. It is as though women sometimes boycott the very terms of political debate.'[43]

Sue Slipman, once president of the National Union of Students, an ex-Communist turned SDP political candidate, put it bluntly: 'Politics is a nasty, bitter, brutal world. It is not full of supportive people who are out to see you do well. It is very competitive and because it is so cut off from everything else, it is also not very rewarding. Very often, for women who are fairly sane, it doesn't seem worth the effort.'

Getting things done was a priority for women. When they did not see that happening, they began to feel that it was a waste of time. And time, as we have seen, was not a commodity that women had in abundance. Indeed, those domestic constraints on women's time might become a positive reason for not engaging in politics, especially at a national level. Harriet Crawley, who fought Brent East for the Conservatives at the 1987 election, was not one for pleading a special case for women, but she told us she knew able women who had decided not to pursue a life in politics because they wanted to put their families first – and the two didn't mix. She talked about the emotional deprivation of not being at home to put the children to bed or read them a story.

It has often been argued, by Mrs Thatcher among others, that women fail in politics because they are not assertive enough, they don't know how to sell themselves, that they are not prepared to push themselves. It is their fault that they are not selected for parliamentary seats, safe or otherwise. They are too humble. But another explanation, suggested by the Labour MP, Harriet Harman, was not based on female inadequacy but rather on positive choice. 'I know loads and loads of women,' she said, 'who've got bags of confidence and a great sense of their own superiority to the men they're working with who don't advance in politics because they don't like the circumstances.' What she was describing was not their inability to get up at a selection meeting and say 'I'm the greatest', but what she called a 'feminist aversion' to that way of doing things. If that was the way to success, women would rather not engage in it.

To suggest that women's behaviour was not aberrant or inadequate, but rather a different – and positive – response to politics, brought an entirely new interpretation to established findings. Until recently it has been conventional wisdom among political scientists to interpret women's apparent lack of political interest and activity as an indication of 'political inadequacy'. Almost invariably, when political views and voting patterns were analysed, women were compared with men on the assumption that men were the 'norm'. The assumed 'normality' of men had become the benchmark for 'desirable' political behaviour. As Cynthia Cockburn argued, this approach had two serious failings. First, it failed to question whether the political behaviour of men was 'normal'; secondly, it failed to consider the political behaviour of women in their own right.[44]

Traditionally, political scientists have paid little attention to women's political behaviour. Murray Goot and Elizabeth Reid, who made a close examination of women and voting studies, found that while women were the subject of very few studies, they frequently cropped up as 'an incidental concern': for example, in an American handbook of social psychology, only one page in a 143-page chapter on 'political behaviour' was devoted to them. Goot and Reid concluded: 'What accounts for both the regularity and the incidental nature of the data on women has little to do with any interest in women as such. Women are of interest only insofar as they resemble, or fail to resemble, men.'[45] Thus, women have remained invisible – unacknowledged and therefore deemed unimportant.

It will come as no surprise to learn that, when women did attract the interest of political scientists, they received less than glowing notices. Women were alleged to be 'less competent than men as citizens'. It was claimed that women were less likely to vote than men, were less interested and less well-informed about politics. If they did cast their vote, they were influenced by the nearest man, most likely a husband or father. Looked at from this angle, the pathetic creatures seemed barely capable of rational thought, let alone able to participate in affairs of state.

Jean Blondel, whose book *Voters, Parties and Leaders* (1963) became a standard text for politics students, listed women along with the very young, the very old and the poor as being among 'the perpetual and occasional abstainers' from the ballot box.[46] He noted that some female abstention may be 'artificial' because some women may be prevented from voting 'at the last moment, by some household chore', but he took it no further than that.[47] Less than twenty years after the publication of Blondel's book, the disparity in voting rates between men and women had almost disappeared. There was world-wide evidence that the longer women had the vote, the more they used it. Abstention by women in Britain was a result of specific conditions which were disappearing. The facts changed, but the idea lingered on.

Women who did manage to drag themselves to the polling station were said to cast their vote under the influence of either their father or their husband. 'The almost perfect agreement between husband and wife,' announced *The People's Choice* by P.R.Lazarsfeld et al., in 1968, 'comes about as a result of male dominance in political situations.'[48] If this were true, then it would be hard to know what to make of another cliché brought to us by political science: that women are more conservative than men – in the sense that they more readily vote for right-wing parties.

On the eve of the 1979 general election, Professor Ivor Crewe, TV election pundit, referred to the 'typical Conservative advantage amongst women'. Yet when the votes were counted, 45 per cent of women voted Conservative compared with 46 per cent of men. In 1987, both men and women supported all three main parties in equal percentages. There was no difference at all between the sexes in party preference when their gender was used as the sole measurement. But when other determinants, such as class and age were introduced, some strange things occurred.

One reason usually given for the traditional gender gap (in which women were seen as more Conservative than men) was the age profiles of the sexes – women lived longer, and older age groups were assumed to be more conservative. However, in the 1987 election, the only age group in which women were more conservative than men was the thirty-five to fifty-four group. In the sixty-five plus group, women were marginally less enthusiastic Conservative supporters than men.[49]

Among the young, meanwhile, there was a dramatic change in voting allegiance between 1983 and 1987. In 1983, men were to the Left of women in all age groups, especially among the twenty-five to thirty-four year olds. In 1987 men were only to the Left of women among the thirty-five to fifty-four age group. In all age groups, a higher percentage of women voted Labour than they had in 1983 and the women in the eighteen to twenty-four age band showed an 11 per cent preference for the Labour over the Conservative Party.[50]

If we look at the class divide, another sort of gender gap is apparent. Although professional, managerial and white-collar voters of both sexes showed a massive preference for the Conservatives in both the 1983 and 1987 elections, the women in the skilled and unskilled manual group shifted allegiance. Between the two elections they swung away from the Conservatives: 43 per cent of women manual workers voted Labour in 1987, compared with 34 per cent in 1983. Female trade-union members showed a similar shift – swinging five percentage points towards Labour over the two elections. While male trade unionists were well to the Left of female members in 1983, there was little to choose between the political allegiance of the sexes in 1987. What seemed to be happening, according to Cynthia Cockburn, was 'a much more dramatic change in women's voting behaviour than men's . . . women are on the move leftwards.'[51]

If women, by the late 1980s, were no longer the conservative sex, it did not necessarily follow that they espoused the same causes and pledged the same loyalties as Left-voting men. (Indeed, it would be hard to find women of any party with an identical political profile to men.) As commentators have begun to discover from opinion poll evidence, women have different political priorities. For example, 'progressive' political views held by women were not necessarily linked to traditional socialist issues like unions and work. Peter Kellner has pointed out in the *New Statesman*: 'On many issues that have little or nothing to do with class struggle against monopoly capital – from social polity to cruise missiles – women tend to be more progressive than men.'

Indeed, women's opposition to nuclear weapons produced the most conspicuous gender gap of all. According to a 1986 Gallup poll, 49 per cent of women believed that Britain should get rid of nuclear arms, whatever anyone else does; only 39 per cent of men agreed with that statement. On the controversial cruise missiles, focus of the Greenham Common women's camp and the revived peace movement of the 1980s, the gender gap was even more pronounced. In April 1981, a Marplan poll revealed that 56 per cent of women opposed cruise, compared with 43 per cent of men. Three years later – when cruise arrived in Britain – a Gallup poll found that 62 per cent of women disagreed with its presence, as against 50 per cent of men.

Shortly before the 1987 election, MORI asked a sample of voters what they believed to be the important issues facing Britain. There was little difference between the sexes about the six most important areas of concern – unemployment came top, followed by the Health Service and nuclear weapons. But a divergence between the sexes became apparent on other issues. Women were more concerned about social matters such as education and AIDS, while men chose defence and 'the economy'. The poll gave a tantalizing glimpse into what matters to women in politics, yet, as Barbara Rogers pointed out in *Everywoman* magazine, in 1987, a whole range of subjects that were likely to be of interest to women were omitted. What would the gender gap look like if the poll had included responses on care of the under-fives, violence against women, social security benefit or the environment?[52]

It is in the nature of the dominant political culture to ignore what have come to be called 'women's issues'. Political scientists operating within that culture have devalued women's political behaviour, interpreting their focus on so-called peripheral 'reform' issues as evidence that women understand politics less well. This was the argument at the core of the slur about women's 'incompetent' citizenship.

Once we reject the conventional view of the political analysts that women are somehow politically inadequate, we can assume instead that women's political behaviour is simply different from men's, but no less rational or normal. Yet women were still excluded from politics by a variety of means – some public, some private, some subtle, some crude. Many women made a voluntary choice to boycott the proceedings – a protest that has gone largely unnoticed. But in spite of all the obstacles, they were making an increasingly significant impact on the political process. In doing so, they were not only changing themselves, but changing the process too. In the following chapters, we chart their progress – both in the margins and in the mainstream.

PART II

Moving the Margins

CHAPTER 3

Lessons from the Coalfields

Talk about panic, I just dried up. My mind was a complete blank. I took a deep breath. I knew there was no way I could make a hash of it now. In my mind I could picture the lads' faces. They were all relying on us.

All my thoughts spilled out. I really let myself go. All our fears, pain and hopes came tumbling out of my mouth. I just had to let them know that we were fighting for our survival. Not only was it our fight, but the fight of every decent person in Britain . . .

The whole room went quiet. You could have heard a pin drop. What had I said wrong? I could feel my face going red, but relief, everyone was now clapping.

This was Norma Dolby's first political speech, delivered to the Great Yarmouth Labour Club in August 1984. In her diary,[1] published three years later, she described herself as 'just an ordinary miner's wife'. She lived with her husband and three sons in a small terraced house in a sleepy Derbyshire mining village. She would meet her friends for a drink in the local pub, do her chores at home and her part-time cleaning job at the Miners' Welfare; once a year she would go to Skegness for a family holiday. She never thought of politics and when she heard rumours of a coming strike, she hoped and prayed her Terry would not have to stop work. On 12 March 1984, she says, 'the Yorkshire pickets descended on our Derbyshire pits just like a plague of locusts.' The men came out, Terry with them. Norma resigned herself, assuming the strike would last a couple of weeks. 'We will just have to get on with it,' she thought.

By the time the strike was in its third month, her attitude

had changed dramatically. 'Getting on with it' no longer meant sitting tight and hoping for the best; it meant total immersion in the politics of the miners' struggle. Norma and other local women set up a group to raise money and provide food parcels. Soon she was out on picket lines, travelling to rallies in different parts of the country, spending whole weeks away from home on fund-raising trips, regularly speaking in public, and being interviewed on television. Her lifestyle, her ideas, her relationship, her sense of herself – all were transformed in the course of the strike. The home-centred housewife became a passionate political activist.

We have already described some of the general mechanisms by which women are excluded from power. Next, we explore the ways in which they overcome this process of exclusion. We look first at the realm of 'extra-parliamentary' politics: community groups, political movements, pressure groups, trade unions. What makes women get involved and what happens when they do?

Norma Dolby's story is remarkable enough. But what was truly extraordinary about the miners' strike of 1984–5 was that her experience was shared by thousands of women all over Britain. A unique event in working-class history, it was the longest-running national strike, and it was the first time a withdrawal of labour at the workplace had been translated into a full-blown political struggle, involving entire communities, and shared alike between the striking workers and their families.

Although the circumstances of the miners' strike were unique, what happened to the women in the course of it was not (apart from the sheer numbers involved). The manner in which they became politicized, and the form and content of their politics were, in many ways, characteristic of the experience of working-class women entering politics at a grass-roots level – whatever the immediate catalyst or cause. Thus, the women's stories that emerged from the strike illuminate a much broader picture of how and why, and in what fashion women begin to exercise political power.

Before the strike, the lives of the women in the mining communities – like so many others – were orchestrated around the workplace needs of their men. In their case, though, the orchestration was particularly finely tuned. Victor Allen, in his book on militant trade unionism, remarked that:

> every detail of the immediate environment of the miners – their leisure, their homes, family relationships, wives and children – has served the structure of their existence, namely the provision of labour power with given skills in required quantities at the right time . . . . In this process, women and wives have been adapted to meet the needs of mining as effectively as miners themselves.[2]

They were thus intimately linked to the politics of mining, yet by the same process rigidly divided from it. Most worked full-time and unpaid at home, or in part-time jobs which tended to be casual and not organized. As we noted earlier, trade-union membership is an established channel through which working-class people gain access to political power. The miners themselves belonged to the National Union of Mineworkers; few of their wives, mothers or daughters belonged to any union, and fewer still were active in union politics. They had no obvious route into political activity of any kind. 'The only interests I had before the strike were my house and my kids,' said Pauline Radford, whose husband Alan was on strike in the Nottinghamshire village of Blidworth. 'I thought I was quite content to be in my own little kingdom, my own little cell, whatever you want to call it, at home looking after the kids, doing washing, ironing and general chores.'

What drove the coalfield women into action was, in one sense, conservative (and in this respect their struggle was unlike many other political initiatives taken by working-class women, which tend to be geared towards changing, rather than conserving, the status quo). They wanted to protect the life they knew, to stop the government tearing it apart. The life they knew was one in which they were subordinate and powerless. And in spite of all that is said about mining communities being 'close knit', the women were, for the most part, isolated from each other before the strike began.

However, in the process of getting together and creating their own organizations, they changed the very nature of what they were fighting for. From the first, they were doing much more than campaigning for men's jobs. They were fighting for their children, themselves and all their futures. What changed was their vision of what lay ahead – and in this respect their struggle *does* resemble others. Their vision came to include a new solidarity among women, a new sense of what women could achieve, and altered power relations between women and men.

The men were on strike to stop the pits being closed and to save their jobs for their sons. They had embarked upon a traditional confrontation to prevent scab workers undermining their bargaining power; this relied on a show of strength, and brought them into violent confrontations with the police, whose methods became increasingly ruthless and disdainful of civil liberties. Margaret Thatcher's government wanted a showdown with the National Union of Mineworkers in order to crush it once and for all; the ground had been carefully prepared, with social security payments to strikers having been cut back. Everyone knew the Tories were hoping that the men would be sent back to work by their wives, in the face of mounting financial pressure. This was said to have been a feature of several earlier strikes, enthusiastically reported by the Tory press who elevated the 'petticoat rebels' to something close to sainthood.

What happened this time was that women in their thousands broke out of domesticity and made it their job to ensure that the strike could go on. From its third month onwards the strike became, increasingly, an endurance test; a show of strength of another kind. It no longer mattered simply whether the men had the muscle to hold scabs from the gates, or foreign coal from the ports. It mattered equally, if not more, that everyone was fed and clothed, that debts were managed, that morale was boosted and that support flowed in from outside the coalfields. The capacity to keep going, against almost overwhelming odds, became an important yardstick by which the impact of the strike was measured. By forming groups to organize the beleaguered villages, to raise funds, to provide food and to drum up support around the country, the women changed the rules of engagement in this industrial dispute. It became *their* struggle – not just for jobs, but for the dignity and survival of their class and their communities.

'If the pits closed, we lost our whole way of life, our children's future was at stake and the villages we called home,' explained Pauline Radford. 'We all knew what happened to mining villages when the pits closed. They became ghost towns; none of us want to see that happening to our homes.'

There had, however, been pit strikes before, in which women had played no significant role – like the one that brought down the Heath government in 1974. What had changed between 1974 and 1984 to bring women to the centre of the stage?

A crucial factor was, of course, that the character of the government had changed. You didn't have to be highly politicized to see that the Tories were bent on destroying the power of the unions in general and the NUM in particular. The stakes were higher in 1984 than in 1974 – and the women knew it. The fact that there was now a woman at Downing Street may also have made a difference. 'Because Margaret Thatcher's a woman we expected something better from her,' Pauline Radford explained. 'When I watch her on television it makes me really angry and I don't think I'd be so angry if she were a man.' The rise of Margaret Thatcher did not make the world of politics seem any more accessible, but it did produce a sharper, more intimate kind of antagonism. She wasn't just a distant authority figure; she was a woman like them, and they would have to show her where to get off.

More significantly, it was during the 1974–84 decade that the Women's Liberation Movement made an impact on the general political climate. It was not a straightforward case of cause and effect. Feminist politics flourished during that time because attitudes towards women were already changing. But women's liberation created a considerable momentum of its own, speeding the process of change, crystallizing and articulating new ideas and helping them to spread. The atmosphere changed, so that in mining villages where no feminist had ever set foot and where 'women's lib' was well beyond the pale, women were, in their own fashion, getting 'uppity'. 'I think women have been gradu-

65

ally asking more and more questions over the last ten years or so,' was how Pauline Radford put it. 'Once you step over the first fence, you want to know what's over the next one and the next .... . The more we found out, the more we wanted to know and the more we wanted to do as well.'

Every woman involved in the strike seemed to share a similar sense of political awakening. 'I used to think that anybody that was political and made political speeches must have read a lot and must know a lot,' recalled Doreen Humber, Pauline Radford's next-door-neighbour in Blidworth, whose husband Pip was also on strike. 'Then I started to realize that I knew a lot too ... things I'd been hearing for ages and trying to ignore were still there in my memory and now they all fitted together and made some sense ... I started to realize I was a political person.' Lynn Beaton has recorded the stories of Pauline Radford and Doreen Humber in one of the best books about the strike, *Shifting Horizons*.[3] The two women first went up to the picket line in Blidworth out of curiosity. 'We were quite timid and stood on the corner a bit away from the main body of the picket,' remembered Pauline. 'Gradually we edged closer and closer. As we got near to the back line we saw there were some other women there as well. We didn't know them then ... one of them said, "Oh it's lovely to see some more women up here."'

Two main factors turned these and other women from nervous onlookers into confident participants: a newly-discovered sense of identification and common purpose with other women – what the women's movement has called 'sisterhood'; and hardship pressing in upon their communities. They acted spontaneously, in direct response to the urgent needs of their families; and it was the collective nature of their action that gave them strength. 'We used to talk to each other a lot on the picket line, we were all starting to get to know each other and there was an excitement in that,' said Pauline. 'By the fifth week of the strike, the hardship was really beginning to tell and the women started to talk about the need to organize some way of feeding everybody.' They decided to have a meeting. 'I liked the idea that I was going to be part of the fight. ... We were all very enthusiastic and determined. In that one week we had learned so much about the situation and our will to fight and win had become very strong, we almost felt as if we could do anything.'

'Setting up a committee' was the first step taken by many of the women's support groups during the miners' strike. This suggests a degree of formality that didn't actually exist. The Blidworth women, like other groups, were responding to suggestions from an outsider. 'A school teacher from Nottingham, Paul Thompson, had been up to the picket line and talked to Annette and Betty about raising funds. ... He'd also talked about the need for organizing a proper committee with a Secretary, Treasurer and Chairperson.'

Paul was a member of the Labour Party and 'seemed to know how to go about organizing things,' Pauline Radford recalls. Untroubled, evidently, by any culture gap between them, he helped the women prepare leaflets and drove Annette and Doreen into Nottingham to distribute them. 'At first they went into a health food shop because Paul wanted to buy some sprouts. ... The people in the shop were very sympathetic and offered to give them some potatoes and food ...' Paul helped them set up an interview with Radio Nottingham and arranged for them to speak at a meeting of the Trades Council. Later, he advised them to elect an 'acting committee', to distribute tasks among themselves, to keep accounts and records. He also told them how to conduct a meeting. 'Paul said that he had prepared an agenda. Most of us didn't know what that was. ... He taught us to go through the Chair every time we wanted to speak, we had to put our hand up ...'

They were grateful for advice and followed instructions up to a point. But for most of the time, they simply made things up as they went along, within a loosely democratic framework. Everyone had a say; some individuals came to the fore as group leaders; there were no hierarchies, no unnecessary procedures. It mattered a lot to them that they enjoyed what they were doing: they took great pleasure in each other's company, in what they dared to do and what they achieved. 'Having a good laugh' was not incidental to their politics; it was essential.

It was the women, chiefly, who carried the campaign beyond the coalfields, linking up with groups of supporters in different parts of the country. This in itself was a crash course in political education. Pauline Radford recalled a holiday she and her family spent at the home of a couple called Sue and Simon, who belonged to a support network in Cambridge. Sue had been a television researcher and was now at home with a small baby. Her house was large and comfortable; she lived in an easy, relaxed atmosphere, surrounded by the trappings of middle-class comfort. The Radfords were given every hospitality and made to feel thoroughly at home. At the end of the week they felt they were leaving 'a very close and dear friend'. But the comparison with life in Blidworth was disturbing.

> Alan was very impressed with what he saw as a calmness in their lives. He saw our life, in contrast, as being full of effort. Everything revolving around work. . . . I started to think about choices and I realized that the difference was that they had choices about what they did, we didn't have those choices. . . . I'd never really thought these thoughts so clearly before but the injustice of the whole system was presenting itself to me. . . . It has to be the whole working class, you've got to stand up and say, no more, we want things different and the sooner the working class find out they are strong enough to do that, then the sooner things will change.

Once the women became engaged in politics, neither their anger nor their enthusiasm could be contained within the immediate struggle. The whole world needed changing. So why not have a go? They had never operated in a conventional political framework, where issues are labelled, partitioned and shelved. They were untouched by cynicism. As Pauline Radford said:

> We all knew we'd never be the same again, that we'd always fight when we saw something we thought was wrong. Already there were other issues which we knew we wanted to get involved in. Mainly they were the peace movement and campaigns against cuts in the health service, but there were lots more. The situation of black people in Britain and the situation in Northern Ireland both worried us now because we knew what was causing those situations and we knew that the only

way they could be solved was by everyone standing up and fighting.

The explosion of political activity among women during the miners' strike has been claimed by some sections of the left as a welcome counterpoint to 'trendy, middle-class' women's liberation. Here were working-class women standing by their men. Here was a struggle pure and perfect, the class united against the forces of capitalism. If women were to dabble in politics (they implied), here was a fine example of how it should be done. This rested on a glib over-simplification of what the women were actually doing. The 'class' was not united, as some women in Nottinghamshire demonstrated when they escorted their husbands through the picket lines; standing by one's man was not necessarily a progressive action.

Nor were the women who supported the strike unequivocally welcomed by the men. They had to struggle to make their own terms and go their own way, in a society which had traditionally excluded them from any part in political decision-making. Many had to fend off opposition from the men – to defy them in order to support them, struggling with and against them at the same time. Suzanne Corrigan and Margo Thorburn reported their experience at the Suachen Bush strike centre in Fife:

Suzanne: The two weeks of the Easter holiday it was pandemonium in that strike centre, because a lot of the men were taking their kids with them for their dinners (the women's group wasn't formed then), and the men were trying to get a game of pool in between picketing and whatever. They couldn't do it for the bairns running about everywhere, so they decided that something would have to be done. That's how the women's group was started. They are not daft, they knew the summer holidays were coming up. They wanted us for marches, to make up their numbers, and they wanted us for this, this and that. But . . . don't open your mouth!

Margo: They wouldn't let us use the minibus [to take the children on outings], it was always going somewhere. We had a big argument about that. It was the strike committee, they

didn't want us there at all. The chairman of the strike committee said that women were only good for one thing, lying
on their backs. ... They really took the piss out of us as if
we were incapable of doing anything. We proved them wrong
and they didn't like that. They just wanted us to serve their
meals and that was that.[4]

Some men were more supportive, and their attitudes matured
during the course of the strike. Many learned to do household
chores, to look after their kids, to respect the women's views
and their contribution to the strike. But there was always an
undertow of resistance. The men wanted help with their strike,
not a women's revolution on their doorsteps, in their kitchens.

The women had gained confidence, independence, female
solidarity. They had travelled, made new friends, new connections, developed new ideas. When Pauline Radford and Doreen
Humber first went picketing, they would take frilly knickers to
wave at the scabs and shout 'Come and get these, you might
as well wear them, they're more suitable for you!' The idea was
to make the scabs feel ashamed that they were 'less than men'
for crossing the picket line. Soon, they thought better of resorting
to 'sexist' jibes. 'We never realized then that we were putting
ourselves down by doing it,' Pauline reflected. 'I suppose we
should have known something was wrong because the police
used to laugh.' As the strike went on, the Blidworth 'ladies'
began to see themselves in a new light.

> We realised that the men were men and not gentlemen and
> therefore we were women and not ladies ... we didn't want
> to be connected to those ladies who sat around and did
> nothing. Although it's only a word, it made quite a difference
> to the way we saw ourselves. We recognised a strength in
> the word women and we recognised our own strength, so
> from that time on we have always insisted on being called
> women.

Beatrix Campbell has pointed out that the emergence of women
into the political arena is sometimes described in a 'tone which
infantilises women, which suggests that women are children

who have finally come of age.' Not so. 'What isn't admitted is that the men of the mining industry have finally been compelled to come of age, to join the twentieth century.'[5] This point was neatly illustrated by one woman's account in a booklet produced by North Yorkshire Women Against Pit Closures:

> I've had a rough marriage. What I had to put up with. He used to knock the hell out of me – he put me in hospital once or twice. I had to wait on him hand and foot. When he got back from work his dinner had to be on the table, or else. But since the strike's been on it's all different. He cleans up now, and washes up. I can go out, and when I come in he'll make a cup of tea for me. I can go and lie down for an hour. I couldn't wish for a better husband, and that's God's truth. And yet before the strike, I sometimes wished him dead. I hated him so much. I shall be sorry when the strike is over, if it's only for our own marriage.[6]

Not only did the women develop a pride in being women and a consciousness of the condition of women; they also challenged the power of men and the meaning of masculinity – not by waving frilly knickers at the scabs, but by redefining femininity and expressing their own power. They found there was a life – and a part to play in politics – beyond their own front doors. By going out and getting on with it, they assigned to men a new role within the home, at least for the duration of the strike.

'The strike was a diving board for a lot of women,' recalls Kim Young of Castleford. 'They were able to say what they actually felt. A lot of women were married to men working shifts who never really realised they had children. Mine actually discovered where the switch was on the hoover.' So women began to 'name their discontent', just as others had done in the consciousness-raising groups of the Women's Liberation Movement. Talking to each other gave them strength. 'I enjoyed being the "enemy within"', says Kim Young. 'I remember one woman said: "I never knew there was life after marriage." That summed it up for me: I realized I didn't want to be married. I wanted to live on my own, do what I wanted in my own time.'

There are optimistic, even triumphant, aspects of the story of the coalfield women. It is also a story of suffering and defeat. As the winter of 1984 drew on, cold and hunger took their toll in mining communities. Christmas brought the added burden of trying to provide something special for the occasion. There were appeals to the public and charity flowed in, requiring a massive amount of extra administration. Many women took the view that if they could get through Christmas, they could get through anything. Inevitably, though, they were worn down both physically and emotionally. As more men drifted back to work, the effort of keeping spirits up was nearly intolerable.

Nevertheless, the women's support groups were almost universally opposed to a return to work. They begged the men to stay out. The crunch came on 3 March 1985. A special meeting of NUM delegates in London voted narrowly, 98–91, in favour of return. No respite had been won for the pits doomed to closure, no amnesty for the miners who had been sacked during the strike. Many of the women felt betrayed. After all they'd endured, after all their efforts, surely the union couldn't give up, with nothing gained? Many of the miners felt the same way, but this was the point at which the women came face to face with the limits of their power. Unlike the men, they'd had no say in the decision to strike a year earlier, and they had no say in this decision either. Their views were irrelevant, they were not even consulted. They were not members of the NUM.

That early sense of omnipotence ('together we can do anything') had failed them. They had transformed the miners' struggle from a short-term physical contest into a long-term endurance test, and they had made history. But in the end endurance had not been enough. They, like the NUM, had overestimated the true extent of support in the trade union movement, and in the country at large. Whatever it took to confound the Thatcher government, they didn't have it. The men marched back to work behind their banners. Women marched with them and cheered them on – a final moment of dignity and solidarity. What was left to them now that it was all over?

Their political consciousness had been awakened – an irreversible process. Friendships and alliances had been established between women that would not be broken. Relations with men had changed, the balance of power had been disturbed and would never be quite the same again. These were significant gains.

Many of the women's groups continued to meet and work, trying to relieve the intense hardship caused by accumulated debts, and campaigning for the reinstatement of sacked miners and the release of those in prison. It was hard to keep up the momentum. There was less time for organizing and no time for travelling, once the women resumed sole responsibility for running their homes and feeding their families. 'We were determined not to drift away home and forget what we had learnt and the friends we had made,' wrote Cath Cunningham of Dysart, Fife in August 1985.

> This was what everybody said at the time, but in reality there have been many women who have not come back to the women's groups. One year on strike (fourteen months in this area) takes its toll on you. Many feel they need a break, a cooling off period. Of course in the majority of homes there is pressure from the menfolk to get back to the way things were before the strike. Many of us are still going through hell to get to our meetings. I think that many women would come too, if there was not the difficulty of transport. There are also their child-care commitments: the men are back on shift-work, so the child-minding is left to the woman.[7]

While some dropped out, others tried hard to maintain the solidarity and spirit of the strike. Women Against Pit Closures, the national body which co-ordinated the women's support groups, attempted to negotiate a relationship with the National Union of Mineworkers which would last beyond the strike. What they asked was that WAPC should have associate membership of the NUM. This would give them no voting rights, or any access to the union's resources. But it would be seen by the women as official recognition of the role they had played, and of their continued involvement in the politics of the mining industry. Once again, they felt the limits of their power; the strike was over and women were no longer participants but supplicants. 'We were told that certain Areas of the NUM threw up their

hands in horror when they first heard about it and weren't prepared to look at the details of how or whether it could work,'
records Dorothy Phillips of Newbridge, Gwent.

> One of the strongest votes against it was in South Wales. . . .
> Yet we *are* part of the NUM, we are *bound* to be part of the
> NUM. I think with the way things are developing that before
> very much longer, the NUM will want our support again –
> unless we have a change of government – and won't find it
> so forthcoming. Because women will say, 'What's the point?
> You only want us for tea and biscuits'.[8]

In Scotland the men responded positively, in 1985 conferring
upon WAPC associate membership of the Scottish Area of the
NUM. The question of national affiliation went to the union's
annual conference. The men said no but eventually agreed to
associate membership in 1986.

The women wanted to continue their political work, to build
on their knowledge and experience, to use the energy that still
flowed abundantly for some – and they wanted to do this in the
mainstream of labour movement politics, alongside the men, just
as they felt they were doing during the strike. Yet in the end there
seemed to be no way that they could get into the mainstream.
The union, bound by its own history of male exclusivity, could
not bring itself to create a space for them. A large number of the
women joined the Labour Party, which was ill-equipped to tap
this phenomenal new political resource. It was compromised by
its own ambivalence towards the strike and – for reasons we shall
discuss later – it was constitutionally inept at relating to working-
class people outside the trade unions. The women found themselves in an institutional vacuum. As a mass organization, they
had nowhere to go. They were left to their own resources, to do
what they could in small groups or as individuals.

They were welcome to join any number of voluntary organizations and issue-based campaigns – and they did. Many fulfilled
promises to support those who had supported them – such as
Health Service workers and unemployed groups. Many threw
themselves into campaigning for nuclear disarmament, building
on links made during the strike with the women of Greenham

Common (of whom we shall hear more later). Some organized around feminist issues. Some got involved with Greenpeace and other environmental groups. Some made connections with groups trying to stop nuclear testing in the Pacific, and with those fighting apartheid in Southern Africa. There were individuals who became school governors and community organizers, some who became party activists – in the Labour Party and other parties of the Left.

In May 1985, Durham Women Against Pit Closures decided to invite women from a range of groups and campaigns outside the coalfields to discuss how they could co-ordinate their efforts. They wanted to help each other in a way that sustained rather than drained their energy, and which minimized competition between groups who prioritized different issues. They set up a network called Links, an information exchange through which groups could publicize their campaigns and draw support from beyond their immediate constituencies – to 'widen the web'. Its first major venture was a protest against nuclear energy in the wake of the Chernobyl disaster. There were demonstrations outside electricity showrooms all over the country and on 25 June 1986, groups of women and children presented petitions and letters to the British government and to foreign embassies in London.

Links was 'about doing it for ourselves,' explained Anne Suddick of Durham Women Against Pit Closures, 'choosing our particular focus and priority and working on that with respect and support and sometimes direct involvement from those specifically concerned in other areas. . . . It meant bypassing the destructive "flavour of the month", demo-hopping mentality fostered by the media who have their own agenda and only notice our needs and struggles when it is convenient – and even then they distort, isolate and compartmentalize what we are doing.' Unlike its midwife, Women Against Pit Closures, Links made no attempt to engage with the political mainstream. Instead, it tried to deal with the consequences of women's exclusion by enhancing the power of groups operating on the margins.

CHAPTER 4

Making Connections

In the story of the coalfield women during the miners' strike and its aftermath, there are certain themes which we found recurring whenever we came across women who were involved in politics at a grass-roots level.

While women in general were excluded from the political process and deterred from taking any kind of action, the numbers who fought back were impressive. Wherever we looked, women were organizing around issues that affected their day-to-day lives in the community. Sometimes with men, sometimes without, usually in small groups, campaigning or taking direct action (often both) – for better housing, better health care, for child care, community centres, street lighting, transport and so on. Our impressions were borne out by Beatrix Campbell in *Wigan Pier Revisited*:

> In all the towns I visited there was a plethora of women's groups fighting their local authority landlords, fighting for nurseries, for better health care for women, organizing mothers' and toddlers' clubs, girls' nights in youth clubs and children's playschemes. ... Women's community politics around housing, health and children – the same preoccupations as united their working-class antecedents throughout the twentieth century – are a continuing indication of women's resilience.[1]

In Chapter 2 we examined the main reasons why women felt excluded from politics. Here, we have tried to trace the paths by which they overcame that exclusion and got involved. We found that women's political priorities were usually different from men's, reflecting the way their lives focused primarily on the sphere of reproduction. (By 'reproduction', we mean not just child-bearing and rearing, but all the work that goes into sustaining human life in the family and community.) Men's priorities reflected, by contrast, their traditional association with the sphere of production – whether or not they themselves were in paid employment.

To engage in political activity wasn't a *normal* thing for women to do, like getting a job or a home or getting married or having children. It represented a break with convention which could be painfully disruptive. The motive had to be strong. More often than not it was a form of crisis-management – a way of dealing with problems or needs that pressed urgently upon themselves or their families. This was what happened in the coalfields when women faced a crisis caused by men going on strike. Other women became politicized through their own industrial disputes. (We deal with workplace politics in more detail later.)

Children's needs (for education, child care, play facilities and the like) were frequently a catalyst. So, too, was domestic violence. Women were sometimes so thoroughly trapped in their homes – without time or resources, or even permission, to go anywhere else – that violence was the only thing that would force them out. And getting out of the house was the first thing they had to do if they were ever to engage in political activity. Among many of the groups we interviewed, we found that violence (unlike politics) was *normal*: being beaten up at home was part of life's routine. Lois Acton, a development worker at the Beormund Community Centre in Bermondsey, South London, told us: 'Almost every woman that comes into the building, their first reason for being here is that they're having problems with the men they live with. They're getting knocked about and they just need to escape for an hour or two a day.' The Beormund put on a range of classes and facilities and made a special effort to cater for local women. Once there, they had a chance to talk to each other, find out they had things in common, build alliances – all essential steps towards becoming more powerful.

A couple of hours' respite was enough for some; others, who needed to stay away for days or weeks, or for good, might find themselves in a Women's Aid refuge, part of a national network of safe houses for battered women which had its origins in the Women's Liberation Movement of the 1970s.

The Women's Aid refuges were an important point of contact between a largely middle-class political movement and working-class women. For some, like Mary Merrin, going to a refuge was a political baptism of fire. Mary's father had been a farm-worker, then a miner. Her family was Labour, she told us, but not political. 'Being Catholic was about the most political thing in my life, going to mass every Sunday.' She worked in factories, got married and had two children. Her husband became so brutal, she fled for her life. 'He tied my hands up and tried to drown me in the bath. He put a plastic bag over my head and tried to strangle me. I had bruises all over my neck.' She ended up in a refuge, and made her first contact with feminism. 'The people in the support groups were very political. I suppose it's the nature of the work; being involved with people who are battered, you tend to be on their side really strongly.'

As a rule, the Women's Aid supporters were careful not to preach or propagandize among the battered women who came to the refuges. For every woman like Mary Merrin, there were no doubt several who rejected the politics, or were too preoccupied to notice. But Mary *did* notice and found – as many women do when they are first exposed to feminist ideas – that her life was suddenly, and quite traumatically, transformed.

> I jumped into it really deeply. I'd been put down for so many years. I was always strong and challenged everything, that was probably one of the reasons why I got beat up so often, because I confronted everything. When I came into the refuge I had to have my say and got involved politically in a woman's way. It was quite instant but I didn't know what I was actually doing for quite a long time.

When she and her two children moved out of the refuge, they started living in shared houses with groups of predominantly middle-class feminists – an experience Mary said she wouldn't recommend for working-class people like herself. ('They had no idea about my life and I had no idea about theirs.') Eventually, she got a place of her own in a housing co-operative. But she felt increasingly at home with feminist politics, and continued working at the refuge, first as a volunteer, then as a paid employee. It was an intensely political environment. She was dealing every day with some of the worst effects of male power and female powerlessness, with poverty and homelessness, with the inadequacies of the law, the police and the welfare state. These were all things she had suffered herself, and she was able to confront them from a strong base of female solidarity and collective self-help. People brought their problems to her and she found she could shoulder more than her share of responsibility. It was all 'quite heavy', she said, but she got a lot out of it. 'After two or three years I sifted out what I wanted and I think what happened to me is good.' She retained her woman-centred view of politics and power. 'Whatever party you're in, women have to go out and do it on their own, and whether you're pushed into it or not, women have to fight on their own or with other women. Men have never helped, they've only hindered.'

Not surprisingly, we found that a fair number of politically active women came from political backgrounds. But we seldom came across working-class women who were simply following a family tradition. This was more common among middle-class women who were inclined to see politics as a career in which they might tread in their parents' (usually their father's) footsteps. Working-class women had to find their own reasons for getting involved, based on their own experience. Once that happened, their childhood familiarity with the nuts and bolts of politics eased the transition. Sheffield city councillor Pat Nelson told us: 'I've always been involved in leafletting and doing things like that, without realizing, in a sense, what I was doing. It's just something that happens. Your home is always used for a committee room, but you don't consider it in any way. It's just part of your upbringing.' It wasn't until after she had grown up, married, had two children and divorced that she got into politics herself.

I decided I wanted to do something other than just being a one-parent family. So I went to college and became a youth worker. I got involved in local issues, things like – we haven't got anywhere for our kids to play. I never considered that writing to council and complaining about this and setting up groups to get a play area was political. Possibly it was in me, coming from a political family. I never thought of it that way.

Janet Hudson, another Sheffield activist, maintained that if you were brought up with politics, it never left you, even if you didn't understand it at the time. She remembered that politics at home were 'very left wing'. Her father was a miner, her mother a canteen manager with British Steel. Both were members of the Labour Party, but Janet says she grew up 'apolitical'. 'I never read much, I was a solid Labour supporter but not really understanding why.' The fact that her dad was a youth leader and 'always did something good in society' was more influential. 'I just thought rather than going out to the club every night, drinking and carding, that it would be much better if I did something useful in society.'

Her husband Paul was active in trade-union circles and through him she became interested in the ideas of the Communist Party. They both joined – to the horror of Janet's parents, who ostracized her for years afterwards. Not wishing to be 'just a card-carrying member' she began, like Pat, to campaign for play facilities on the council estate where she lived. 'I put a notice in the shop window and had a meeting every week and got twenty to thirty women involved . . .' Once she'd started, there was no turning back. Time passed, she moved to Leeds, had children, but there was always something that needed changing, and it was usually right on her doorstep. 'Often I felt, oh god, I wish it didn't bother me, I wish I could be like everybody else and go to a night club and have a good time and forget about it, but once you become political you can't suddenly switch off. You might have a year out, but you come back.'

The influence of the Women's Liberation Movement could be detected almost everywhere women were organizing. It was seldom acknowledged to be influential, and the effect could be subtle or slight. But there it was: a change in the atmosphere, a change in the way women perceived possibilities, a changing sense of what was natural and right, and what was not. It is impossible to measure the extent of it, but the influence of women's liberation, directly or indirectly, tipped the balance for many women between organizing *within* subordination, and organizing *against* it. We look more closely at women's liberation later on.

A theme which cropped up regularly in the accounts of women organizing was the intervention of an outsider. Usually middle-class and well-educated, often public-sector workers, these individuals would form a kind of human bridge of information and ideas. Sometimes, they would be acting in a purely voluntary capacity – like Paul Thompson, the Nottingham school teacher, who happened to take an interest in the struggle of the miners' wives of Blidworth. In other cases, the intervention was an extension of the outsiders' paid employment – depending, it seemed, on how the individual interpreted the job.

Tony Oliver and Roy Crowder, Adult Education workers, featured in Jan Burrows' account of setting up the Five Arches Community Centre. Jan met the two men through the local school, where she and some of her friends took an Open University course. 'Tony came to talk to us on classes in the area. Our first reaction was "who does he think he is?", but he was a key figure in our change.' When the women began to meet regularly at Jan's house, he and Roy often popped in. 'They never forced any of their ideas on us,' said Jan, 'but they continuously gave us support and encouraged us to organize ourselves.' Tony and Roy were on hand when the women decided to occupy the disused school buildings. 'They helped with organizing the legal side of the fight. They told us who to contact, councillors, local authorities, newspapers, radio, etc. . . .'

For the women who attended the Beormund Community Centre in South London, Lois Acton and her co-workers did more than simply enable them to escape from home and attend classes. The centre was a political place – not party-political, but connected with local issues and campaigns. Women who passed through its doors were exposed to political ideas and actively encouraged to develop political skills. 'We put microphones up in the hall two or three times a week so that anyone can have a go,' said Lois Acton. 'We want to demystify the business of speaking in public. You can see people blossoming.' Similarly, the Women's Aid feminists played a key role in developing political awareness and skills in women like Mary Merrin who came to their refuges.

In some instances the intervention came through official channels – a deliberate effect of local authority policy. When we met Rose Thomas, Yvette Adams and Sharon Felix in Huddersfield, they were working together to set up a day nursery on their housing estate. All were black single parents who had been surviving on social security and, when they were lucky, on part-time jobs. What they all said they needed most was financial independence – decent jobs so they could provide for themselves and their children. That's why they wanted a nursery. 'We might just be sat here saying we need more nursery spaces, not knowing who to approach,' said Rose Thomas. What had broken that impasse for them? They had attended a training course, funded by the local authority, which was specially designed for black women with children, to help them set up their own businesses. While they were on the course, they had a meeting with an officer from the local housing department, who talked with them about what could be done to help black people on their estate. It was out of this session that the nursery project emerged: a need translated into a plan of action. 'It took some convincing for me to believe we could do it,' Rose told us. 'The course gave us the opportunity of feeling that we're just as capable of doing things as men are. It worked on our self-confidence, our awareness, it taught us about computers. We don't doubt ourselves any more.'

These outside interventions might have provided the beginnings of a political education for women who were in no position to get it anywhere else. They filled a vacuum left by the failure of political organizations to develop any real links with working-class women whose lives were centred on their homes and families, rather than on paid employment. They were sometimes patronizing or even manipulative, but they were seldom unwelcome. Women always felt they were starved of knowledge and weren't fussy how it was served up. They learned how to sort out what they needed. But the process was utterly haphazard. A woman's chances of encountering an outsider who would show her the ropes, and the quality of the advice she received, would depend on her own circumstances, on the political sensitivity of the individual concerned, and on where she lived.

Where women set up their own organizations, they tended to favour loose, non-hierarchical structures and procedures, based on co-operation rather than competition and on informal consensus rather than on voting and majority rule. Their style of organization echoed that of the Women's Liberation Movement and, like the women's groups of the late 1960s and early 1970s, it was based not on any established political formula, but on a tradition of female-centred community activity (jumble sales, children's parties, church bazaars, knitting circles, etc.) that had existed for generations. We would not wish to imply that all women are perfect democrats (or anarchists, depending on your point of view); the literature of the women's movement has produced many instances of women being overbearing, inconsiderate, even tyrannical towards each other in small, informal groups. But our evidence did suggest that, left to their own devices, groups of women were not inclined to reproduce the formal, hierarchical structures that were associated with men's politics; they were more likely than men to favour a relaxed, sociable approach, to be open to 'everyone having a say', to be unimpressed by precedent or ceremony, to recognize only minimal distinctions in status between themselves, and to be deeply suspicious of anyone putting on airs. It could be argued that these are not political virtues, but merely a symptom of powerlessness: if you're running the world, you need correct procedures, brother. The case remains unproven, since women have never had that privilege.

The link between pleasure and politics was also a common theme. Women liked to enjoy their politics. This wasn't simply an indulgence. It was the way they generated energy and harnessed enthusiasm. They had fun, laughed a lot, took pleasure in each other's company. Perhaps it was because there were so many other claims on their time and energy, and because their lives already offered too much hardship. Pleasure was an integral part of the political process for them, because it helped make life worth living in the present, while they struggled to make it better in the future.

There was often trouble from men where styles or interests clashed within political groups. Cheryl Brown told us what happened when a group of men approached the women at the Five Arches Community Centre.

> About six came and they all wanted this tenants' association. We thought it was a great idea. We set up the association and it came to choosing the officers didn't it? But they'd already worked it out that a man would be the chairman, the secretary, the treasurer – and we would do the typing and answering the phone and all this. One or two of them, as soon as they realized they weren't going to be officers on the tenants' association, we didn't see them again.

It was hard for men to accept women organizing autonomously – unless it was done in such as a way as to leave no ripples on the surface of their own lives. It was harder still to accept women taking the lead in joint political actions. (The miners had been able to accept what happened during the strike because the women's actions served the men's interests as well as their own, and because the period of the strike was understood to be a temporary interruption of life's normal pattern.) When men began to intervene in a Liverpool housing co-operative, the effect was disastrous – as one of the women founders recalled:

> They thought the thing had just happened. They never thought we'd given half our life to it and sat up till four in the morning working on it. There'd been no animosity before, then they moved in and tried to reorganize everything and introduce committees. It happened when the money started coming and things started happening, but I don't know where they were when we were marching.

There was often a utopian idealism about women's political vision, seldom found among seasoned politicians. It was this kind of vision which inspired Links, the network set up after the miners' strike. Apartheid in South Africa, nuclear power, police powers, racism, sexism, health and environmental hazards, unemployment, Third World poverty, nuclear weapons – all were part of the same system of 'exploitation, male violence and capitalism,' wrote Anne Suddick, in an article setting out the philosophy of Links. 'Human and civil rights and freedoms are the first victims sacrificed to the arms race, the profit motive and nuclear development. That is why we must make common cause with struggles for peace, freedom and independence throughout the world.'

Women had no vested interest in existing power relations. They were unconstrained by the conventions of masculine politics, where established procedures dictated the pace of the action. They seldom felt they were part of any political tradition (the history of women's politics having been suppressed) and so they carried little or no political baggage. This could be a weakness and a strength. Lacking experience, they could be naive. Unencumbered by knowledge of past defeat or disillusionment, they were hopeful and fearless. Less preoccupied with the trees, they were sometimes better able to see the wood.

But another recurring theme was this: no matter how successful women were at organizing at a grass-roots level, their power was limited while they remained outside the circles where key policy decisions were made and implemented.

CHAPTER 5

The Impact of Feminism

The influence of the Women's Liberation Movement could be detected almost everywhere women were organizing. It would be hard to overstate its importance in relation to our subject. The very questions we are exploring – about how and why women begin to exercise power – are themselves part of the same political development.

This is not the place for a full account of women's liberation. What we aim to do here is to examine its role as a political catalyst for the women who participated, and to explore its wider influence on political ideas.

The term 'women's liberation' describes a distinct phase of the continuing women's movement (which has a much longer history). It grew out of the 1960s and flourished during the 1970s – an independent venture, outside the political mainstream, but outside through choice rather than necessity. The desire for political autonomy was one of the key elements of the Women's Liberation Movement.

When it began to take shape in the late 1960s, feminist politics was not in the culture at all. Which isn't to say that it was new. Mary Wollstonecraft and others before her had had many of the same ideas and fought many of the same battles. Yet the news had not travelled down the years, because women lacked the power to determine what was 'history' and what was not. An important achievement of the Women's Liberation Movement was to rediscover the history of feminist politics. But that took time and in the early days there was no sense of precedent. The new feminists had to start from scratch.

Many of the ideas which seemed outrageous then are now familiar, if not orthodox. It was, for instance, highly controversial in the late 1960s to demand that women should have a legal right to equal pay for equal work, or be admitted to jobs on an equal footing with men. It was no less contentious to claim that women should read the news on national radio or television – they were not considered to have sufficient 'authority'. Anyone who said that a woman should be prime minister would have been greeted with howls of derision on all sides.

It was outlandish to argue that women and men should share housework and child care. It was utterly novel to suggest that the use of women's bodies to advertise products was politically oppressive rather than simply morally offensive. And to propose that women should meet together without men and construct their own independent political forms was . . . well, *weird*. There wasn't even a vocabulary to convey some of these new concepts. 'Sexism', 'consciousness-raising', 'male chauvinism' and 'sisterhood is powerful' were all coined for the purpose.

What made it happen? Social and economic conditions had changed substantially since 1945. There had been a dramatic expansion of higher education for young women as well as young men, with the opening of the new universities in the mid-sixties. The arrival of the contraceptive pill gave women, for the first time, a degree of control over their fertility. More women were going out to work than ever before (at least, since the war), while the spread of fast foods and labour-saving domestic appliances eased the burden of work in the home. The economy was sufficiently strong to suggest that horizons would continue to expand. Yet there was no correlation between the possibilities that were opening up for women and the prevailing view of how women *ought* to behave. This view would have it that 'real' women stayed at home to care for their homes and families – venturing out only to shop diligently with their husbands' money and to decorate the environment. It was not surprising, in the circumstances, that women were inclined to be discontented with their lives.

There was, meanwhile, a growing political turbulence in the United States and Europe, with civil rights marches, anti-war demonstrations, sit-ins and strikes, culminating in the dramatic events of 1968, when students and workers took to the streets of Paris. Conditions were ideal for fermenting women's discontent into rebellion – especially among the young, urban middle classes. Many of them had been on the fringes of student politics; they had breathed the air of the libertarian counter-culture. 'Freedom' was a word on everybody's lips, yet it didn't seem to apply to them. Young men championed the causes of Vietnam, of blacks and workers everywhere, preaching 'free love' and 'power to the people', but were apparently blind to the subordination of women in their own organizations and families.

Spontaneously (it seemed), women turned to each other and began to discuss what was happening to them – first in the United States and a couple of years later in Britain. They discovered that problems they had once thought to be personal and private (and usually their own fault) were shared by women in general, and this set in train a process of placing women's shared experience in a political framework which challenged existing power relations between women and men.

'The personal is political' was a phrase invented by the Women's Liberation Movement to describe its basic approach, which flew in the face of convention. 'We regard our personal experience, and our feelings about that experience, as the basis for an analysis of our common situation,' declared an early manifesto from the radical New York Redstockings. 'We cannot rely on existing ideologies as they are all products of a male supremacist culture. We question every generalization and accept none that is not confirmed by our experience.'[1] Small, informal discussion groups became the primary units of the movement. 'Our first priority isn't to get over information, but to know what everyone in the room thinks,' explained the first UK women's liberation magazine, *Shrew*. 'We believe in getting people to interact, not to listen to experts. We want them to *themselves* make an analysis of their situation, which will lead them to action.'[2]

In some ways, the effect of the Women's Liberation Movement in the late 1960s and early 1970s resembled that of the miners' strike on the coalfield women in the mid-1980s. It was a sudden, intense, exhilarating and often painfully unsettling encounter with a political struggle which bore directly on their immediate personal circumstances, and which transformed their sense of themselves, their relations with women and men, and their attitudes to the world around them.

Sally Hutton joined one of the early women's groups in London: 'I had studied politics for my degree, but it was always remote, it didn't have anything to do with me,' she recalled. 'I suppose feminism was what brought it home.' Sally's parents were both teachers and she had graduated from Sussex University in 1969. Shortly afterwards, she became pregnant and married, leaving a job she enjoyed on a local newspaper and moving to London, where her husband was training to be a doctor. 'I was at home all day and I hated it. I loved the baby, and even wanted another one. But I was lonely and I really felt I'd messed things up. I started to panic that my brain would never work again.'

What kept her going were her friendships with two other women who lived nearby, both with children the same age as hers. When a curious notice about a meeting of the 'women's liberation workshop' appeared on the local library notice board, the three women went together to see what it was about.

> I was spellbound; I'd never seen a group of women all together like that before. They were talking about the role of the family and why we needed to find alternative ways of living. Someone said it was important for small children that they didn't spend all their time in female company. I'd never thought of that before.

Sally and her friends took home a pile of leaflets and offprints of articles and discussion papers. Before long they decided to meet regularly to discuss what they were reading and to invite other women to come along.

> We talked about our husbands, our children, about equal pay and family allowances and orgasms and make-up and high-heeled shoes. We read avidly, a lot of stuff from the States as well as Germaine Greer and Juliet Mitchell. We questioned everything, we told each other our troubles and built up a really intense group feeling – friendships that would last a lifetime. It was such a passionate time. We were meeting once

a week and going to other meetings and conferences and demonstrations. We just couldn't get enough of it for a time. The ideas were so completely new, unheard of. It was like finding hidden treasure. They were all about us, intimately about us. And at the same time they were about all women and all men, about the way the country was run, about – literally – changing the world.

The first national women's liberation conference was held at Ruskin College, Oxford in February 1970. This and subsequent national conferences, held once or twice a year until 1978, brought together women with a great diversity of views. There were some, who became known as radical feminists, who traced women's oppression to the biological distinction between women and men. Others, mainly socialist feminists, argued that male supremacy was a social and economic, rather than a biological, phenomenon. Some were essentially reformers, campaigning for legal and practical changes. Others were Trotskyists, Leninists, Maoists. All managed to unite behind a set of basic political demands – for equal pay, equal education and job opportunities, free contraception and abortion on demand, and universal and flexible nursery care. These were the four original demands of the movement, but in fact they conveyed little about its real nature. It was far more than a pressure group and reform was not its chief preoccupation. Above all it was a movement to increase the power of women in both the public and the private spheres.

Following the Ruskin conference, the Women's Liberation Movement began to take on a distinctive character and form. It became a loose federation of autonomous groups. There were no leaders or hierarchies and, after some preliminary faltering, there were no men at meetings or conferences. The new feminists had no respect for established procedures or structures. They wanted to create the kind of power that would grow organically, rather than to seize the citadels that men had already constructed. It meant finding ways of organizing which encouraged the participation of ordinary women and facilitated open discussion, both to ensure that their aims were rooted in women's experience, and to spread the power of decision-making. As Sheila Rowbotham argued, the conventions of many political organizations on the Left would inhibit rather than increase the power of women:

> If you accept a high degree of centralization and define your-selves as professionals concentrating above everything upon the central task of seizing power, you necessarily diminish the development of the self-activity and self-confidence of most of the people involved. Because, for the women's move-ment, the development of this confidence and ability to be responsible for our own lives was felt to be a priority, this became part of the very act of making a movement. ... We had to learn to love ourselves and other women so we could trust one another without falling back on men.[3]

The approach was not unproblematic: an open, unstructured organization did not necessarily function in a fair and democratic way.[4] Nor was it new. 'Participatory democracy' had a long tra-dition, from early dissenting religious groups to the anti-authori-tarian movements of the late 1960s, and even without the influence of women's liberation, women's groups tended to-wards informal, non-hierarchical ways of organizing. However, the new feminists developed this way of working probably further than any other movement or organization before them. They studied its problems, adapted it in various ways and per-sisted with it, insisting on – and demonstrating – the interdepen-dence of form and content.

As a political apprenticeship, involvement in the Women's Liberation Movement was a uniquely rich experience. It led women to develop a theoretical perspective on male power and the forces that sustained it; by analysing 'patriarchy' as a system of male power which pre-dated capitalism and helped to form its character, they gained new insights into the causes of female subordination. Women's liberation also enabled them to explore new ways of organizing with other women. Maureen McMahon was training to be a teacher in Leeds when she first joined a Women and Education group, which combined informal discus-sion with research into sexism in schools. 'I learned to value the company of women in a way my mother's generation never did,' she told us.

> It was far more enlightening and interesting than being with men – and it was funnier. We shared a complex, conspiratorial, anarchic, rude sense of humour. I'd never thought of meetings as being a place for laughter, rather the reverse. But we made a big thing of being open and letting everyone play an equal part and building each other's confidence, and that's what made it relaxed and easy.

This wasn't just a hedonistic impulse. It enabled them to build up a sense of solidarity and that made them more powerful.

> We gave each other so much support, we were able to confront what was going on – in our relationships at home as well as in the education establishment. We started going round to schools giving talks, and we always went in twos and threes. It was all pretty basic – like why boys seemed to be better at science. But it was early days and this was fresh ground. We got through to a lot of people.

Through consciousness-raising groups, through issue-based networks like the National Abortion Campaign and Women's Aid, through groups working in various ways around education, child care, psychology and the arts, through community-based women's centres and self-help groups – through all these and countless other channels, women learned about the possibilities of gaining more control over their lives and wielding more political power. They discovered that if they got together they were stronger. A group of North London feminists who set up a women's centre at Essex Road in 1974 wrote a leaflet explaining.

> When we find that we do share experiences, it's not only a big relief, but it makes it easier to try and change things that need changing – whether it's the planning of the street you live in, or whether it's about contraception or child care, schools, problems at work, etc. We think that women are in a really strong position to change things – because they are close to the root causes of day-to-day living, both in the house and at work.[5]

Many had their first opportunity to develop the conventional political skills of organizing meetings and demonstrations, writing leaflets and press handouts, speaking in public and lobbying councils and parliament. 'I didn't know at the time that I was becoming what you might call a "political animal",' Maureen McMahon told us. 'But that's what it was. We had to find out how to put pressure on the local education authority. We organized public meetings and we managed to get some of our ideas across in the local media. We also found out about the barriers and pitfalls – like how you can be stonewalled by the council, or made to look a complete idiot in the press. We were very naive at first but we weren't stupid; we tried to learn from our mistakes.'

One difficulty that dogged the Women's Liberation Movement was the distance between its egalitarian goals and its organizational base. It was, from the outset, committed to liberating women of all classes. 'We identify with all women,' declared the Redstockings' manifesto. 'We define our best interests as those of the poorest, most brutally exploited women. ...' But it remained a predominantly middle-class movement, vulnerable to accusations of being out of touch with the majority of women.

There is no doubt that middle-class women built the movement. Its politics were based on analysis of personal experience, and it was therefore inevitable that the movement would reflect, first and foremost, the needs and problems of the women who formed it, and those of working-class women only as they were perceived by middle-class women.

On this last point it resembled many left-wing organizations in Britain, Europe and the USA, whose goals were based on the needs and problems of working-class people as perceived by their male and predominantly middle-class leaders. Where it ceased to resemble those organizations was in its commitment to participatory democracy and to building power organically; it was not in the nature of the Women's Liberation Movement to swoop in and tell the working classes what to think and whom to follow, or to seize control of existing organizations. All it could do was make connections, on the understanding that working-class women would find their own routes to liberation.

It was wonderfully useful for men to dismiss women's liberation as 'middle-class'. Men of all classes and political leanings employed the slur, to undermine a movement which sought to diminish their own power and privilege. But while it was true that the groups and conferences which gave the movement substance were predominantly middle-class, the ideas and goals that gave it political momentum were not. Women of all classes wanted more money, better jobs, less time spent on domestic work, decent nurseries, more choice in matters of reproduction, freedom from violence and sexual coercion, respect from their fellow beings and, in general, more control over their own lives. Even if middle-class feminists *had* been entirely preoccupied with themselves and had never troubled to make connections with working-class women, they could hardly have failed to raise issues that were vitally important to them. In fact, only a minority were too busy either trying to politicize their navels, or climbing career ladders raised in the name of equal opportunity, to care what happened to sisters beyond their own field of vision.

As Lynne Segal pointed out in *Beyond the Fragments*:

> Many of the initiatives of the women's movement in Women's Aid, rape crisis centres, nursery campaigns, cuts campaigns like the one to defend the Elizabeth Garrett Anderson hospital in London, and others, clearly do involve working-class women. The women's movement did mobilize in defence of the Trico women on strike for equal pay, and the Grunwick strikers who were demanding union recognition. Many feminists have been active in trades councils and tenants' associations . . . .[6]

One of the earliest campaigns involved members of London women's liberation groups in leafleting office blocks in the early hours of the morning, in support of a move by women cleaners to organize themselves into a union. As time went by the trade-union movement became the main site where connections were made between women's liberation and working-class women.

But making connections across classes was not an easy matter. Women's liberation involved changing consciousness, building a new awareness, and there weren't any short cuts. Every time a new individual or group became involved in the process, it was necessary to begin at the beginning, with every woman going at her own pace. Feminists who had been in the movement for some time, who knew the language, who were familiar with the arguments, who wore the clothes and the hairstyles that became associated with the movement, could be awesome to newcomers of any class, and positively alienating to working-class women who did not even share their pre-feminist experience. It took a rare combination of political sensitivity, understanding and empathy on the part of middle-class feminists to overcome this problem and build mutually beneficial links with working-class women. Some had what it took; some didn't.

A more serious problem was posed by an apparent conflict between working-class politics and the Women's Liberation Movement. Most working-class women who came into contact with feminist ideas and understood that they were subordinate as women within their own class, nevertheless had a sense of divided loyalties, for it was evident that the men in their families and communities were also oppressed – as they were themselves – by the class system. As we saw with the coalfield women, they had to struggle with and against their men at one and the same time. And there was bound to be a hesitancy about lining up with a movement that was predominantly middle-class. Ethnic minority women faced similar difficulties, as we shall see.

Socialist feminists, who represented a strong current within the Women's Liberation Movement, argued (convincingly, in our view) that there was in fact no conflict between the goals of feminism and the goals of socialism. After all, wasn't socialism about the redistribution of power and resources, on an equal basis? Surely, then, it couldn't be grafted on to a patriarchal system in which men had more power and more resources than women – and used those privileges to hold women in subordination? Women's liberation was the rock on which socialism had to be built. As Lynne Segal put it:

Women are central to the struggle against capitalist social relations not only in the workplace but also in the home. We are demanding that men change themselves, that they change their relations to women, and to children, and take on some of the nurturing and caring work which women have always done. . . . This is the way in which we want to transform the nature of working-class politics, and overcome the divisions within the working class . . . a Marxism which does not base itself on feminism, which does not recognize that the division within the working class and society as a whole necessitates a strong and autonomous women's movement, is not what we call 'socialist'. It will not liberate women.[7]

All the same, middle-class women who were committed to socialist as well as feminist goals had a relationship to men in their own communities that was significantly different from that of working-class women; they could struggle to change their men in the interests of women's liberation *without* at the same time struggling to defend them in the interests of their own class. They could understand the need to fight with and against working-class men *without* having to confront them in their own kitchens. This unavoidable distinction – rather than any actual conflict between socialist and feminist politics – was perhaps the main reason why class remained problematic for the Women's Liberation Movement. The movement could not dissolve class barriers; most working-class women continued to feel distanced from it.

It would be misleading, however, to measure its value or its impact by the numbers who were directly involved. The Women's Liberation Movement was more than the sum of its groups. It exerted a far wider influence – on political life and on the public consciousness.

First and foremost, women's liberation was a celebration of womanhood and the company of women. It helped put about the idea that women could become more powerful by organizing together ('sisterhood is powerful'). Women's caucuses and committees in trade unions, political parties, local authorities and other bodies multiplied in its wake.

It also created a critical momentum behind the campaign for equal rights, which led to the enactment of equal pay and opportunities legislation in the mid-1970s. The campaign had its roots in the 1950s, but it was not until the late 1960s that it made any significant impact – with the first 'equal pay strike' at Ford's. Women sewing machinists at the Dagenham and Halewood motor factories came out in support of their claim to be re-graded as semi-skilled, rather than unskilled, workers. In the end they had to settle for 95 per cent of the male semi-skilled rate, staying within the unskilled grade, but they had brought production at Ford's to a standstill and put equal pay on the political map.

In the House of Commons, meanwhile, the first Private Member's Bill to outlaw discrimination against women was introduced by Labour MP Joyce Butler in 1967; it was followed by a succession of similar bills over the next five years. The Equal Pay Act was passed in 1970, with implementation delayed for five years. As employers used the interlude to segregate male and female workers, thus avoiding the intention of the new law, it became increasingly clear that, without a parallel law against sex discrimination, the Equal Pay Act would be worse than useless.

The climate of the late 1960s fuelled the militancy of women in the labour movement, just as it helped to inspire the early women's liberation groups – and each drew strength from the other. The new feminists took up the call for equal pay and opportunity, which reached its height in 1973 when two Private Members' bills seeking to outlaw sex discrimination were passing through parliament at the same time. There were mass lobbies of parliament, angry demonstrations, packed meetings and torchlight processions down Whitehall. By the time the Heath government fell in 1974 there was a sufficient head of steam behind the campaign to make the new Labour government bring in legislation of its own.

Laws enacted in 1975 and 1976 not only outlawed some forms of sex discrimination in employment, education and provision of goods, facilities and services, but also provided limited maternity and pension rights. They did little to shift age-old patterns of discrimination and disadvantage, and it has been argued by some that they simply kept the lid on women's discontent. But they did improve conditions for some individual women and they did contribute to a major shift in public opinion. It was no longer controversial, by the end of the 1970s, to claim that women should be admitted to jobs on the same footing as men, and be paid the same as men for doing the same kind of work. The idea was abroad that women could do what men could do (including combining parenthood with paid employment) and should be given a fair and equal chance. Even though this did not reflect the reality of most women's lives, it disturbed the consensus about what that reality should be.

Women's liberation was responsible for developing a body of ideas about systems of male power or 'patriarchy' – how these came about, how they operated and how they interacted with economic relations. These questions remained controversial within the women's movement as well as among men. But the important thing was that they had been put on to the agenda.

The idea that there was a political dimension to women's personal experience spread well beyond the early consciousness-raising groups, giving a much wider range of women new confidence in their own judgement, which enabled them to express their discontent and seek solutions. Previously 'hidden' problems became public knowledge: domestic violence, for example, had been considered a private matter which should not concern the state until it became the subject of feminist campaigns.

This new perspective gave rise to strong criticism of the traditional division of labour – an arrangement which designated men as the main family breadwinners and women as secondary wage-earners whose primary role was to look after home and family in an unpaid capacity. What began as an expression of discontent by mainly middle-class women on both sides of the Atlantic, housewives who were feeling bored and unfulfilled at home, had far-reaching political implications. The division of labour was a determining factor in wage bargaining and the provision of benefits; it was also one of the basic building blocks of male power and privilege. By conferring on women the 'double burden' of combining unpaid work at home with paid work outside the home, it trapped them in a cycle of relative powerlessness and poverty. By conferring on men economic power within the family, it held in place a web of conventions about the way men and women led their lives and saw themselves and treated each other – not just at home, but in the world at large.

The new feminists affirmed the *economic* importance of domestic labour, observing that without it there would be no reproduction, let alone production – a fact which had been ignored by generations of economists and politicians. They also pointed out that domestic labour was not a *natural* female function, and that the present arrangement was a political artifice which benefited men *vis-à-vis* women and capital *vis-à-vis* labour. In doing so, they exposed a conflict of interest between women and men within the working class – a heresy to the orthodox Left, but one which couldn't be dismissed.

More broadly, women's liberation helped to change 'common sense' about what women and men were like and how they behaved. The new feminists challenged prevailing patterns of male and female behaviour in all aspects of life: in bed, in the streets, in the kitchen, in the school room, in the workplace, in the media, in conversations and representations, in meetings, conferences and council chambers. They sought a new understanding of how meanings were attached to 'femininity' and 'masculinity', and introduced the possibility of changing those meanings. They argued, for example, that it was no more natural for men to be aggressive, loud and long-winded than it was for women to be submissive and silent; the idea that authority and leadership were 'masculine' attributes belonged to a political construction of gender which served to enforce the power of men.

Many of their arguments remained controversial. What changed was that the controversies created by women's liberation entered the culture. New generations grew up to whom they were accessible, if not familiar. Feminist views cropped up regularly in glossy women's magazines, in national newspapers, in television and radio programmes; increasing numbers of women who worked in the media were themselves feminists. There was a great outburst of women's publishing, creating a whole new body of literature – theoretical and documentary works as well as fiction. All the while, there was a strong current of male resistance, and the dominant view continued to endorse male power and privilege. But women's liberation made a deep and lasting impression on the landscape of ideas.

It is hard to be precise about when that distinct phase of the women's movement passed into history. After 1978 there were no more national conferences, but women's liberation did not so much *die* as *scatter*. Since the early 1970s, it had grown in strength and confidence; consequently, by the late 1970s, energies that had been focused inwards, on building a new politics, began to shift outwards and diversify, making connections with other struggles and changing in the process. What emerged in the 1980s was a new phase of the women's movement, inspired and still profoundly influenced by women's liberation, but more diffuse, less certain on some issues, less hopeful and sometimes less angry; it was also broader and more deeply rooted, more accessible, more experienced and in some ways more respectable.

One feature of that new phase was that feminists began to move into mainstream politics. From the late 1970s, increasing numbers joined the Labour Party. Women who had become politicized through women's liberation had learned both the value and the limitations of operating in small, autonomous groups within an unstructured political movement; they could change themselves, they could influence ideas, but when it came to changing the way the country was run, they had to rely on those in power giving way to pressure. Clearly, the powerful could not be relied upon. Nor could they wait any longer for the power of women to grow organically through consciousness-raising and participatory democracy. It was time to engage with power directly. They were no longer prepared to hover on the sidelines, watching new generations of articulate, well-educated, middle-class men dominate the field.

In the Labour Party, they revitalized women's sections, campaigned for constitutional changes that would give women more power in the party, and lobbied to get women's issues on to the agenda. Gradually, in some policy areas, what the party said began to reflect the influence of feminism. In 1983, some feminists joined the new Social Democratic Party and made similar efforts there – with some success. A few found a place among the Liberals, while the Conservatives nurtured their own breed of feminist. We shall return to the political parties in Part III.

CHAPTER 6

Black Women Organise

Afro-Caribbean and Asian women built their own political movements during the 1970s and 1980s. They saw that women's liberation was largely a white women's movement – and since it was committed to basing its political analysis and objectives on the personal experience of its participants, it had little to offer black women, whose history and whose lives were so different. They had to find their own ways of becoming more powerful.

Afro-Caribbean women had a long tradition of organizing to defend their communities. In the late 1940s and 1950s, when new immigrants to Britain were faced with poverty wages, abominable working conditions and some of the worst housing the country had to offer, it was the women who took it upon themselves to find collective ways of making life more bearable. Beverley Bryan, Stella Dadzie and Suzanne Scafe record in their book, *The Heart of the Race*:

> The hairdressing salon ... served many Black women as a meeting place and more often than not the 'salon' would be based in somebody's front parlour. ... Going along to have your hair pressed or relaxed was a social event, an opportunity to meet and exchange stories with other women. And the woman who was the best source of information was, of course, the hairdresser who was well-placed to give advice, support and reassurance to others.[1]

Out of this kind of informal networking, so typical of women's grass-roots activity, the 'Pardner' system developed – a self-help scheme for collective saving. 'Nine of out ten of the pardner schemes had a woman in charge of them. It was done on a village or family basis. Whoever's needs were greater, they got the deposit on a house . . . . It helped pay the mortgage, but it also provided us with somewhere to go.'[2]

Increasingly, Afro-Caribbean women became active in the struggles of the black community against mounting racial discrimination and abuse. They mobilized alongside men in the Black Power movement, which was inspired by Malcolm X and other radical black leaders in the United States, and which identified with liberation struggles in Africa. It was an intensely political time. By the late 1960s there were organizations and pressure groups up and down the country who pursued with a new militancy the fight for black people's rights. 'Demonstrations, boycotts, sit-ins, pickets, study circles, supplementary schools, day conferences, campaign and support goups – all had become commonplace activities, exposing both young and old to their politicising influence.'[3]

As their political awareness grew, Afro-Caribbean women became more conscious of how they were constrained, as women, within their organizations, and how this limited their political effectiveness. One account, recorded in Bryan et al., tells how women members of a youth group were undermined and overshadowed by the men, who regarded each female newcomer as sexual prey:

> In that atmosphere, you felt vulnerable and exposed as a woman. The men certainly didn't understand anything about women's oppression. In fact, they didn't have the faintest clue about it. . . . Some women were badly mistreated, but the way the leadership tried to deal with it was similar to the way they tried to get new ideas through to the membership generally. Brothers were hauled up and disciplined when what they needed was political education – to read, study and discuss the woman question and to confront their own sexism. No attempt was made to take seriously women's issues, they just weren't considered immediately pressing.[4]

Whatever else was different, there was little to distinguish the behaviour of black and white men towards women in political groups. 'The brothers used to be busy making all the decisions, taking all the initiatives, and we got to take the minutes, make the coffee, that sort of thing.'[5] Sexism was shared quite equally, it seemed, across the racial divide. For black women, however, the question of how to respond was a far more complicated business. They needed to assert their own voice, define their own goals and wield power as women. Yet they could not afford to break ranks. Ultimately, the extent to which they could become powerful depended on the strength and solidarity of the black community as a whole. (To a degree, white working-class women – the miners' wives, for instance – were in a similar position, but there were crucial differences. The black community was embattled not only by economic disadvantage, but also by racism – and that came from sections of the white working class as well as from the middle class and the state.)

Afro-Caribbean women saw how their brothers, sons, husbands, fathers and lovers were being criminalized by oppressive laws and policing methods, as well as by economic discrimination. Their struggle against the sexism and violence of those same men had to be carried on with backs turned against a white state, which might otherwise exploit divisions between them. For example, white women who were beaten up at home might sometimes feel they could call on the police for protection; for black women this would mean handing over their men to a force that represented an institutionalized form of violence.

The first caucuses of Afro-Caribbean women were formed during the early 1970s. They began to discuss their common experience of racial and sexual oppression and to organize around issues of particular concern to black women – such as child care, housing and work. They felt themselves to be influenced less by white feminism than by African women engaged in revolutionary struggles in Mozambique and South Africa: 'Those sisters weren't just picking up a gun and fighting – they were making demands as women, letting it be known that they weren't about to make all those sacrifices just so that they could be left behind when it came to seizing power.'[6]

In some respects, the political goals of the Women's Liberation Movement seemed to conflict with the needs of black women. One of its chief campaigns, for example, was to defend the rights of women to abortion, yet black women were often under pressure to terminate pregnancies they wanted to keep, or to be sterilized before they were sure they did not want any more children. Many also took the view that white women, who shared racial privilege alongside white men, were part of the problem black women faced, and that the white women's movement took no responsibility for its own inherent racism. It was not surprising, then, that when they began to organize, they could not simply *join* the existing women's movement, but had to create a movement of their own.

'There were no models for us to follow, no paths laid out,' recalled members of the Brixton Black Women's Group, set up in 1973.

> We just had to work it out as we went along. We were very wary of charges that we might be 'splitting the Black struggle' or mobilising in a vacuum or imitating white women. These were the kinds of criticisms Black men were making at the time. We couldn't be – in fact, we never were, anti-men in that sense. But it was so good to be in a group which wasn't hostile and didn't fight all the time. That sense of autonomy, of woman-purpose was something everybody felt at the time, though.[7]

This group, and others formed in the same period, mobilized around black women's needs and at the same time were in the forefront of struggles involving the whole community – for instance, against the notorious 'sus' law, which was being used by the police in some areas as a form of racial harassment. The Brixton women also made links with women in Africa and with Asian women in Britain.

Inevitably, the experience of Asian women was quite distinct from that of Afro-Caribbean women. They had different histories and traditions. Their communities tended to be organized differently, with more emphasis on small family-based businesses and private housing, so they encountered different forms of institutionalized racism. Many Asian women, especially in Muslim families, were confined to their homes for almost all purposes except education and paid employment, so they had little or no opportunity to organize. And Asian families suffered particularly acutely during the 1970s from Britain's racist immigration laws.

Consequently, the catalysts that drew them into political activity were of a different order. Although they were severely restricted at home, many Asian women were forced by economic necessity to go out to work – and it was in the workplace that they developed a sense of solidarity and self-reliance. Asian women were in the forefront of a number of important industrial disputes during the 1970s, including those at Imperial Type-writers, Grunwick and Chix. After three months on strike at Imperial Typewriters in Leicester in 1974, Shardha Behn recalled that the women had won few concessions from the management, but a great deal for themselves:

> The first day I got back to work, my foreman asked me what I had gained in the last twelve weeks. He was making fun of me I know. . . . I told him I had learnt how to fight against him for a start. I told him he couldn't push me around like a football from one job to another. . . . In the past when I used to get less money in my wage packet I used to start crying at once. I didn't know what else to do. I told the fore-man, 'Next time I won't cry, I'll make you cry.'[8]

Disputes over the immigration laws were another important politicizing influence. Anwar Ditta was one of many who had to fight for the right to live in Britain with her own children. Born in Birmingham and brought up in Rochdale, she first went to Pakistan at the age of nine, when her parents were divorced. She grew up, got married, had the first three of her five children, and returned to Britain in 1975. Her husband followed, and she expected their children to join them soon. 'I never realized there would be a problem – I am a British citizen,' she told us. 'I was just an ordinary housewife then. I wasn't involved in anything, just doing the cooking, working as a machinist, living in Roch-dale.'

She applied to the British embassy in Pakistan. They wrote requesting further information and gradually it dawned on her that she would have to fight. First, she attended a meeting of a defence committee set up to help Nasir Begum, another Asian woman who was having trouble with the immigration rules. She told them her own story. Next, she spoke at a public meeting in Rochdale on the Immigration and Nationality Act, and soon afterwards travelled to Manchester for the launching of the Anwar Ditta defence committee. 'The main skill I required was writing – I couldn't read or write properly then. But now I have learnt to read every single pamphlet, even if it takes me two hours. If I don't know a word I look in the dictionary.'

Anwar Ditta spoke at nearly 400 public meetings during her campaign. With her defence committee, she organized demonstrations, pickets, conferences, petitions. Granada Television took up her case. She travelled to Pakistan to find relatives and midwives who would testify that she was her children's mother. Only when Granada's 'World In Action' organized a blood test that proved her maternity beyond reasonable doubt did the Home Office relent and allow the family to be reunited in Britain.

When we met her eight years later, she was still working as a machinist in Rochdale, doing out-work with an industrial sewing machine in the back room by the kitchen. But now she also had an extremely busy life as a voluntary adviser, public speaker and campaigner. She had joined the Labour Party, but had declined invitations to stand for election as a councillor. 'I don't like the label "leader",' she told us. 'We can see what happens to them. I just want to help.' When her street found itself without water in the middle of the night, it was she who was called upon to contact the council and report back to the neighbours. There was so much to do that she had begun to worry about neglecting her family; they had no time for holidays or outings.

But she was not the only one who had changed. Campaigns like hers – and there were many of them – helped to change the mood among Asian women. As Parita Trevidi commented in *Feminist Review*: 'Through the political experience of campaigning and participating in important struggles, Asian women have broken away from the set roles prescribed to them by society'; at the same time, they 'provided essential organisational support and political back-up to individual women who are fighting for independent political status in this country.'[9] Anwar Ditta confirmed that impression. 'In the community I used to be isolated.

No one came on the demos, very few were in the defence committee. After the campaign, I find there are changes among Asian women. Some will talk about politics now. A lot of them are participating in the community. My campaign had a lot to do with it.'

Like Afro-Caribbean women, Asian women have had a complex and contradictory set of battles to fight in order to establish their own political demands, on their own terms. Family relations were especially problematic for them; as they began to organize, one of the things they did was to set up refuges for Asian women fleeing domestic violence or unwelcome arranged marriages. But their experience could not be explained in terms of white feminist theory, as Parita Trevedi pointed out: 'Within a marriage, it is not just the relationship that the Asian woman has to her husband that is a source of tension and inequality. The relationship of the woman to her husband's parents, brothers, sisters, lends a totally different dimension to the kind of force and violence she experiences.'[10]

For Asian women, domestic violence could not be dealt with in isolation from economic and racial discrimination. 'Very few have the necessary resources to contemplate life on their own with anything but trepidation,' wrote Trevedi. 'With employment prospects grim, welfare benefits inadequate, it is above all fear of economic insecurity that drives some women back to the marital home and not cultural traditions.' The tendency of Western women to see Asian women's oppression in terms of their culture and traditional practices suggested the problem was somehow one of backwardness. 'The solution which flows from this is that "modernity" – the change in attitudes to correspond with industrialised mores – is what is needed. This analysis is inadequate . . . .'[11]

One of the first Asian women's groups in Britain was Awaz, whose activities peaked between 1978 and 1980.

Amrit Wilson recalled what happened at that time in her book, *Finding a Voice*:

We took up and campaigned over immigration cases, we organized pickets over the issue of sexual harassment of Asian women at airports (virginity testing as it was called). We also organised a major national demonstration against state racism, and we supported women in struggles at work and were involved in setting up an Asian women's refuge. But in most of these things we worked with other groups – long established ones like the Indian Workers' Association of Great Britain, black women's groups and the then newly-formed and very male dominated Asian youth movements.[12]

For a brief but critical period between 1978 and 1982, Asian and Afro-Caribbean women joined forces in OWAAD, the Organization of Women of Asian and African Descent. Like those who built the Women's Liberation Movement, the women who formed OWAAD strove to create a non-hierarchical structure.

By devising a system of rotational representation, to take account of childcare demands and other commitments, it was possible for women to choose whether and when to participate in the overall running of the organization. Although the system was by no means flawless, it represented a new and self-determined approach to political organisation which remained unhampered by leaders or appointed spokeswomen.[13]

Three hundred attended OWAAD's first conference in 1979. Never before had there been such a gathering – with women of all ages, representing a great variety of backgrounds and politics. 'It really broke down that isolation, because black women realised from going there and seeing all those other women that there were a lot of us in the same position. So a lot of the difficulties we had as women started to be shared and discussed. . . .'[14] The effects were to ripple through the black community for years to come. Many of the participants were inspired to set up local black women's groups, some of which outlived OWAAD for several years. Others took back political demands which had crystallized during the conference and began to organize with men around specific issues.

Education, for example, emerged as an urgent priority. A group of parents in the London borough of Haringey, concerned about the high suspension rate of black children in their area, was prompted by the OWAAD conference to set up a Black Pressure Group on Education. They investigated the procedures used in different Haringey schools, publicized their findings in the local press and were eventually invited to meet the Local Education Authority. When the LEA attempted to side-step the issue by setting up disruptive units or 'sin bins' within schools, the group went into action again.

> We spent a lot of time visiting local parents, leafleting the community, writing to local schools to let them know our feelings about disruptive units and generally raising it as an issue within the community. ... To cut a long story short, we eventually won that battle, and the idea of disruptive units being attached to every secondary school in the borough was dropped. That was a really important victory for us.[15]

The fact that black women were active and involved was not, of course, without precedent. What *was* new, as Bryan et al., have pointed out, was that black women 'had begun to articulate *demands* as an organised *body*, with the assurance which could only come from a strong sense of self-knowledge and mutual solidarity'.[16] OWAAD quickly developed into a network of groups, campaigns and projects, liaising through a newsletter, FOWAAD. Afro-Caribbean and Asian women supported each other in campaigns against virginity testing at Heathrow Airport, against ethnic record keeping, in defence of those arrested during the Southall demonstration against the National Front in April 1979, against the 'sus' law, the racist use of the contraceptive Depo Provera, the immigration laws. ... The principle of Afro-Asian unity turned out to be more problematic in practice than in theory, according to Bryan et al., but 'Black women proved it could be done.'[17]

Unavoidably, there were differences of opinion within OWAAD – and disagreement was especially acute over the question of feminism. Some black women refused to be associated with the term, which in their view represented an ideology that was unacceptable, both because it was part of a white supremacist culture and because it was (or seemed to be) anti-men: 'If you're a Black

110

woman, you've got to start with racism. It's not a choice, it's a necessity.'[18] Others, meanwhile, set about redefining the term and claiming it for themselves: 'This has meant developing a way of organising which not only takes account of our race and our class, but also makes our struggles against women's oppression central to our practice.'[19]

Disagreement over this question caused deepening rifts in the organization that eventually led to its demise. In its short life, OWAAD had achieved a great deal. 'It brought Black women out of isolation and turned us into a force to be reckoned with in our own right,' declared Bryan et al. 'It became a forum for us to discuss and articulate our demands. And it represented a period of intense growth and learning for all Black women in this country, the repercussions of which can still be felt today. . . .'[20]

Far from being the end of black women's political organizing, the passing of OWAAD marked the beginning of a new period of activity. Many had their work cut out dealing with the aftermath of the 1981 inner-city 'uprisings' – setting up defence committees and police monitoring units and generally closing ranks in a tense and hostile atmosphere. Lord Scarman's inquiry into the causes of the Brixton 'disorders' recommended that funds be injected into deprived inner-city areas where black people were living. 'Almost overnight, a spate of new ethnic welfare projects, self-help groups, black women's centres and police monitoring committees appeared on the scene,' recalled members of the Brixton Black Women's Group, 'and because they were often the very provisions we had been demanding for years, our immediate response was to welcome them.'[21] Many black women became deeply involved in these new projects, bringing to bear all the political skills they had learnt over recent years. This development was not without problems: the paid workers were accountable to the state, not to the people; there was always a danger that state funds would neutralize the militancy of the community without helping to solve its problems. And while the state could give, it could also take away. By the mid-1980s, black communities found themselves bearing the brunt of government spending cuts – as conditions worsened in housing and local services, and as funds were withdrawn from community projects on which they had begun to rely.

Some five years after the demise of OWAAD, we met two groups of black women in Southall, West London. Until recently they had been operating as a single group. Both received funds from Ealing Borough Council. The reasons for their parting clearly echoed the disagreements within OWAAD: they had different views about their relationship to feminism and about their choice of political priorities and strategies. They also had a great deal in common. The differences between them – as well as the similarities – helped to illustrate some of the distinctive features of black women's politics in the late 1980s.

Sylvette Collins and Cynthia Alexander belonged to a group known as the Southall Black Women's Centre. Both felt they had been spurred into political activity by their experience of racism. Cynthia had grown up in Ladbroke Grove, the daughter of first generation immigrants from Sierra Leone who, she told us 'still had this thing that you've got to be humble'. She saw for herself how black people were victimized and bullied. 'I always said if ever there was an opportunity to stand up and say how I feel and try to stop other black people going through what I went through, I would do it. I can't change the world, but I can work towards it with other people who are also part of the same cause.'

Sylvette had come to Britain from the Seychelles – in her words, 'as a black servant'. She was already aware of the position of black women in this country before she came here, she told us. She had expected life to be hard and it was. The turning point came for her when she went on a march in 1981 organized to protest at the way the authorities had handled the New Cross fire – where thirteen young people died in what was thought by many to have been a racist arson attack. 'Women and men had come from all over the country. It was the first time I ever realized that we black people together could do something. Also, I was looking at the racism of the police.' (There were violent clashes between demonstrators and the police during the march.) 'That was what changed my life completely. I got involved from then. Coming here, to this group, has made me more positive in my action. What's helped me is finding other women who feel as I do.'

Neither woman would call herself a feminist. 'We don't fight against men as such,' Cynthia explained. 'If a woman comes to us for help – if she is a victim of domestic violence, for instance – our support is for her. We give no thought to the man. As black people we've got to work together. You've got more women organizing than men in the black community anyway, so if women didn't support the men, they'd be in real trouble.' Sylvette added 'If me and Cynthia walk down the street we are seen not as two women but as two blacks. So obviously you fight racism first.'

Their priority was to provide a place where black women could go if they needed advice, help or just company, in order to combat the effects of racism. They ran drop-in sessions for local women and their aim was to respond to whatever needs were expressed by the women who came to the Centre. Most often, that meant tackling domestic violence, racial harassment, and problems connected with immigration, housing and benefits. They helped women to find out what their rights were and to negotiate with the authorities. 'We leaflet housing estates, to get women to come forward and speak their mind,' Sylvette explained. Their strategy was to *enable*, rather than *direct*. They were equally willing, they said, to organize bingo or sewing classes, if that was what women wanted. The crucial thing was for women to get together in a supportive atmosphere. 'We are here to develop our abilities as black women,' Sylvette told us. 'So that we can feel as though we are someone, instead of feeling inferior. Then, together as one, when we have all acquired those qualities so that we are on the same level as anyone else, we can use them to challenge the barrier of racism which blocks our view. That is how we become more powerful.'

Pragla Patel and Rita Din belonged to the second group, Southall Black Sisters. As its name suggests, this was an overtly feminist organization, whose priority was to campaign around women's issues. It had been set up in the early days of the black women's movement, not long after the Brixton Black Women's Group was formed, and well before the two women we met became involved. Both were from middle-class Asian families; they had started to become politically aware while they were students: Rita had studied English and history at college in Winchester. Pragla had studied sociology at Liverpool. Ideas about racism and feminism, first discussed at college, were thrown into sharp relief when they returned home to Southall. They found solidarity and an outlet for their political energies in Southall Black Sisters.

'We feel we could do casework day in, day out,' Pragla told us, 'but it wouldn't change what's going on.' Domestic violence had become the main focus of their campaigning, which they pursued on behalf of women as a means of changing relations between women and men in the black community. In one case, they had read in the local newspaper about an Asian woman who hanged herself after enduring years of violence at home.

> We organized a picket outside the coroner's court. The inquest was over in five minutes – a lot of things didn't come out in the hearing. So we decided to protest outside the man's home. This kind of tactic is adopted in India. If a woman dies in mysterious circumstances, women in the area will get together and protest outside the house of the perpetrator, to publicly embarrass the family. We leafleted the street where the family lived and marched through Southall. Women who had gone through violence themselves took part. It wasn't a massive demonstration, but it made an impact.

Part of the strategy of Southall Black Sisters was to make links with white feminists and with campaigning organizations – black and white – in other areas. On one hand, they felt it was essential to organize around domestic violence and arranged marriages, because these were the main areas of conflict and oppression within the Asian community. On the other hand, they wanted to stress that the subordination of women within the family was not specific to their race or culture. 'We want the support of white women because we don't want it to be seen as an Asian phenomenon. We want to make the link to show that it happens to all women, Black and white, and across class as well.'

An important reference point for them was the women's movement in India, where the fight on women's issues was not confused by the 'double struggle' going on in Britain. 'When we are fighting racism we end up condoning some of the practices that take place within the community,' Pragla explained. 'We say our culture's fine, extended families are fine, we must keep our families together because the immigration laws divide us. Whereas in reality, those very practices are often oppressive to us women who live within them. In India and Pakistan you can see those things clearly.' They were unlike many black women, they told us, in not giving priority to the struggle against racism; for them, the struggle against women's subordination was equally important. And they were especially critical of whites who paraded their 'understanding' of sexist practices beneath the banner of anti-racism. 'When we go to social services – for example to try to get help for a woman who needs to escape from her family – people there who are trying to be aware say, "Oh, but in your culture you do things this way, maybe that's the best way, see how anti-racist we are." That attitude forces the woman back.'

They believed they had made some impact on the council's attitude: 'Domestic violence is suddenly on their agenda. They're thinking more about what women go through and what they should be offering to women.' But they also recognized how difficult it was to get through to local women. 'We've tried leafleting door to door, in translation. Southall is a very working-class area, the majority of women are from the Punjab and don't necessarily speak English. A lot of them are housebound.' They were committed to involving local working-class women in the management of the group.

> What should take an hour takes four hours. We have to interpret for them. These are not docile women, they make their comments. They are very supportive. It's just that they are not familiar with the structure, they don't know the jargon, they ask a lot of very obvious questions. It's awful at times when you are in a crisis and you have to take quick decisions, but it is the only way.

When we asked how they could become more powerful, they

replied that it would help to have more funding, wider recognition of groups like theirs and 'strong women on the council'.

There were striking differences between Southall Black Sisters and the Southall Black Women's Centre, but there were also important areas of shared commitment and experience. Both wanted to be identified with the working-class movement in Britain. Both were critical of white feminism. Sylvette Collins put it this way: 'Black women have to break away and make their own way if they are going to breathe, because white middle-class women tend to become managers of working-class womens's lives. They take the role of husbands, telling you what to do and how to think.' 'Some white feminists don't have a clue about racism,' said Rita Din. 'It is something I experience every day, so it is something I have to take on.'

Both groups insisted, too, that black women had to organize for themselves, because black men were at best non-supportive and, at worst, thoroughly hostile. 'A young Asian girl got raped, not long ago, in the underpass,' Sylvette told us. 'None of the men did anything about it. But if the National Front comes in and one of the men gets hurt, they all expect the women to come and support them.' Pragla Patel cited another, earlier case: 'An Asian woman had given birth to five girls and because of this her husband burned down the house; she was there with her five daughters. Nobody batted an eyelid. Women decided to come together, because they weren't getting solidarity when they asked for it, from men they were marching alongside.'

The two groups shared a dim view of black male councillors. 'They look upon us as though we don't know what we are talking about. We are too radical,' said Cynthia Alexander. 'The majority don't recognise the right of Black women to organise,' Pragla Patel confirmed.

Both organizations were primarily concerned with the same range of practical, everyday problems: violence, housing, health, poverty, child care. They were equally dedicated to empowering black women, and aware of the limitations of being a pressure group, sharing a sense of being held fast in the margins, unable to cover the great distance that separated them from real political power. They supported the Labour Party with equal scepticism and a deep distrust of politicians. They would vote Labour because there was 'no choice', but wouldn't join a party that had introduced racist immigration laws, and whose leaders were opposed to black sections. They agreed on the need for more black women to occupy positions of power in local and national government, but, as Sylvette Collins put it, 'In the end, being black is not enough. It's the policies that count.' Pragla Patel remarked that she had seen too many people whose politics had changed when they entered the mainstream: 'A lot of them are in there because they want to further their careers.'

What counted most to both was making sure that the voice of ordinary black women was heard and heeded by those in power. 'It's a long-term thing,' said Rita Din, 'getting more radical thinking in the black community, so that women begin to see themselves as assertive, independent, having a right to live as they wish.' Sylvette Collins explained:

> If black working-class women had a voice, they would attack the issues that affected them. Like child care and education. Like how come there is not enough housing, how come the streets are not well lit? How come the black families are in tower blocks and the white families are not? How come black battered women stay longer in refuges before they get rehoused? Working-class women can come here and draw strength from each other and talk as they want. By the time they finish they can stand up, even in front of Neil Kinnock, and say what they think.

For the Southall Black Women's Centre, the key to building up the voice of ordinary black women was to be 'ordinary' themselves, to keep a low profile, to avoid labels or tacics that might frighten anyone off, and to be a presence in the community that would slowly – they hoped – promote a sense of collective strength. Although they did not turn their backs on white feminists, they believed that an alliance with black men would ultimately prove more fruitful. 'If we move away from men, that means we are leaving them again in ignorance. By working with them together we can re-educate them to realize – come on, brother, we here too.' For the Southall Black Sisters, the key was to raise the profile of black women's politics; to demonstrate and campaign in order to raise awareness; to confront and to challenge; to make themselves heard in the community in a way that would alter the climate of opinion. They wanted to anchor their politics among local black women, but they were keen to make alliances across the race barrier.

> A lot of black women say to white women, 'go away and sort out your racism, leave our problems for us to resolve.' That's fine up to a point, we do want to determine as black women how we organize, what issues we take up, but when we ask for support, it's because we feel that white women should also recognize the things we have in common.

The two approaches represented a difference of emphasis rather than any profound disagreement. They could be seen as complementary rather than contradictory. They echoed some of the differences of emphasis among white women in the Women's Liberation Movement – and they continued to coexist, each giving strength to the black women's movement.

CHAPTER 7

The Spirit of Greenham

On 27 August 1981, a small group of women set out from Cardiff in South Wales to march to a spot near Newbury in Berkshire which was to be the first cruise missile base in Europe. Hardly anyone had heard of Greenham Common then. Nor did anyone – not even the women themselves – guess that this was the beginning of a major new focus of political activity: a women's peace movement. There were thirty-four women on the march, accompanied by four men and a handful of children. They covered a distance of 120 miles, declaring themselves 'Women for Life on Earth'. When they arrived, some of them chained themselves to the fence of the airbase – a decision taken during the nine days of the march. They delivered a letter to the Base Commander, explaining who they were and why they were there:

> We wish to be neither the initiators nor the targets of a nuclear holocaust. We have had enough of our military and political leaders who squander vast sums of money and human resources on weapons of mass destructions while we can hear in our hearts the millions of human beings throughout the world whose needs cry out to be met. ... We represent thousands of ordinary people who are opposed to these weapons and we will use all our resources to prevent the siting of these missiles here. We want the arms race to be brought to a halt now – before it is too late to create a peaceful, stable world for our future generations.[1]

The Commander came out to have a look at the women and told them: 'As far as I am concerned, you can stay here for as long as you like.' Had he known what was to happen in the following months and years, he would surely have eaten his words.

Heartened by the support they received, as news of their action spread, the women decided at the end of the first week to set up a permanent picket at Greenham Common. They called it a peace camp. Gradually, women from all over the country began to visit them – and were caught up in their enthusiasm. Wendy Franklin came from the Isle of Wight to join in the first rally: 'They reached out to us with their hearts surprising themselves and celebrating with us their new-found strength. We began to understand that the message of Greenham was "No one can do it for you, you have to do it for yourself." ' Some left, more stayed and the camp became established. 'Some of us had a private agreement that we would pack up the week before the CND October rally, walk to London and call it a day,' recalled Caroline Taylor, who arrived just a few days after the marchers.

> But support kept coming in the form of visits, presents and letters so that peace-camping became an end in itself, and our enthusiasm for it waxed rather than waned. Our arguments became more refined as we learned more. We all read books, many of us for the first time. We got more horrified at the extent of the arms race and rapidly became more radical as our 'normal' lives receded and we immersed ourselves in full-time 'public relations' work to get across our views. The idea of 'giving up' became impossible. . . . Within a few weeks I was no longer going home for visits. Greenham was my home.[2]

In this fashion, through any number of spontaneous decisions and actions, the character of 'Greenham' – no longer just a place, but a political phenomenon – was formed. People turned up with caravans, tents, a portakabin. One weekend, fairly early on, a visitor painted a big sign which said 'Women's Peace Camp'. Yet it was not until several months later that the women agreed to ask the men to leave. It was a highly controversial move at the time, but – contrary to the expectations of many women as well as men – it seemed to strengthen, rather than weaken, the camp's support. Through wind, rain and snow, through evictions by the local authority, through multiple arrests and escalating harassment by vigilantes, women held their ground and spread their message – not just across Britain, but around the world. A national network of Greenham support groups sprang up – again, spontaneously – of women who campaigned for peace and disarmament in their own neighbourhoods, as well as regularly visiting the camp.

The women were determined to be in control of their own action, and to do things their own way. They organized in an open, informal and non-hierarchical manner, much in the style of the Women's Liberation Movement, and resisted attempts by the media to focus on individual spokeswomen.

One of the main reasons why they had asked the men to leave the camp was that they were worried – especially as they planned their first major blockade – that men would more readily engage in violent confrontations with the authorities. The women themselves made a public commitment to non-violence. For some it was a strategy chosen for its practical advantages, as Barbara Harford and Sarah Hopkins explained in their book about Greenham: 'After all, we cannot match the resources that could be used against us and our non-violence makes it difficult for the forces of law and order to legitimise any mistreatment, especially if the world is watching.'[3] For others, it was a philosophy, in the spirit of Mahatma Gandhi and Martin Luther King. 'Violence breeds violence and damages those who resort to it. Means and ends have to be consistent.'[4]

They were also in revolt against the traditional style of peace campaigning – described by one woman from Sheffield:

There's a table at the top with three guys sitting behind it. There are rows and rows of seats. We all sit down, we're informed, and we find ourselves talking to the backs of each others' heads. ... They're all going on about SS20s, missiles, rockets, the next demonstration, all kind of political things I don't understand. ... They don't seem to *feel* about it. All they seem to do is work with their heads.[5]

The Greenham women created their own repertoire of non-violent direct action, both to draw attention to their protest and

to disrupt activities at the base. They lay down in front of bull-
dozers. They formed a human barrier to stop incoming vehicles.
They spun webs of coloured wool across the gates and these
became an international symbol of women's action for peace.
They 'keened' – a wailing lament, to express deep feelings of
distress and anger. They danced and sang: 'You can't kill the
spirit/She is like a mountain/Old and strong, she goes on and
on and on . . .' They used surprise to great effect, first to block
the gates when least expected, then to make sudden incursions
into the base itself.

On Boxing Day, 1981, a second peace camp was set up at
the air base at Molesworth, in Cambridgeshire – also due to
receive cruise missiles. By June the following summer, camps
had been established at nine other military installations around
Britain. Men were involved in some of them, but the women
of Greenham had taken the lead and set the tone. Peace-camping
was primarily a women's initiative and a women's activity. The
Campaign for Nuclear Disarmanent drew fresh strength and
energy from the women, and took on a whole new lease of life,
its membership swelling to unprecedented levels.

Greenham women (a phrase which described not just the
peace-campers, but their supporters too) became internationally
famous. They were deluged with requests to speak at meetings
at home and abroad, and visitors came to the camp from all
over the world. They received a huge amount of media attention
– some of it hostile and downright misogynist, some grudgingly
sympathetic.

In November 1982, eighteen women who had broken into the
camp and occupied a sentry box were tried at Newbury magistrates' court for 'behaviour likely to cause a breach of the peace'.
Defending themselves, they claimed the right to stop the British
and United States governments from contravening the 1968
Genocide Act, calling expert witnesses to explain to the court
why nuclear war amounted to genocide. The magistrates, who
were not persuaded, convicted the women and gave them a
choice of fourteen days' imprisonment or being bound over to
'keep the peace' for a year. The women pointed out that it was
not they who needed to be told to keep the peace. There devel-

oped a pattern of arrest and imprisonment reminiscent of the days when suffragettes were gaoled under the notorious 'Cat and Mouse Act'.

Meanwhile, the scale of protest escalated. On 12 December 1982, 30,000 women converged on Greenham Common to 'embrace the base', linking arms around the perimeter fence, which they hung with webs of wool and banners, children's clothes and toys, and photographs of loved ones. 'There was nobody giving orders or telling us what to do,' recalled Chris Mulvey who'd come from Dublin. 'We'd each had a message from the Greenham women, to bring a hymn to express why we were here and that was all. The rest was left to us.' Tents were put up, tea made, the fence decorated – an intuitive act of mass co-operation.

> Sometime during the day we joined hands and began to sing. Hand in hand in hand for nine miles we formed a living chain to lock in the horrors of war, to stand between them and our world and to say: we will meet your violence with a loving embrace, for it is the surest way of defusing it. How strong I felt when I joined my voice to the waves of voices shouting Freedom and when the echoes from so far away drifted across the base. . . .[6]

On New Year's Day 1983, forty-four women climbed over the fence and danced in a ring on top of a cruise missile silo. On 1 April, CND organized a human chain of 77,000 linking Greenham to Aldermaston, while 200 women staged their own April Fools' Day protest, invading the base dressed as furry animals for a Teddy Bears' Picnic. Later that month they padlocked all four gates with indestructible bicycle locks. In June, they sewed a four-and-a-half mile dragon, to weave in and out of the base. On Hallowe'en, they took down four miles of the fence with bolt cutters. . . .

But Greenham cannot be explained simply in terms of protest. It was also about community and co-operation, about the ways in which women acted together and interacted with each other. At the peace camps, they had to learn how to live together in adverse conditions, how to cook and wash and pass the time and look after children and take decisions in a manner which involved and satisfied – and above all *sustained* – as many individuals as possible. Creating an appropriate *style* of operation was as vital as keeping up the action.

Within the support network there were groups whose members combined a wide experience of both women's liberation and mainstream Labour movement politics, and who were able to distil that knowledge into their peace movement activities. 'We take a lot of care of each other,' explained members of the Common Singers, one of the Hackney Peace Groups. 'Our main thing is imaginative, non-violent direct action. It's always explicitly feminist and very supportive. We are determined that any political activity is not alienating. We've all had experience of that.' Most of them had served time in trade-union or Labour Party branches and they were committed to finding ways of organizing that enhanced their energies, instead of draining them. 'Within the group there's an agreement that you can drop out or not come to meetings and come back whenever you're ready. We all have busy lives, some of us have children and we need space for those things. It's the tale many women tell about keeping several plates spinning in the air at once.' The actions they planned often had an anarchic, theatrical quality – like dressing up as woodland animals for a mass trespass on the Trident base at Faslane – and were invariably intended to be fun as well as to make a point. If they didn't take care of each other, if they weren't able to have fun, they believed, they would burn themselves out and be much less effective in the long run. They were also strongly committed to making explicit connections between different political issues:

> A local hospital was being closed and we worked out that the cost of keeping Trident at sea for two weeks could keep St Leonards open for a year. 'Make the choice!' was what we put on our banner. So we were supporting the campaign against the health cuts, but bringing our own perspective to it.

In spite of all the efforts of the Greenham women, the first batch of cruise missiles arrived on 14 November 1983. Far from giving up at this setback, they adapted their strategies to demonstrate that cruise was not only deeply unpopular with the people of Britain, but that it would not work. On 11 December, 50,000 embraced the base, using mirrors to reflect it back on itself. Protests, arrests and imprisonments continued.

The new transportable missiles were supposed to be shifted around the country in deepest secrecy. A network of 'Cruise-watch' groups ensured that they never moved unnoticed, and that every flaw in the system received maximum publicity. They gave advance notice of the routes to be followed. They pursued the weapon launchers to Salisbury Plain. They even climbed on to the launchers and painted them. They were ready with cameras to record breakdowns and other technical failures.

By this time, also, the Greenham women had broadened their perspective very considerably from the days when their campaign had focused simply on the siting of cruise in Britain. They made links with campaigns in other parts of the world – with women from the South Pacific who were protesting against nuclear tests, with women struggling to free Namibia and stop uranium mining there, with Italian women trying to keep cruise missiles from the Cosimo base in Sicily, with campaigns to end the scandal of Europe's food mountains. They supported the coalfield women during the miners' strike, as we have seen, and campaigned with them against nuclear power and nuclear dumping. They fought a legal battle to establish that Greenham Common was, indeed, common land – in order to challenge the right of the military to build a base there in the first place. They identified and publicized a total of 160 British bases used partly or wholly by the United States Air Force ... and much else besides.

In 1984 a Gallup poll showed that 62 per cent of women and 50 per cent of men in Britain were opposed to cruise missiles. Peace movements elsewhere in Europe – inspired at least in part by the Greenham women – had also made an impact on public opinion. When the Soviet leader, Mikhail Gorbachev, signed the Intermediate-Range Nuclear Forces (INF) Treaty with US President Ronald Reagan on 8 December 1987, Greenham women could justifiably claim that they had helped to create the necessary climate for this small but significant step towards nuclear disarmament. The Treaty agreed to remove land-based cruise and Pershing missiles from Europe. This was not, however, the end of Greenham: there was too much scepticism about the effect of the treaty and too much alarm at what NATO could do instead – such as stepping up the numbers of air- and sea-based missiles. There was also the continued presence of US military installations in Britain, to which most Greenham women were strongly opposed, and the wide range of other campaigns in which they had become involved.

Greenham was far more than a pressure group or a single-issue campaign. It was a mass movement which drew thousands of women into political awareness and activity during the early 1980s. It introduced many of them to feminism; those who had missed the high tide of discovery and invention that launched women's liberation in the seventies made similar connections through working with other women for peace. It also propelled many who were already feminists towards a new range of political concerns – and thus revitalized the women's movement, which drew energy and inspiration from Greenham, as did CND.

It was never a working-class movement; indeed it was, like the Women's Liberation Movement, predominantly white and middle-class. To leave home and family, to live (even temporarily) in a peace camp, to put oneself in the way of arrest and imprisonment was extremely hard, involving great risk and sacrifice. It was not lightly undertaken even by the most independent and fancy-free of women. For a working-class woman with husband and children, a paid job on which the family depended and heavy responsibilities at home, it was unimaginable. But the emphasis of Greenham shifted as women became increasingly aware of these limitations. 'The early simplicity of "women give life/men build death" could not sustain a movement for ever,' Barbara Norden commented in *Spare Rib*.[7] 'The sort of feminism that saw the nuclear arms race as a direct expression of patriarchy has tended to give way to a more diverse brand of socialist feminism which has enabled Greenham to make links.' Without those links – perhaps especially those with Women Against Pit Closures, which gave many their first close encounter with working-class struggle – the life of Greenham as a political movement could not have been sustained.

The politics of Greenham shared many features with the politics of the coalfield women, and with other groups of women active outside the political mainstream: the spontaneity with which their movement developed; the loose, informal structure and the absence of hierarchies; the disrespect for conventional forms and procedures which bred its own inventiveness; the commitment to making politics pleasurable; the impulse towards radicalism which sprang from a sense that the whole world needed changing . . . all these bore witness to a strong and distinctive tradition of women's politics which spanned divisions of class and culture, as well as generations.

CHAPTER 8

Up the Organisation

One critical factor which distinguishes a political movement from a political party or organization is that its substance and momentum are gathered solely from the energy and enthusiasm of the people involved. As long as these are abundant, it is healthy and strong. If they falter, it rapidly declines. It may limp along on residual loyalties. Sometimes it can be revived by a transfusion of new energies. If not, it must die. It has no immune system to defend it against the onslaught of apathy.

An organization, on the other hand, is sustained by its structure and its conventions. It can run low on energy, free of spontaneity, yet still maintain its presence in the world. It can stay in passably good health through regular exercise of its component parts. This may be dull and repetitive, but keeps it ticking over. Even if it does fall ill it need not die, because it has its own life-support machine. It can lie moribund for a time and then, as conditions change, resuscitate itself.

Movements have played an important part in enabling women to find a voice and become involved in political activity. They are an appealing vehicle for women, especially as they tend not to be organized in any formal sense: they don't have procedures or rituals that exclude or intimidate; they tend to be open and flexible, uncluttered, unfettered, responsive to immediate circumstances. A movement demands no more from the individual than her own enthusiasm dictates. Nor does it limit or control her part in it. She can interpret it for herself.

Thousands can be inspired and mobilized by a political movement, but it only works for those who ride on the crest of its waves. It may give you a sense of belonging, while it lasts; but it cannot provide a sense of security, or continuity or place. You are more likely to get that from an organization – that is, if it is the sort that doesn't make you feel excluded or marginalized because of your sex. Women's organizations have, in their own way, played a vital role outside the political mainstream in helping women to become more powerful.

The largest and most enduring of these groups has been the National Federation of Women's Institutes (WI), now with more than 340,000 members, grouped together in some 9,000 branches. It does, in fact, call itself a 'movement' and not without justification – if a movement can be defined as a spontaneous combination of individuals on a mass scale, expressing a common feeling towards a common purpose. But unlike the other movements we have dealt with so far in this book, it has a constitution and a structure; it has leaders and rules and accounts, a national headquarters with thirty professional staff, an annual turnover of nearly one million pounds, capital assets worth more than one million pounds and its own residential adult education college.

The first WI in Britain was launched in Anglesey, Wales in 1915, at the instigation of a Canadian, Mrs Alfred Watt. She was a member of the Canadian WI, which had been founded in 1897 by a Mrs Adelaide Hunter Hoodless. The fourth child of Mrs Hunter Hoodless had died in infancy, poisoned by contaminated milk, and she was determined that other women should be better informed about health and hygiene and more skilled in the domestic sciences, so that they and theirs wouldn't suffer a similar fate. She was one who believed that the 'ultimate development of organization' was socialism, and she maintained that the way to achieve the 'highest degree of advancement' for each individual in society was to 'develop to the fullest extent the two great social forces, education and organization'.[1] Such were the radical roots of the WI.

By 1917, there were 137 Women's Institutes in rural England and Wales. They sent sixty delegates to the first national conference in London, where they formed themselves into a National Federation, adopted a constitution and elected their first chairwoman. The purpose of the WI was not only to inform and educate, but to provide a congenial meeting place for country-dwelling women. As one early member recalled:

> The institute has brought together in our very rural village women of all classes in true friendships. Women who have lived together as total strangers to each other not perhaps from any unkind or class feeling but from sheer want of opportunity for meeting and making friends. Women who have never ventured out to church or chapel or village entertainment now come eagerly to our meetings, forget their shyness in opening up their minds to new ideas and welcome opportunities for developing their hidden talents.[2]

The organization flourished, with membership reaching a quarter of a million by 1927. Denman College, an imposing Georgian mansion set in seventeen acres of parkland, in Marcham, Oxfordshire, was opened in 1948, after a two-year campaign to raise £60,000 – no mean feat in those times of post-war austerity. Membership peaked at 462,000 in 1956. Since then it twice extended its conditions of entry, first to allow the formation of institutes in places with more than 4,000 inhabitants, and later to include 'country-minded women wherever they live – in towns, in the suburbs, on housing estates and even in London.'

Rather as the Greenham women acquired a public image through the media (as dirty lesbians, Soviet stooges, irresponsible wives and mothers, etc.) which distorted and belittled their real achievements, so the Women's Institutes have been relentlessly caricatured as a band of jam-makers in jolly hats. Jam they have certainly made – tons of the stuff. What that represented, though, was not a quaint pastoral hobby, but one small part of a massive exercise in developing skills in food production and processing which helped pull the nation through two wars. In peace-time, those skills were channelled into a thriving commercial enterprise – a network of WI co-operative markets, at which members (and non-members) sold home-made produce. By 1987 there were 564 such markets, with a combined turnover of more than £7 million, returning £6.5 million to a total of 55,000 shareholders.

There is a chronic hunger among women (which we noted

earlier) for knowledge and self-improvement. They tend to feel they are living on the edge of the 'real world', which they do not properly understand. The work they do – both in and out of the home – seldom encourages self-esteem; their skills are under-valued and they don't have much opportunity to feel they are making progress. And women generally have less opportunity than men for higher education and training. One of the great attractions of the WI was its capacity to feed that hunger where it was most acutely felt – in rural communities. Through its own local meetings, through lobbying the authorities for adult education classes, and through the residential courses at Denman College, the WI provided women with education and training – not only in home-based crafts, but also in poetry, drama, fine art, health, ecology, technology, law, finance and basic political skills. Courses at Denman College in 1987 ranged from 'Flower Painting' and 'Hedgerow Basketry' to 'Self-Defence for Women' and 'Making the Most of Your Word Processor'; from 'Shakespeare and His Times' and a 'Choral Weekend' to 'Leadership Training', 'Women and Money' and a beginners' course in public speaking.

By offering social contact and solidarity, and by providing opportunities for education and self-improvement, the WI helped to establish the basic conditions in which women could begin to wield political power. It was also a public-spirited organization, through which women could express a collective responsibility for improving the world they lived in. It believed in 'truth, tolerance and justice' and concerned itself with an increasingly wide range of social and environmental issues. It had a long-standing commitment to 'international understanding and co-operation' and raised many thousands of pounds for development projects in the Third World. A change in the constitution in 1971 allowed local WIs to take up 'matters of political or religious significance, provided the movement is never used for party-political or sectarian propaganda.'

Individual institutes and county federations became involved in local campaigns – resisting, for instance, the closure of a sub-post office or school, or saving a threatened bus route or hospital. They would also clear footpaths and be vigilant about enforcement of local speed limits. One of the main ways the WI made its influence felt locally was through the election or appointment of WI members to various administrative bodies – such as parish and district councils, health and education authorities, school boards of governors and magistrates' benches.

At a national level, resolutions passed at its annual general meetings became 'mandates', which every member of the organization was pledged to support. Mandates accumulated over more than seventy years reveal the WI's distinctive political character. It demanded stronger punishments to deter crime, especially in cases of child abuse, and 'higher standards' with less violence on film and television. But these were the only respects in which it might be said to comply with the traditional stereotype of women as 'naturally conservative'. The WI was consistently and passionately concerned with improving standards of health, education and welfare through the facilities and services of the state. It took a close and detailed interest in conservation and rural planning, in animal welfare, in combating environmental pollution and raising standards of nutrition. It made a firm commitment to equal opportunity, to increasing the participation of women in many aspects of public life and to improving the conditions of women's daily existence.

In 1921, the WI called for more women to serve on juries, and in 1943 it demanded equal pay for equal work. In 1954, it launched the Keep Britain Tidy Campaign; in 1961, it pledged support for the international Freedom from Hunger Campaign; in 1973, it urged the government to provide free family planning; in 1975, it came out in favour of equal opportunity and legal status for men and women and pledged itself to work to achieve those goals; in the same year it voiced concern about domestic violence and called for immediate action to provide alternative accommodation for battered women and their children. In 1987, it urged the government not to legalize the irradiation of foods, and to raise the earnings level of supplementary benefit claimants. These are just a few examples from the WI's broad portfolio of progressive policies.

Carrying a resolution was never a casual or precipitous affair. The WI prided itself on 'informed opinion' and set great store by its own system of democracy; local institutes received background briefings on each proposal that went forward, so that they could discuss it in detail before the Annual General Meeting.

In its own discreet fashion, the WI then lobbied the government of the day to meet the demands of its mandates. 'What we do depends on the topic,' explained their officer in charge of Public Affairs. 'We write letters to Ministers, we seek meetings with Ministers, we write to selected MPs.' On some issues they prompted mass letter-writing campaigns to all MPs, or formed alliances with other organizations. Sometimes ministers took the initiative and invited them to meetings. 'We are lucky being able to operate at all these levels. By and large, we are likely to get a meeting with a Minister if we seek one. Another indication of how seriously we are taken is the length of replies we get – usually two good sides of A4, carefully argued. Ministers are anxious to explain their case to us.'

The WI was prepared to call itself a political organization, but abhorred any association with political parties. Its status as a registered charity prohibited party-political activity, but that was not really what held it back. It shared that belief, so common among women, that politics was a dirty business, unnecessarily prone to conflict, above which the voice (*its* voice) of reason must rise. The official 'biography' of the WI put it this way:

> Power in the WI is exercised by the constant application of pressure and by reasoned argument. They reflect the deep-rooted belief of most people that it ought to be possible, for instance, to devise a sensible rural bus-service without making it a political issue ... they hold a trusted position as the wise voice of ordinary reflective people and any demonstration of aggressive strength would erode that position.[3]

The WI relied for its political effectiveness upon two main factors: size and respectability. The Queen, the Queen Mother, the Duchess of Gloucester, the Duchess of Kent and Princess Alice all belonged to the WI, as did countless members of the landed aristocracy and gentry. It was part of the British establishment – where its voice was heard and tolerated as the gentle urging of a sensible wife.

By virtue of its size, it could claim to be not just a pressure group, but a representative body – speaking for a broad swathe of 'country-minded' women. It had succeeded in breaking through some of the rigid social barriers of rural Britain, bringing together a substantial range of women – from the tenant farmer to the primary school teacher; from the shop-keeper to the district nurse – as well as countless wives, mothers and grand-mothers working at home, and a small but conspicuous con-tingent of titled ladies from the shires.

The survival of the wi was partly due to its structure – which was loose enough not to stifle, but sufficient to maintain momen-tum in changing times; it was democratic in a way that prized the individual and encouraged members to participate, and it had substantial, independent means. No less important was the fact that the wi organized itself primarily around meeting women's needs. Women joined because it offered them what they wanted and couldn't get elsewhere: a chance to get out of the house, to make friends, to learn, to develop skills, and *to have a good time*. In those conditions wi members developed a collective voice which was political in their own terms, in a way that made sense to them and did not jar with the rest of their lives. It did not make them *very* powerful, but it enabled them to be *more* powerful than they would have been as isolated individuals, or even, in some respects, as subordinate members of a mixed-sex political organization.

It did have its limitations, however. The wi was broad, but not classless. It worried about the rural poor – and tried to help them – but somehow never managed to embrace them as equals. Moreover, the wi could only hope to be influential as long as it did not step out of line. Scored deep into its personality was a desire to be moderate and inoffensive, 'nice' and acceptable. As politics in Britain became increasingly polarized, this might prove to be unduly restricting for an organization which had the interests of women at heart.

Abhorring conflict and prizing its respectability, the wi pass-ively resisted any change in the circumstances of women's 'pri-vate' lives. It was not within the tradition of the wi for members to talk about personal problems, to admit that anything might be troublesome on the domestic front. There was a tacit assumption that members led 'normal' lives in nuclear families; power relations between women and men in the private sphere were not challenged. Perhaps this kept the Royals happy, but it might also have contributed to the WI's failure to attract younger women into membership.

In spite of efforts to broaden the appeal of the WI, age took its toll. In just two years between 1986 and 1988, the WI saw a net reduction of some 10,000 members and 150 local institutes. In 1988, it embarked on another membership drive – an uphill struggle for an organization whose roots were firmly embedded in the first half of the twentieth century. The WI was powerful not just because it was respectable, but because it was *big* – indeed, the biggest. If it could not move with the times, it was in danger of realizing what one elderly executive member described as 'our greatest fear . . . that we shall cease to matter'.

Its smaller urban sister, the National Union of Townswomen's Guilds, was formed in the late 1920s by veterans of the constitutional suffrage campaign. They wanted to create a new kind of organization which would carry the women's movement into the era of universal franchise, and they wanted to ensure that women were sufficiently educated to make the best of their new vote. 'Our programme was comradeship, arts and crafts and citizenship,' recalled the late Dame Margery Corbett Ashby, one of the founders. The Townswomen, like the WI, had a formal, hierarchical structure, with limited autonomy for local Guilds. They combined social contact with self-improvement and public-spiritedness, and helped to give some urban women a collective, non-partisan voice. They, too, generally took a progressive stance on such matters as the environment, health and women's rights, while following a less than liberal line on crime, violence, public morals and related issues. They set great store by their respectability – with the Princess Royal as their patron – and steered a cautious, moderate path, leaving undisturbed the traditional relations between women and men.

Like the WI, the Townswomen's Guilds were predominantly middle-class; their formative years were the 1930s and 1940s, and they since suffered a decline in membership, from a peak of around 250,000 in 1971 to 110,000 in 1981. They saw an upturn in the 1980s, with membership at 120,000 in 1988, but continued to be troubled by the difficulty of attracting younger women. In the long term, this could prove a tougher challenge in the towns, where social conditions changed more rapidly, and where more married women had paid jobs, leaving less time for extra activities outside the home. A crucial question for both the wi and the Guilds was not whether they could survive, but whether they could continue to offer enough women what they wanted, in order to keep membership sufficiently high to safeguard their political influence.

One organization that grew apace during the 1970s and 1980s was the National Childbirth Trust, which began in the late 1950s to promote a particular method of natural childbirth and developed into a much broader network of groups aiming 'through education and mutual support' to build 'confidence and enjoyment of both childbirth and parenthood'. In 1988 it had some 330 branches with 35,000 local and 11,000 national members. A registered charity and strictly non-political in its demeanour, it nevertheless served an important political function, by enabling women to get together and help each other gain more power over those critical areas of their lives.

On quite a different level, the Fawcett Society was a lobbying organization dedicated to doing away with 'all forms of sex discrimination'. It derived its political weight not from its size (it had 500 members in 1988), but from its reputation as the longest-surviving feminist organization, having started life in 1866 as the Kensington Ladies' Discussion Society.

The veteran feminist writer, Mary Stott, remarked that:

One of the oddest notions that people have about people is that women cannot work together. In the UK they have been working together in organized groups for at least 150 years. . . . They have banded together for political purposes; to fight oppressive laws and economic conditions; to raise the status of women from that of criminals, bankrupts and minors; to succour the deprived; to achieve improvements in the education, health and welfare of women and children; to give one another support in their trades and professions; to widen their own horizons; to have an escape from the confining four walls of home. And they have banded together for company and friendship, because, contrary to a powerful old myth, they *like* being together.[4]

Yet it is not only through women-only organizations that women have been influential *as women*. An interesting phenomenon of the 1970s and 1980s was the 'feminization' of pressure-group politics. Women became increasingly involved in mixed-sex voluntary organizations and issue-based campaigns – and brought with them the insights and objectives of the women's movement. One reason why this began to happen was that more women than men were prepared to accept the low wages that were endemic in the voluntary sector; the nature of the work tended to attract those who were already politicized, through involvement in women's liberation or the labour movement. As time went by, some of them moved into senior jobs, often in charge of predominantly female staffs.

The power of pressure groups is limited, as we have already noted, but that is not to suggest that they are insignificant. MPS are generally starved of resources for carrying out their own research, and pressure groups play a vital role in informing political debate. In the 1970s and 1980s, they were open to women in a way that other mixed-sex political organizations (such as parties and unions) were not; entry generally depended on a willingness to work hard for little or no money; success depended on building up expertise rather than on drinking in the right bars, or talking louder or longer than anyone else. Most of these organizations were relatively new and the culture that built up around them reflected the balance of women and men who worked in them; there were few, if any, exclusive practices or traditions.

The National Council for Civil Liberties was one of the first to be affected, developing a women's rights unit with a women's officer in the early 1970s. The Child Poverty Action Group's campaign for Child Benefit was increasingly influenced by ideas developed in the women's movement, notably in its criticism

of the 'family wage' (a concept, popular with trade-union negotiators, that family income should depend upon the earnings
of a male breadwinner). In the work of Shelter during the late
1980s, the housing needs of women, and the effect on women
of new housing policy gathered emphasis. In 1989, women occupied the top jobs of Director or General Secretary in the National
Council for Civil Liberties (Sarah Spencer), Shelter (Sheila
McKechnie), The Child Poverty Action Group (Fran Bennett),
the Joint Council for the Welfare of Immigrants (Anne Awers)
and The National Council for Voluntary Organizations (Usha
Prashar). These individuals were not single-handedly responsible for promoting a 'women's agenda'; they were, rather, an
outward sign of a process that had been going on for some years,
in which the presence of women and the influence of feminism
had spread through many of these organizations.

CHAPTER 9

Workplace Politics

The year 1988 saw another turbulent phase in the continuing battle between Health Service workers and government over the state of the National Health Service. Nicola Baines, a student nurse at the Maudsley psychiatric hospital in South London, was among hundreds of members of the Confederation of Health Service Employees (COHSE) who took part in one-day strikes and an overtime ban to step up pressure on the government to put more resources into the Health Service. As low pay and poor conditions had driven more and more nurses out of Health Service employment, even relatively wealthy hospitals like the Maudsley were forced to bring in casual labour from nursing agencies. That was bad enough in any hospital, Nicola told us. 'But in psychiatry it's ridiculous. You need commitment and continuity, not casuals – there one day, gone the next.'

She was wholeheartedly committed to the dispute and, as well as picketing and attending rallies, marches and countless meetings, she had been drumming up support among local workers – including bus drivers, who were members of the Transport and General Workers' Union. A tough-minded individual in her mid-twenties, who had been in women's groups at college and was now an experienced trade-union activist, Nicola had gone along to address the drivers' branch meeting and ask them to come out on strike in sympathy with the nurses. She'd expected Neelam, another student nurse, to be there with her, but Ian, the COHSE branch secretary, turned up instead. 'I was so glad he was there. I felt completely intimidated – a room full of men. I didn't speak at all. I tried butting in a few times, but to no avail. And they didn't direct any questions at me. If Neelam and I had been there on our own, I'm sure the whole atmosphere would have been different.' How so?

> More flirtatious and friendly, but they wouldn't have taken us seriously. When the branch secretary of the bus garage, who was all in favour of going on strike, made his summing-up speech, he pointed to me and said – 'just look at that little scrap of a girl there, not a ha'p'orth of flesh on her, what more can I add?' Well, I could think of a thing or two, but you have to be polite if you're asking people to help you!

If there's one route, more than any other, by which ordinary women learn to become more powerful, it is surely trade union-ism. Yet the culture and traditions of the British trade-union movement are profoundly masculine. It's at once a spur and a shackle for women. It provides a means for them to get together and fight for changes they need. At the same time, it can make them feel – as Nicola Baines felt – marginal, incompetent and relatively weak.

We met Nicola with fellow student Neelam Choksi and Carol Symes, a staff nurse at the Maudsley. All three were in their twenties, none had ever belonged to a political party – nor did they now. 'I did some leafleting for the Labour Party during the election campaign,' Carol told us. 'But we feel we've had no support from the leadership over this dispute. Neil Kinnock says he's not in favour of nurses going on strike. What does he know?' They had no patience with parties to the left of Labour, whose banners were prominent on the picket lines: 'The SWP are the bane of our lives, always trying to get their oar in, tell us what to do,' said Carol 'And the others – the RCG, the RCP – they all drive me mad.' 'I do want to join some sort of party,' Nicola said, 'but I can't find one I like.'

For all three, then, it was a union rather than a political party that provided a route to politics. And the Health Service dispute was their first major venture into political activity. 'I did my training in Bath, where nurses weren't aware of what was going on outside.' Carol explained. 'We were being trained to think of ourselves as "professionals", and I didn't notice any cuts. I was concentrating on me and just getting on with my life. It was only when I got to London that I saw there were massive cuts being imposed and I realized unions could do something about it.' Neelam told us: 'I've had quite a sheltered upbringing. Women don't become politically active in my culture. I just took the role I was brought up to. But working at the Maudsley and being amongst other women who were active spurred me on.'

Now, the union and the struggle for a better Health Service dominated their lives. 'I spend up to thirty hours a week on union activities,' said Carol. 'That's on top of the thirty-seven and a half hours of nursing.' 'It's changed my life,' was how Angela put it. 'Everything is lost to the dispute and my efforts in that. It's affected my relationships – I find it hard to get on with people who don't wholly support what we are doing. I only want to be with people who are involved too.' And clearly, it was an enriching experience; they got a buzz out of it. 'It's very challenging,' said Carol, who'd spoken at a couple of big rallies. After joining COHSE, she'd become involved in other political campaigns too. 'Against the Alton Bill [which sought to limit the right to abortion], the education march – anything that's going!' As Neelam said: 'I feel more powerful now that I am part of a body that is doing something about these ward closures.'

The three women believed they had a chance of winning at least some concessions from the government – and late that year, when the government allocated extra funds to the Health Service so that nurses got a pay rise and more permanent staff were engaged at the Maudsley, they felt their actions had helped to make it happen. And they'd learnt a lot – how to hold meetings, speak in public, organize. 'I feel a lot more grown-up, a lot calmer,' Carol said. 'When we suddenly had to ballot everyone for our overtime ban, I didn't panic. I knew what to do.'

But their achievements were circumscribed. None of them had husbands or families to look after. 'I don't think I've got time for a relationship, let alone children,' said Nicola. They knew of one woman with children who'd been active in the dispute. 'Her husband helped her with the kids. But she's away on maternity leave now.' Carol told us:

141

There's a group of women who are active, but it's very hard to get any others involved. We've tried everything – question-naires, special working parties on special issues, you name it. I think it shows how badly people feel about the Health Service. At the end of the day, they've had enough. They want to go home and forget all about it.

They were often exasperated by the way they were perceived as union militants – both by the public, via the media, and by fellow trade unionists. As she went round the bus garages asking for support, Nicola was told, 'If you'd come in your uniform we'd go out on strike for you, darling!' Working in a psychiatric hospital, they didn't wear uniforms, and at the start of the strike press photographers and television crews turned up and asked disappointedly where they could find uniformed nurses on a picket line.

Carol had been asked to speak at the Hackney Empire, where more than 2,000 were gathered for an evening's entertainment – organized by COHSE and Red Wedge as a morale-booster during the strike. She had mixed feelings about it. 'Why had they picked me? I had spoken at a rally before and it went across fairly well; that's good. But I was the only woman speaker among all these national officers and I felt like a little toy. "There's Carol in her trendy gear" – it was what I looked like that counted for them.' Activist or sex object? It was a touchy subject, she said. She felt angry and yet implicated – unable to rise above a sense that she was somehow to be blamed for what made her feel demeaned. On another occasion, she had been one of two nurses picked out to pose for photographers during an all-night vigil at Downing Street. 'It went on for half an hour: "Can you look this way, darling?" "Can you look that way again, love?" "Can you look pathetic?" You want to help the strike but you know you're being exploited. Where do your loyalties lie?' By the time we met them, all three had been interviewed by television crews. They knew it was all edited: they'd be noticed and listened to because they were not 'political' – they'd never been on strike before. And if they looked good, they were noticed all the more. 'If you're not good-looking, you're just seen as this no-hoper, an aggressive person who probably can't get a boyfriend and that's why you're involved,' said Nicola. 'There's more power behind being pretty.'

Much of what they said about their union and their place in trade-union activities suggested a sense of being children in an adult world: younger, weaker, less able, not ready, vulnerable, intimidated. This was due less to their actual youthfulness, it seemed, than to the fact that they were having to enter a world that didn't belong to them. Most members of their union (79 per cent) were women, yet there were only five women out of twenty-six on COHSE's national executive committee. On their local branch executive at the Maudsley, there were eighteen women out of twenty-eight. The chair and secretary were both men, Carol told us, 'but that's not to say these two people want to be at the top. I'm assistant secretary and I've been holding back from taking more responsibility. It's very hectic and these men are very experienced. COHSE members feel safer with them being there. I think it would be a bad thing for me to take over now, because I am less experienced.'

They all felt there was a problem about getting into – or even close to – the mainstream of the union. 'It's like being a student nurse; you're right at the bottom of the hierarchy,' Carol remarked.

You have the staff nurse above you, then the sister, the clinical nurse manager and unit general manager. If you've got a little problem or you want to do something, you've got to go all the way up for a decision and it takes for ever. It's the same within COHSE. We're lucky to have a good branch here at the Maudsley, but if we need a decision taken higher up, it's got to go to the regional office, then the head office in London, or the sub-committee of the London Co-ordinating Committee, then the London Co-ordinating Committee, then the National Executive and the General Secretary.

Nicola added:

The structure is created by men. But it's not just a structure, it's a way of life. When you approach the organization, it's like you have to speak another language, go into another culture. I'm pretty confident about these things, and yet I find that intimidating, so it must be a lot worse for some. It's not the same when I am with women: I feel I can slip up, say the wrong thing and it doesn't matter. But with men I feel I've got to get it right, or I won't be taken seriously. I've got to know so much more. With women I'm more likely to be accepted for what I am.

Neelam told us that as a newly elected branch steward, she'd been invited to a union day course. 'I really wanted to go, but someone told me it was a typical trade-union thing, all men – and that really put me off. I had this vision of not being taken seriously.' The union ran courses for women only; Neelam and Nicola both expressed interest in those, but they weren't sure it would help them get any closer to the mainstream of the union. 'The trouble with women-only things,' said Nicola, 'is how much power do they really have?'

Few would deny that in the last decades of the twentieth century women have kept the British trade-union movement on its feet. Between 1970 and 1979, women's union membership increased by 41.7 per cent, compared with only 6.1 per cent for men. Even since 1979, when unions have been in decline with membership falling by nearly three million, women's share of membership has continued to expand. It now accounts for about one third of the total. But the number of women joining the labour force – potential members – has been even higher. Two main factors have brought this about: first, the historic shift in the post-war period from manual to non-manual work, and second, the more recent growth in part-time work. From 1961 to 1981, non-manual employment increased by 20 per cent, while manual employment fell by 2 per cent. During that period, the number of clerical jobs increased by 36 per cent. In the twelve years to 1984, the number of full-time jobs fell by 2.3 million, while part-time jobs increased by 1.3 million. Overall, 88 per cent of part-time workers were women. In 1985 women part-timers held 17 per cent of all jobs, and this was expected to rise to 22 per cent by 1990. Women were expected to secure two-thirds of all new jobs created by the mid-1990s. However, the 'density' of women's trade-union membership – that is, the proportion of women in paid labour who actually joined unions – was only 60 per cent of men's. Evidently, unions were failing to take full advantage of the growing numbers of potential female recruits.

Old habits die hard. The history of British trade unionism is deeply marked by men's efforts to prevent women from competing with them in the labour market and – to that end – to keep them out of their workers' organizations. At the inauguration in 1829 of the 'Grand General Union of the United Kingdom', the cotton spinners stipulated that 'the union shall include only *male* spinners and piecers'. But as Emma Paterson, founder of the Women's Trade Union League, commented some years later: 'So long as women are unprotected by any kind of combination and are consequently wholly at the mercy of employers for the rate of their wages and the length of their working hours, working men not unnaturally look with suspicion on their employment.'[1]

Women set up their own work-based organizations – some as early as the 1780s, but more commonly towards the end of the nineteenth century. The Women's Trade Union League, originally the 'Women's Provident and Protective League', was founded in 1874 to promote trade unionism among working women. By 1886, between thirty and forty women's societies had been established; eighty or ninety more sprang up over the next two decades. By the turn of the century, men's unions had begun to organize women, either admitting female members or setting up allied women's societies. The textile unions led the way, followed by printers, cigar makers, steel smelters, pottery workers, and later the new 'black-coated' and general workers' unions. 'Their object . . . was not entirely disinterested,' commented Barbara Drake, whose classic history of women in trade unions was first published in 1920. 'The men's object was not so much to exclude women entirely from employment – an aim generally viewed as impracticable – as to confine them to certain branches of the trade and to certain districts. Under the circumstances, some degree of sex antagonism was almost inevitable, and did not tend to make organization easier.'[2]

Women faced hostility from men, who feared their capacity

to undercut wages and saw organization as a means of controlling them, as well as from employers, 'who saw in each attempt to organize them a threat to their vested interest in "cheap and docile" female labour'. Not a few were willing to join – a total of 166,000 women belonged to unions by 1906 – but organizers, male and female, found them hard to recruit. 'We shall become part of an organization over which we shall have no control,' complained Miss Henshall in 1906, on behalf of seventy-two felt-hat trimmers who were resisting overtures from the National Union of Journeymen Felt Hatters to join its allied women's society, 'and it will be of no benefit to us whatever, so far as we know.' The male hatters responded: 'Like children who object to go to school, although it is for their good, and afterwards bless their parents who had to force them to go, many trimmers are in their infancy as far as trade union organization is concerned.'[3]

Many of the obstacles to women's trade unionism encountered in the early twentieth century bear a close resemblance to those we recognize today – which suggests how deep and intractable they can be. Mr Will Thorne, secretary of the Gasworkers' and General Labourers' Union, remarked that women did not 'seem to grasp the real need of trade unions' or 'attend to the branch business as well as the men (and they are bad enough in many places)', but he glimpsed a reason why: 'When a man has done his day's work he becomes free, and that is not so with women.'[4] Miss I. O. Ford, honorary secretary of the Leeds Society of Work-women, considered the struggle to organize women 'a most disheartening and painful one,' but felt certain the fault did not lie with women themselves.

> Those women who really grasp the aim of trade unionism grasp it, I think, more firmly than men, because more religiously. Trade unionism means rebellion, and the orthodox teaching for women is submission. ... Society encourages selfish indifference amongst women, in that it considers a woman's home must make her sacrifice to it everyone else's home and all public honour.[5]

Mary MacArthur was all too aware of the problems of recruiting and then keeping women in union membership. She was secretary of the Women's Trade Union League from 1903, and later general secretary of the National Federation of Women Workers, a general women's union founded by the League in 1906. The main cause she identified was women's relatively low standard of living: 'This sounds paradoxical, but it is nevertheless true that, while women are badly paid because of their unorganized condition, they may be unorganized mainly because they are badly paid.'[6]

Slowly but surely, the National Federation of Women Workers built up its membership from 2,000 in 1906 to 80,000 by the end of the First World War. It had fifty women organizers and accounted for more than 13 per cent of all female trade-union members. Barbara Drake commented:

> Uniting so far as possible in one body all classes of women for whom there are no appropriate trade unions, and so pooling their slender resources . . . it has overcome the extraordinary difficulties of organization. In power of numbers, in the variety and substance of its benefits, in financial stability, in the wisdom of its counsels and the distinction of its leadership, in negotiation or disputes with the employers, in public influence and in its status as a trade union, the Federation loses nothing by comparison with any other general labour union, yet it retains the advantage of an all-women's organization. Not only are women obliged to come forward and manage their own affairs, but the concentration of its members on women's problems has led to the formation of an exceptionally matured women's opinion. . . . At Trades Union Congresses and Labour Party Conferences, on Government and statutory bodies, at public meetings and demonstrations, it is recognized by common consent as the leading authority on women's questions, and fills a place in the trade union world which could be filled in no other way.[7]

In spite of its success, it came to be seen as something of an anachronism. The idea of single-sex unions belonged to an earlier and less mature age of trade unionism, so it was thought, and 'progress' led inexorably towards joint organization. At the Fed-

147

eration's 1920 conference, Mary MacArthur argued that it should merge with the National Union of General Workers, to become 'a great industrial organization of men and women, in which women are not submerged but in which they take as active a part as the men'. The terms for the merger were that the Federation should keep its own executive council and become a 'district' of the NUGW, with special officers to cater for women. But all signs of separate identity swiftly disappeared. Within three years, the separate women's district had been abolished; the number of women's officers fell from sixteen to one and, by 1930, the voice of women was so thoroughly silenced that the NUGW did not send a single female delegate to the TUC Conference.

'For the Federation to give up its present task of voicing women before these are effectively represented by joint-organizations would mean a loss to the industrial women's movement, of which the gravity is almost impossible to over-estimate,' Barbara Drake had warned in 1920. 'In the meantime, the management of joint-organizations is for all practical purposes in the hands of men.' The causes could be found, she said, in the same 'complex of circumstances' which made it hard for women to join unions in the first place.

> The inferior grade of worker to which women members mostly belong ... their comparative youth and inexperience, the tradition of social and economic dependence ... one or all of these factors have contributed to place them in a subordinate position in the union. The burden of home duties, from which young girls are by no means exempt, further hampers them seriously in active public work ... they are backward in attending branch meetings, and for this reason alone tend to lose their chance of nomination for responsible office.[8]

There was also the problem of women officers occupying a subordinate position, Barbara Drake explained. It was harder to recruit women from among the membership, so they tended to come from non-industrial backgrounds, often from universities, to the disapproval of the men who ran the unions: 'Snobbishness is not peculiar to one class.' Moreover, the burden of work was almost intolerable: 'The most serious drawback of the trade union service is the habitual overwork which is apparently involved, and women who are over-conscientious, and take things less easily than men, suffer most from the strain.'[9]

Seventy years later, such problems as these were still much in evidence. The nature of women's paid employment, their domestic responsibilities and the traditions and practices of trade unions were all seen as reasons for women's relatively low level of involvement in trade unions in the 1980s. 'It is characteristic of women's work that it is often casual and temporary,' Cynthia Cockburn observed in her Fabian pamphlet *Women, Trade Unions and Political Parties*.[10] That meant they were less likely to feel it was worth committing themselves to union membership; or they worked in low-grade posts where they weren't allowed to leave their work stations to discuss union business, or get paid time off for union work, or obtain information from management. They felt more vulnerable to victimization in lower-grade posts. A survey by the white-collar union ASTMS (which later became part of a new, merged union, the MSF, the Federation) showed that women felt employers would withhold promotion and make life difficult for a union activist.[11] Part-time work, which was almost exclusively women's domain, did not in itself stop women joining trade unions, according to Kate Holman in *Organising Women Trade Unionists*, but other factors associated with it made organization difficult: 'small, isolated workplaces, different employers; and a low level of existing unionisation'.[12]

A major factor was women's unpaid work at home, which already competed with paid work for the hours of the day. 'To be active in a union introduces a third responsibility into women's lives which many may feel will be the straw to break their backs,' said Margaret Prosser, National Women's Officer of the Transport and General Workers' Union. She agreed that the biggest deterrent to women's involvement was the shortage of time. 'We would argue and defend the democracy of the trade unions. The difficulty with democracy is that it is bloody time-consuming and women haven't got an awful lot of time.' The TGWU elected their regional committee members from different sections of industry, she told us, so for instance a candidate from the Health Service, standing for the South-East regional committee, would have to be elected not just by their own hospital, but by others as well. 'You need time to get around, to meet people in other workplaces. Although it's democratic, because it ensures that people know something about you and your politics before they vote for you, it excludes women because women are not in a position to get themselves known in that way.'

A 1985 MORI poll compared levels of union activism among women and men. Only 56 per cent of female union members had been to a union meeting, compared with 79 per cent of male members; 18 per cent of the women had put forward a proposal at a meeting, compared with 37 per cent of the men; 43 per cent had voted in a union election and 8 per cent had been a shop steward, compared with 66 per cent and 21 per cent of men.[13] Cynthia Cockburn pointed out that men's greater propensity to join unions and play an active part in them was often read as a sign of men's 'more developed political consciousness', but that was open to question:

> Men's greater political activity is predicated on turning a blind eye to the extent to which their own freedom to engage is the result of women's longer working hours, when home work and paid work are taken into account, and from the generally supportive role women play to men in both spheres. It could be said therefore to be a narrow and sectional conception of the political.[14]

Men ran the unions, and women felt the unions didn't 'belong' to them: that was the verdict of several studies carried out in the 1970s and 1980s. 'Women workers are still not seen as the norm, even by many trade union men,' Cynthia Cockburn observed. 'The typical member of the workforce is seen as a male, white, full-time, life-time worker . . . the same hierarchy of power that exists in employment is allowed to exist within many unions. Because women are not "important" employees they are not seen as important union members.'

One survey measured the gap between the numbers of women holding key positions in major unions and the numbers there *would* be if they accurately reflected the proportion of women in the membership. It found, for example, that the TGWU would need to employ an extra sixty-six women full-time officials, the GMB would need a further twelve women on its Executive Committee; and the National Union of Teachers would need to send another seventeen women delegates to the Trades Union Conference.[15]

Of course, women could not increase their share of power without men reducing theirs, so in order to keep the ratios accurate, there would need to be (respectively) sixty-six, twelve and seventeen fewer men. But any real shift in power was bound to be resisted by men. As Margaret Prosser told us:

Some men who've been involved for a long time see it as their right to get elected to the regional committee, not as something they have to continue to work for. If they get knocked off their little pedestal, they don't look to themselves and say 'where did I go wrong?' but see it as a personal attack by someone who is out to do them down. That complacency has grown up in what we might call 'the good years' when unions didn't have to work very hard to get members in. You wouldn't find that kind of complacency among women.

Black and Asian women were more inclined to join unions and participate in union activities, according to a 1984 report,[16] but less likely to hold positions of power. Thirty-four per cent of white women workers belonged to trade unions compared to 57 per cent of West Indian women and 38 per cent of Asian women; 9 per cent of white women had attended a union meeting in the last six months, compared with 19 per cent of West Indian women and 10 per cent of Asian women. But only 2 per cent of all three groups held an elected post. The higher level of union activity among ethnic minority workers was shared by women and men alike. Why it existed remained a matter of speculation, but in 1982, when the most recent survey on the question took place, it may have reflected a stronger trade-union tradition among first-generation immigrants, stemming from their countries of origin; there was no evidence of the pattern being repeated among young ethnic minority women or men born in Britain. Easier to explain was the shortage of black and Asian women in positions of power. A TUC report in 1987 commented:

> Racism not only prevents black and ethnic minority women and men gaining employment in the first place, it also militates against union activity to improve their position in employment and within the union. Additionally, often, racism and sexism go hand in hand: black women therefore face the sex discrimination faced by white women, together with the racism faced by all black people.[17]

The report recommended a number of measures to combat racism and sexism in unions – including the collection of statistics on gender and ethnic origin, special training, and 'positive action' measures to help and encourage ethnic minority women.

Again and again, we heard that women – whatever their ethnic origins – 'lacked confidence'. When the shop workers' union, USDAW, surveyed their members, they found that considerably more women than men felt they 'didn't really understand how the union works', did not have enough confidence to get more involved, and did not relish going to meetings on their own. Cynthia Cockburn commented:

> What lies behind the confidence factor is intimidation by the masculinity – both in terms of sheer presence and of style – of union committees, branches, conferences. The role model for unionism is male. Even women activists, it has been found, are more likely than non-activists to have fathers or husbands who have had a tradition of union belonging. It was seldom their mothers that passed the union tradition on to women![18]

Unions held meetings at times and in places where it was harder for women to attend. Their agendas were shaped by male rather than female values: 'Men talk about the size of their cars, who gets the top jobs and who gets extra staff,' said a woman member of APEX. 'We talk about maternity rights, contracts, new technology, much more immediate issues.'[19] There was a tendency to overlook the way in which employment was inextricably bound up with the rest of life – reflecting men's narrow preoccupation with paid as opposed to unpaid work. Unions consequently saw the worker in limited terms and failed to cater for the 'whole human being'. They used coded jargon and procedures; their style of operation often seemed very 'masculine' – aggressive and confrontational rather than seeking consensus. Not all unions were guilty of all these faults, but all these observations were regularly made by women exploring the reasons for their relatively low level of participation.

In the 1980s, as in the 1920s, it was widely accepted that life as a trade-union officer involved 'selfless' dedication to work – including long hours away from home and the capacity to respond instantly and wholeheartedly to crises. For women trying to keep their footing in a man's world, often struggling against prejudice, the burden of work could be even heavier. That ruled out most who had family commitments and thus most ordinary working women. Those who struggled on still found it hard to assert themselves. As Cynthia Cockburn pointed out, 'Men are used to regarding each other's opinion as significant and often fail to pay attention to women and to what women say.' Women were in an impossible bind: they had to be 'manly' enough to get their voices heard, yet their credibility depended upon retaining 'femininity'. 'If you're strong enough to speak your mind, then you are thought of as aggressive rather than assertive,' said one member of the Inland Revenue Staff Federation. 'If a woman wants a seat on the executive, then she can't be a "normal" woman.'[20]

Ivy Cameron, national negotiator with the Banking, Insurance and Finance Union (BIFU), pointed out that the power to turn union policies into practice lay chiefly with the national negotiators, and the shortage of women at this level was critical. As unions developed more enlightened policies on women's issues, there remained 'an institutionalized gap between the new policies and any commitment to put them into practice'. Some men wanted to try, but there was no cultural support for them.

We hammer employers on their selection and interviewing procedures, to stop them filtering out the women from key jobs. But the same thing happens in trade unions. Women tend to get syphoned off into the support jobs – research, education, training, administration. There's a macho culture and until there are more women in front-line jobs, that will be very hard to change.

It wasn't just a matter of men keeping women out of key jobs. 'Reasonable, sensible women look at trade unions and say: "I don't want to do one of these jobs." And some of us make terrible role models, running round like headless chickens trying to keep up with men. We need to change, work more normal hours, get away at weekends, make our jobs more humane.' Part of the trouble, Ms Cameron said, stemmed from an old-fashioned approach to trade-union business.

> There's a silly emphasis on a macho way of negotiating. It's bad for the health of the individuals concerned and it doesn't tackle the really important issues like low pay. A lot of time is wasted in rituals: the big build-up to the annual pay round and months spent haggling over half a per cent. Would it not be better to go in and talk about job evaluation, flat-rate increases, restructuring, equal value? And what's the point of shouting across the table in the archetypal way? There are other ways of bargaining – more co-operative and less confron-tational – which take less time, create less hostility and tension, require a lot less heavy drinking and get better results.

The future viability of trade unions, in Ivy Cameron's view, depended not just on accommodating women, but on drawing upon female values to create a new trade-union culture.

During the 1980s, some unions began to make more of an effort. In Manchester we met a group of three women employed by a mail-order firm, distributing electronic goods. They belonged to the Union of Shop, Distributive and Allied Workers (USDAW), which has the fourth-largest female membership among all British unions. Moira McDonald, Teresa Scanlan and Sue Cullinane had been working for the firm for between five and eleven years. Their ages ranged from thirty to forty; Moira and Teresa each had a grown-up child; all had been divorced, and Teresa had remarried. Moira was in the Labour Party; Teresa and Sue did not belong to any party. They formed a close-knit group who clearly enjoyed each other's company. They had become heavily involved in union activity – going to national conferences, attending courses and, in Moira's case, chairing the divisional women's committee in her area. The union gave them a sense of solidarity, a means of improving conditions at work, and a route to political education and self-esteem. 'It's made me much more aware of what's going on,' Sue told us. 'I never used to read a paper. I listened to the news, but I was in my own little world.' Teresa said, 'In the union I'm going to all different types of schools and I'm really enjoying it. It's my little life now, it's different – nothing to do with my family.'

For these women, unlike the nurses we met earlier, it wasn't a dispute which had politicized them but the continuing experience of being in a union that was taking a positive approach to its female membership. All three agreed that it was common for women to have to 'choose' between union activity and marriage. 'My first husband wouldn't let me go out,' said Teresa. 'If I'd stayed with him I wouldn't be here now.' Moira made a similar point: 'Unions can lead to marriage break-up. With one partner getting educated, the other not being supportive, or whatever, they can have nothing in common any more. That's what happened with my husband and me.'

In the early 1980s, USDAW had begun to feel the impact of a growing women's lobby within the union. Although the majority of its membership was female, its power structure was still dominated by men and there was no recognition of women as a distinctive constituency with its own needs and opinions. By 1986, USDAW had set up a network of divisional women's committees with a national women's committee, and had taken on a full-time women's officer, Bernadette Hillon. 'I think it was the debate on abortion that first got women galvanized,' Bernadette told us. 'In 1980, USDAW was a fairly conservative and Catholic union and it was saying abortion was a bad thing. The women began to say – "We're browned off with the union telling us what we should think and feel, and we're not having it any more."' The union responded – and not just out of the goodness of its heart: its leaders sensed that the future lay in recruiting low-paid and often part-time women workers, whose identity couldn't be submerged in the male-defined mass. 'A while ago, the union would have been ashamed to admit it organized the lowest-paid workers in Britain. Now they're coming out with it and trying to fight for them,' Moira McDonald told us. 'All the unions are doing it. The TGWU wouldn't have touched them with a barge pole five years ago, but they do now, because those are the only people who are left who are getting jobs.'

The new women's committees identified four major issues for USDAW to work on: the growth of part-time and casual, flexible working; equal pay; reproductive risks for VDU operators; and health screening. They set up training workshops, issued leaflets, surveyed the membership to find ways of increasing women's participation, took on more new issues – including sexual harassment – monitored progress and generally set about reshaping the union's priorities and style of operation. Gradually, these measures seemed to be making some impact. 'More women delegates spoke from the floor than men this year,' Teresa Scanlan remarked of the union's national conference.

In their own branch, Moira, Teresa and Sue had been trying – with some success – to encourage other women to get involved. 'We try to bring up things that would be relevant to them, rather than just discuss bureaucratic issues. We've had speakers from the Health Service, and we've discussed equal pay. Now the union's getting something done on cancer screening and on VDUs. There was nothing up till a year ago.' The union had paid for them to go on an assertiveness course. 'You sit there and go through what you've done against terrible odds – husband that's violent, no money, no job prospects, but you've kept a family and a home together. You realize it's a tremendous achievement,' Moira said. 'A woman who's overcome all that and then set out to educate herself has reached a higher point of consciousness than someone who's been to university – she's more knowledgeable because of her experience.'

Developments like these in USDAW were part of a general shift among trade unions which began in the mid-1970s and continued into the 1990s. Unions introduced special measures – such as setting up separate women's structures, reserving seats for women on key committees, providing women-only training, campaigning around issues such as equal pay and opportunity, parental leave, sexual harassment, child care and cancer screening, organizing crèches at conferences, negotiating work-time meetings, issuing pamphlets, posters and other propaganda material, and recruiting actively among part-timers. In 1979, the Trades Union Congress issued a charter, 'Equality for Women within Trade Unions', which gave the official nod to measures of this kind, urging unions to take positive steps to increase women's participation.

Performance was patchy; some unions approached the task more wholeheartedly than others. In 1975, the National Union of Public Employees, two-thirds of whose members were women, introduced five reserved seats on its national executive for women. The effect was to encourage more women to stand for unreserved seats as well, and by 1986 women held a total of eleven seats. In 1982, finding that changes to the executive committee were having little impact on women at branch level, NUPE set up a network of women's advisory committees, appointed a women's officer and launched a programme of women's training courses. Between 1974 and 1984, the proportion of women shop stewards in NUPE increased from 28 to 42 per cent. Meanwhile, the print union SOGAT '82 (one of the few with a female general secretary) had commissioned research into women's participation, which was published in 1985. The researchers found 'substantial under-representation of women ... in decision-making roles at all levels', not least because of a union rule which required five years' continuous membership for candidates for election to national or branch office. The media union BETA, in which women make up 44 per cent of the members, had only two women out of twenty-two executive members in 1986. But the National Union of Tailors and Garment Workers (in which women make up 90 per cent of the membership) increased the number of women on its executive from three to eleven between 1978 and 1986.

What was once highly controversial – to treat female members differently in order to break down ingrained patterns of discrimination – became almost commonplace. The one thing women seemed to value most among all the new measures was the opportunity to meet without men. 'If more women could get together in small groups like this one and go through study courses together, or just talk informally, that would build up confidence,' said Moira MacDonald. 'We couldn't have spoken freely if men had been here,' said a NUPE member on a women's weekend school. Another said she had discovered for the first time that other women shared her ideas and feelings: 'I used to think it was just *me!*'[21] But there was scepticism in some quarters about how far separate meetings and structures could help women become powerful. As one member of the Society of Civil and Public Servants commented: 'Even though there is a really thorough women's structure inside the union, there is no real change in the power structure in that men are doing the important jobs and they discuss the important issues down in the pub, when there are few women around.'[22] In unions, as in other institutions, those who hold power seldom surrender it willingly.

According to Ivy Cameron of BIFU, the next ten years would be a crucial testing time for the unions. Women's employment and women's needs had to be put at the top of the unions' agenda – because that was where the main action was going to be in the field of industrial relations. Failure to take account of this could undermine their influence and effectiveness. 'Women's low level of participation has always been seen as a women's problem. It's not. The survival of the trade-union movement depends on women. Men will have to change themselves.'

Clearly, women in trade unions have been deterred from exercising power by many of the same factors that put them off other kinds of political activity. They are also provoked or encouraged to participate by many of the same factors that provoke and encourage them elsewhere – in extra-parliamentary movements and organizations as well as in community politics. As in the margins, so in the mainstream. In the following chapters, we turn to the field of electoral politics, looking closely at women's relationships with political parties at a local and national level.

PART III

Into the Mainstream

CHAPTER 10

The Women's Party

As election day drew near in the winter of 1918, groups of women began arriving in the Midlands town of Smethwick. Many were veterans of the pre-war struggle for the vote but now they were gathering for a different purpose: to organize the election campaign of a new and unique political party. With characteristic enthusiasm, the women sallied forth into the Smethwick streets to support their candidate. She was, after all, famous throughout the land, and her audacious oratory had once inspired thousands to join the suffrage cause. Christabel Pankhurst was her name, and she was seeking to represent the citizens of Smethwick for the Women's Party, under the robust watchwords: Victory, National Security and Social Reform.

Women were voting for the first time in a general election. Seventeen were standing for parliament. One had been selected as a Conservative Unionist candidate, four for the Liberals, four stood for Labour and seven were Independents. That left Christabel, the first and only candidate ever to stand for the Women's Party.

Formed in 1917, the new party had grown directly out of the Women's Social and Political Union, the Pankhursts' powerful suffrage organization. Up to then, the established parties had exhibited such hostility to women's enfranchisement (except, to a certain extent, the Independent Labour Party) that it must have seemed a logical move to create a political party for women. 'While the Women's Party is in no way based on sex antagonism it is felt that women can best save the nation by keeping clear of men's party political machinery and traditions which, by universal consent, leave so much to be desired,' declared the party manifesto in 1918. It was signed by the suffrage veterans,

Emmeline Pankhurst and her daughter, Christabel, Annie Kenney and Flora Drummond.[1]

The Women's Party campaigned on a programme of broad social reform which incorporated many feminist ideas of the time: equal pay for equal work, equal opportunity of employment, the reform of the marriage laws, improved maternity and infant care. It also offered what, at first sight, looked like a remarkably radical vision of co-operative housing – estates for workers with communal restaurants and laundries, crèches and nursery schools, central heating and hot water for all.[2] Christabel's deep-felt commitment to women had not deserted her – such communistic arrangements could, she believed, end the drudgery of women's lives. But these schemes of the Women's Party were designed with benevolent industrialists in mind; they were not intended to inspire any move towards changing economic relations between classes – indeed, strikers were urged to return to work to end the misery of their womenfolk.

The Women's Party had a greater and more glorious mission. Christabel's grand passion was patriotism, and when war was declared, the WSPU suspended its 'civil war' against the government. 'As suffragettes we could not be pacifists at any price,' declared Christabel. 'We offered our service to the country and called upon our members to do likewise.'[3] She urged men to be militant and to fight for King and Country – after all, the women had proved themselves to be militant in their war for the vote:

> It is true that we have never had to face the sudden blow of the enemy which may lay you dead in an instant; but you must remember that, on the other hand, you men who decided to fight have a wonderful backing . . . everybody is supporting you. When we Suffragettes began our fight we had public opinion against us, and, as you all know, that is harder to face than the guns of the enemy.

The men must prove themselves against the 'German peril': only then could their wives and their nation be proud of them.[4]

In many respects Christabel's politics, like her mother's, but unlike her sister Sylvia's, were Conservative and jingoistic. 'We must in future have not only Britain for the British but a Britain worthy of the British,' she said in her election address. And her attacks on the Labour Party were neatly, if simplistically, condensed into an electoral choice between 'the Red Flag or the Union Jack'.[5] Her concern for the working class was laced with an authoritarian intolerance of the messy business of democracy. 'We want all our women to take their instructions and walk in step like an army,' she once said.[6] No wonder she relished aspects of war-time life.

Christabel's fervour for the war effort found favour with the Prime Minister, Lloyd George. He supported her candidacy at Smethwick (in effect, she fought for him on a coalition ticket) because he recognized the effort of the Women's Party in dampening down dissent in 'the centres of war industry'. Christabel spread her anti-socialist, anti-strike message in the industrial heartlands and, in November 1918, Lloyd George wrote to the Conservative politician, Bonar Law: 'The Women's Party, of which Miss Pankhurst is the leader, has been extraordinarily useful, as you know, to the Government – especially in the industrial districts where there has been trouble in the last two very trying years.'[7] Christabel believed that the Women's Party mission was vital because of what she perceived as sinister attempts 'to lead the women electors politically astray and exploit them in the interests of Compromise Peace with the Germans and their allies.'[8]

Despite its name, its roots in the suffrage movement, its leaders' track record and an impressive chunk of its manifesto, the Women's Party was not essentially interested in creating gender-based politics. It was as much an anti-pacifist party as a pro-women's party, and the newly-christened *Britannia* (previously *The Suffragette*), the Women's Party newspaper, made that clear. It was also, quite simply, a vehicle for the Pankhursts' parliamentary ambitions. 'To Emmeline Pankhurst it was as natural as breathing that her daughter should become the first woman MP,' remarked Barbara Castle in her short biography of Christabel and Sylvia Pankhurst. 'Was she not the leader of the Women's Party that had done so much to help win the war?'[9]

The Women's Party's belligerence and its simmering fascism had little to offer (and much to offend) women whose politics had been inspired and shaped by socialism or liberalism. Among its critics was the trade unionist Mary MacArthur who visited Smethwick to speak for the Labour candidate. And Sylvia Pankhurst bluntly declared: 'Here is obviously a Tariff Reform, Tory, Imperial jingo organization and we who are socialist and internationalist have other ideas.'[10] For Sylvia, her sister's politics represented a bitter rejection of all they had gone through together in the past. When, during the war, she read of the recruiting campaign being planned by her mother and sister, she wept: 'To me this seemed a tragic betrayal of the great movement to bring the mother-half of the race into the councils of the nations. "Women would stand for peace!" How often, how often had they and all of us averred it!'[11]

The campaign in Smethwick did not go with a swing. Christabel went down with flu and her Labour opponent, a union organizer, appeared more at ease with the working-class voters. Nevertheless, on election day Christabel did well enough to demand a recount: in the event she had lost by 775 votes. A little over six months later, after a brief attempt to raise funds and attract more workers, the Women's Party was no more. The first and last attempt by women in Britain to establish their own political party had failed.

Perhaps it was the wrong moment. By 1918 the campaign for the vote which had united women of so many political persuasions had almost run its course. It was time to re-group, to reassess objectives and strategies – surely not the best time to launch a women's party, especially one spiced with Christabel's crankiness. But would there ever be a right moment? History does not relate.

In this section we examine the role of political parties. What do they offer women? How do they help, and how do they hinder the efforts of women to gain access to political power? We examine the machinery of party politics to see how in each party women fit – or do not fit – into the framework. We explore the extent and the shape of women's power in party structures and examine the impact of women's presence on party philosophy. But first let us consider why, in sixty years, no one has seriously revived the idea of a women's party.

It is fair to assume that such an experiment would be likely to occur at a time of intense feminist activity. After the suffrage movement, the next major wave of feminism came with the Women's Liberation Movement of the late 1960s and 1970s. Why did no women's party emerge during that time?

In the early and middle years of women's liberation, feminists were not primarily interested in engaging in a battle with parliament, parties or any of the other manifestations of man-made politics. They had other priorities, for they had discovered that feminism could be applied to parts of the body politic that other ideologies had never bothered to reach. Women's agitation was everywhere. But it was deliberately not organized to contest formal political power; the ways and means of a political party were – for a time, at least – antithetical to a feminist consciousness.

As the ideas of the women's movement took root and multiplied, feminism was no longer a fringe preoccupation. Its diversity became part of its strength, but that also made it vulnerable as a distinct political force. By the early 1980s, it was clear that no one political grouping could 'possess' feminism. It was to be shared (and contested) by many. Women from all parts of the political spectrum came to claim it (even the ones who were heard to say, 'I'm not a feminist but . . .'): they could dismantle it, remake it in their own image and ride off with it into the sunrise of their own political dream. Feminism in its broadest application appeared to be something that shifted and responded to outside conditions – it was not immutable. It could be the means to many ends and women could adapt it to fit their own needs and a variety of political cultures. This was not the stuff of which a political party could be built.

From the mid-1970s, the emphasis on a separate 'women only' politics began to lose a degree of its attraction. For many feminists who had learned their politics from the women's movement it gradually became clear that nothing was going to change unless power was challenged – and only those who sat at the table would get a slice of the cake. The way forward was to infiltrate male-dominated power structures and take on the men at their own game.

The desire to join with men was not simply pragmatic. For many, it derived from a political outlook that transcended sexual divisions. Only a small minority of feminists believed that men were entirely dispensable and could be expunged from the future; for the rest, the feminist project was ultimately about building a world that women and men could share, to the best interest of all. That could only be achieved by fighting alongside men and trying to change their attitudes at one and the same time – a difficult enough task, but one that could not be attempted from a separate women's party.

So for women who wanted to join a political party, there was no alternative but to join one with men in it. Almost invariably, it meant joining a party built mainly by men, in which men remained the dominant sex. That was no less true in 1989 than it was in 1919. Women were, however, *present* in the parties – and, increasingly as the 1980s drew to a close, they were making their presence felt.

The Conservative Party had around one and a quarter million members; the proportion of women was unknown, but informed guesswork would put it at around 40 per cent. Labour had just under 300,000 members in 1987 and, in the 1960s (when figures were last available), women made up around 40 per cent of its membership. Before the merger of the two centre parties, the Social Democratic Party had 58,000 members, 40 per cent of whom were women. The Liberals did not keep records of the gender of their 80,000 members.

A great majority of these women worked in the rank and file of their parties. Alongside men (and sometimes separately), they slogged away in the constituencies, year in year out, supporting and criticizing party policy, organizing, socializing, educating, boosting party funds and, come election time, fighting for 'their' candidate to be returned to Westminster or the town hall. A few held positions which gave them some personal power, locally or nationally. Most were content to feel that they were part of an organization that was, or might become, powerful. But what made them choose one party rather than another?

CHAPTER 11

Labour and Equality

For some women, as for some men, party allegiance was untroubled. Cultural loyalties made party membership as much of an obligation as dusting the family nicknacks. This attitude found its clearest expression in the 'traditional' wings of the parties of both Left and Right. 'I always used to argue for Labour even when I worked in an office. I'd always hated the Tories because that's how I'd been brought up,' explained Janet Hudson of Sheffield. 'Where I was, in a mining area, if you put a donkey up as Labour, they'd vote for it.' Similarly, the Tories had their 'natural' supporters whose party allegiance shone as brightly and as clearly as household silver.

Behind what appeared to be blind party loyalty – reinforcing a sense of belonging to a particular class or set of values – could be found, in many, a positive endorsement of party policies and party codes. Those members felt comfortable – as women – enjoying what party life had to offer. Yet there were others who were exercised about the role of women within their party and who would chide and challenge the party orthodoxy. Talking to grassroots activists across the country, we found profound belief that political parties were failing women. Few admitted that their party was 'good' for women – although all believed that their party was better for women than the others.

There was a shared assumption among women from all backgrounds and political perspectives that women's power *as women* in the parties was tenuous and individual, rather than entrenched and collective. The shape of their powerlessness took a different form and made different patterns in each of the major parties.

The Labour Party, more than any other, seemed to offer a

'natural' home for women because of its identification with egalitarian goals. Labour had inherited the mantle of nineteenth-
century socialist movements, which, as Eric Hobsbawm has
pointed out, 'provided much the most favourable public environment for women . . . to develop their personalities and talents.
But more than this, they promised a total transformation of
society which . . . would be required to change the ancient pattern
of the relation between the sexes.'[1]

There was, however, a contradiction between Labour's egalitarian goals and its origins as a party. It was set up with the
explicit purpose of representing the trade unions at Westminster,
to speak for the organized male, white, industrial working class.
Its personality was formed in an exclusively masculine, produc-
tion-based culture. Its political priorities reflected the needs of
those with power in the party – and the unions, who provided
most of the funds, were assured, through the block vote, a com-
manding position. Labour was committed to redistributing
wealth and power, but for those whose voice was loudest, that
meant a redistribution from the capitalist class to the working
class, where men remained firmly in control. It was assumed
that the unions provided the party with all the working-class
connections it needed, and so Labour never developed any
organic links with people who were not organized, paid workers.
For most women, that meant their relationship with Labour was
oblique, and relied on a class loyalty that took no account of
their relative powerlessness.

More recently, however, the party showed signs of change.
In the mid-1970s, Harold Wilson's Labour government carried
through a substantial programme of equal rights legislation; it
seemed to be responding to a new mood among women, recognizing that they had needs that were distinct from men's, and
votes that mattered. Still, the old atmosphere of a dominant male
culture hung about the Party like smoke from the leader's pipe,
but by the end of the decade that, too, was beginning – just
slightly – to fade. Women were playing a part in the process
of change, which gathered pace in the 1980s and gradually
shifted their relationship with the party.

When we met Cath Potter, she was chair of Manchester City

Labour Party. She belonged to a new generation of young, left-wing activists whose ideas were transforming the style and content of local politics in many a traditional Labour stronghold. It was a wet summer afternoon, and in Manchester's cathedral-style town hall she was running a 'Justice for Mine Workers' stall as part of a fund-raising day for Puerta Cabeza, Manchester's 'twin' town in Nicaragua. Cath's own journey to politics was from a working-class, Labour-voting background, but primarily through her involvement in the Campaign for Nuclear Disarmament as a student at technical college in Oldham. She joined the Labour Party during Tony Benn's fight for the deputy leadership in 1982. (This was a period of general recruitment of men and women who had decided it was time to come out of the margins and campaign for radical politics *within* a political party.)

Party members like Cath Potter saw Labour creating a crucial platform for their ideas, because 'women can't get anything done without it' and 'Labour can't win without women'. She saw women being drawn into the party through example: the Greenham Common peace camps and the miners' strike – both, she believed, showed it was possible for women to create a political role for themselves outside a male orthodoxy. 'The visibility of women in the mining districts motivated other women. We had sixty to seventy support groups in Manchester during the strike and a high proportion of women were involved; often it was their first experience of politics. Some of them joined the Labour Party after that.' CND and Greenham inspired a similar response from women, said Cath Potter, 'because there were large proportions of women in leading positions. The more women organize, the more women want to join the party. In the past, the odd woman did well, but the mass of women were not seen to make a contribution.'

Neither development was part of any Labour Party programme, nor did they always find favour with the Labour leadership. Yet these movements successfully propelled women into Labour's rank and file. These women were to join another group of recent arrivals to the party, women who were also new to formal party politics, whose ideas had influenced both the miners' wives and the Greenham women, and whose impact on the Labour Party was to be considerable. These were feminists – a loosely knit group of largely urban, middle-class women. Some were veterans of student politics in the 1960s; all shared some experience of the Women's Liberation Movement, whose intellectual and political energies had been directed towards the contemporary 'woman question'.

Feminists began to join the Labour Party towards the end of the 1970s in response to several developments. One was that the Labour Party itself appeared to be changing. This was partly because Labour after 1979 – in opposition rather than in government – offered a focus for campaigns against a fiercely right-wing government. The Labour Party in opposition also appeared more attractive to 'alternative', anti-authoritarian groups than it had in government – it was no longer the 'establishment'. At the same time, discussions about constitutional reform were taking place inside the Labour Party. The campaign for the mandatory re-selection of MPs was seen as a way of making the Party more accountable and democratic. The desire for a more open Party was also part of a move to build political alliances beyond Labour's traditional bases. All this had an attraction for feminists whose ways of thinking and organizing depended on a participatory and non-hierarchical framework. The Labour Party was beginning to look to be a more fruitful place.

By this time, the women's movement itself was in something of a crisis. It was time for socialist feminists to come in from the cold. Lynne Segal, academic and London-based socialist feminist, was one of those who found a home in the Labour Party at this time. 'Those who believed that reaction to a government of the far Right would be to mobilize resistance could hardly have been more wrong,' she commented later.

In 1980 some feminists, including myself, were travelling around the country trying to unite what we called the 'fragments', hoping to build up and co-ordinate networks of women and men active in any progressive struggles without abandoning our feminist perspectives and ways of working. We too failed to foresee the extent of the disarray and despair the Thatcher government would succeed in creating. As the political climate shifted to a defensive protection of the inadequate incomes and services we already had and were about to lose, many feminists gradually began (often with considerable reluctance) to test out the only remaining political forum still speaking even the language of reform. We joined the Labour Party.[2]

Sarah Perrigo, a political lecturer in the School of Peace Studies at Bradford University, joined the Labour Party in the late 1970s. Writing about women and the Labour Party in *Feminist Review*, she, too, drew attention to the hostile political and economic climate that seemed to be threatening the women's movement. 'It seemed,' she wrote, 'imperative that alliances be made with other movements similarly threatened if gains won were to be defended and the movement progress.'[3]

The effect of these shifts was to bring into the Labour Party a small but highly articulate group of mainly white, middle-class women. 'Many of us,' wrote Sarah Perrigo, 'had gained enormous experience and confidence through our involvement in feminist politics and felt more able to enter (or in some cases re-enter) the more formal arena of Labour Party politics and make our voices heard.'[4]

At the same time, Labour felt the impact of changes in the trade-union movement, where more women were joining and becoming active. Increasing numbers of blue-collar and white-collar women who had gained political experience in their unions became visible in the Labour Party and played a part in the process of change. Many had been influenced by women's liberation, although they did not always see eye to eye with the non-union-based feminists, as we shall see.

Women too young to remember the early Women's Liberation Movement also saw in the changing Labour Party something attractive. Ellen McLaughlan from Glasgow came from a working-class, Labour-voting family but had never bothered to have any links with the party until she joined in 1983, at the age of twenty-four. 'My image of the Labour Party was that MPs and important people had all the power, so there was not much point in people like me getting involved. Then with all the changes and the campaign for democracy, I thought ordinary members would be able to influence the party and how policies are made.'[5]

The sense that the Labour Party had opened up and that Party policy could be influenced from the grass roots was an important development, not least for working-class women who had viewed with unease – and from afar – the traditional Labour Party with its powers firmly fixed in Westminster and the unions. There was also a growing sense that it was possible for women to make their mark in the Party. A few more women's voices were being heard, a few more faces seen. The idea that more women should be selected for council or parliamentary seats was beginning to affect the attitudes of ordinary members. Julie Donovan, a working-class woman active in community politics in South London's docklands, told us:

> I used to think I couldn't work for the Labour Party, the leadership is so insincere and hopeless. But now I think you've got to. Get more and more women in, more women on the council, eventually a woman parliamentary candidate, and gradually you can change it. It's the only place there is for working-class women to work for change.

This 'changing' Labour Party also began, at a local level, to make alliances with Afro-Caribbean and Asian women and men who worked as teachers or as social workers and administrators in local government, or who were part of the burgeoning black voluntary sector. Some joined the Labour Party as a strategy for influencing policy in local government and making waves in town halls. Historically, the ethnic minority communities had been denied any power in the political process; the Labour Party had complacently counted on the black and Asian vote, but had offered little in return. Sylvette Collins of the Southall Black Women's Centre commented: 'Labour has used black people's votes – just as they're using mine – but they never do anything about it.' The trade unions had made little effort to recruit ethnic minority workers, or to identify the particular problems of the immigrant communities – indeed, trade unionists had marched from London's docklands in 1968 to support Enoch Powell's 'rivers of blood' speech.

Anwar Ditta, a working-class Asian woman from Rochdale who became politicized through her own experience, commented:

> No one party is going to be 'fair' about immigration. The immigration laws will always be tough. My case taught me that there are racist laws in this country, one for black and one for white. But I came to a decision on political grounds that I had no choice but the Labour Party. Cyril Smith, the Liberal MP here, dropped my case. It was a good lesson for me, that, and for the Asian community, because it's always said that he does a lot for the black people. I joined Labour because it has a better deal for black people and for women. If you live here, it's the only party you can join.

Anwar was perhaps not representative of the Labour Party's ethnic membership, but her views on Labour's immigration record were typical of many women who had somewhat reluctantly found a home with Labour.

To understand how Anwar Ditta or Julie Donovan, or any of the other women who joined, fitted into the Labour Party, it is worth a glance at the delegates who gather for the Party's annual conference. There are three major groupings. First, the trade-union delegates, descendants of those who built the party; by and large these are bulky, soberly-suited, middle-aged men (only 12.9 per cent of union delegates were women at the 1987 conference). Clutching papers and briefcases, they are seen to prowl the corridors fixing deals with fellow unionists, colonizing bars and foyers, eager to exchange a word in an ear or a slap on the back. These delegates possess the crucial block votes representing 90 per cent of any card vote on conference resolutions; it is a mechanism which gives them status and power. The unions have 40 per cent of Labour's electoral college, used for electing the party leader and deputy. They also control the purse-strings, for their six and a half million members contribute £5 million annually to the party's funds, which represents 80 per cent of the total.

Then there are the MPs, the members of the Parliamentary Labour Party, who don't vote on resolutions to conference but control 30 per cent of the electoral college, their power to choose party leaders having been reduced in favour of the constituency delegates. In 1989, out of a total of 227 Labour MPs, 22 were women. The MPs are rather more diverse in appearance than the union delegates – some look as though they might have come from the senior common room of a university or from barristers' chambers, although others – with regional accents and union-sponsored parliamentary seats – do come from working-class backgrounds.

The third grouping is made up of constituency party delegates, who have 30 per cent of the electoral college and about 10 per cent of card votes at conference. More of these are women than in the two other categories – 31 per cent in 1987. This group is more casually dressed; many, especially those from Southern constituencies, are middle-class, working in further education or in the media, as social workers or local-government officials. Some are children of the 1960s and hold fond memories of those libertarian years although they are now in their early forties. They speak forcibly and articulately and sometimes scowl at the men in suits who leave the conference hall when the subject for debate turns to the rights of women or gays. They are often the target of the Tory press in its tireless crusade to discredit the so-called 'Loony Left'.

On the platform, the great and the good of the party preside; and here, again, is a row of men in suits. Occasionally a woman can be seen among them – an MP or a member of the National Executive. More rarely, a woman chairs a session of the conference. The leader's wife also appears from time to time, kisses her husband and is given a bouquet of flowers amidst affectionate applause. . . .

The body politic of the Labour Party continued to be sturdily male, however much it tried – and try it did on occasions – to make a genuine appeal to women. The most prominent female role model it had to offer in the late 1980s was the leader's wife. Glenys Kinnock was already a forceful and intelligent woman in her own right, with her own political life working with CND and women in the Third World. However, her official role in the Labour Party was firmly established as that of wife and mother, symbolizing traditional family values. This was the image that was clearly defined in Labour's TV political broadcasts during the 1987 general election campaign. It reflected the actual experience (or, if not, the ideal) of most Labour leaders – who had made their way in politics with a good woman behind them. But what did it signify for women who were striving to move in the same direction? Anna Wyatt, as chief executive of South-wark Council, was a senior figure with a highly demanding job. She told us:

> I find it difficult to relate to the way all those male politicians live in their houses and have their wives, and their wives look after the children and do part-time jobs. It presents a clash because most women who are influential in the party aren't coming from that background at all. Even the women who are married are independent people and are there in their own right. The men are really locked into the notion of women being the support system.

Women were not image-makers in the Labour Party in the late 1980s, except in a wifely capacity. Gone from the hierarchy were figures such as Barbara Castle and Shirley Williams. Jo Richardson was the only woman in the shadow cabinet until a new rule introduced in 1989 opened up more places for women. Before that, Jo Richardson had been grafted on as shadow Minister for Women. Her arrival was the result of a hard-fought campaign, and she had taken on the burden of securing a place for women's issues at the heart of the Parliamentary Labour Party. But the Ministry for Women was not considered an area of expertise like Employment or the Treasury, imbued with gravitas and status. It was, in spite of the enormity of the task, considered rather marginal and light-weight.

It was not just in the Party leadership or in the House of Commons that the male presence was overwhelming. The same was true at the bottom of the power pyramid, in the local constituencies. In 1986 the women's committee of the South-West Region of the Labour Party carried out a survey of the region which revealed that, at ward level, women made up 42.2 per cent of all members, but were under-represented in proportion to their membership in all posts, except in the purely clerical jobs of minutes secretary and secretary. Only 13 per cent of chairs and 16 per cent of treasurers were women.[6]

The feminist incursion into the Labour Party brought with it a challenge to the domination of men. Feminists queried the efficacy of the Party's methods of stimulating support and enthusiasm at the grass roots and started to ask just what Labour was doing for women. Angela Trikic was a socialist feminist who chaired a Labour Party ward in the leafy constituency of Withington, South Manchester. She was brought up in Leicester in a working-class home where her Yugoslav immigrant father imposed strict codes of conduct on his teenage daughter. A veteran of university politics and a former member of the International Marxist Group, she went on to teach at a further education college and became a single mother of two boys. As ward chair, she had noticed that women members were not coming to ward meetings. To find out why, she held a meeting for women only on a Sunday afternoon in a local community centre. The time, the place and the agenda all broke with the usual conventions of the ward. She discovered that evening meetings were difficult for some women to manage because of domestic problems, and that some Asian women did not attend because the meetings were held in a pub. The women also told her that they found meetings too full of routine 'business' procedures and too preoccupied with passing paper resolutions which left no time for political discussion. Finally, the women felt that the party members failed to get out and about in the community. All these problems were underlined by a feeling that party meetings 'were so male in the way they operated'.

It is hard to escape the conclusion that men had for years been unable or unwilling to recognize how the patterns of political life – even at the grass roots – excluded women. The result was continuous undermining of women's participation in party life at local level – the point at which formal participation in the political process began. 'You just feel that your opinion, your experience, your brain don't count because of your sex,' commented Lois Acton, a community organizer and long-time Labour activist in South-East London. 'There's this in-built resistance to listening unless you come from a particular background – you've got to have your full accredited stable behind you, you've got to have done your time. Most women can't do that, they can't get their full card of political activities ticked, so they don't get to be taken seriously.'

Up and down the country, women were relating the same kind of experience. Their verdict was that meetings and Party activities were unfriendly and intimidating to women, and remote from practical politics. 'People come along to meetings, and they don't know what anyone is talking about, so they go away,' was a typical comment. The preoccupation with passing resolutions and conducting party 'business' to the exclusion of political education, campaigning or, indeed, enjoyment was particularly off-putting to women. As Glenys Thornton, chair of the London Labour Party, said: 'Anyone who goes to branch meetings and continues to go deserves a medal; they can be really quite dire.' Part of the problem, she observed, was that Labour had lost its direction as a social and educational force; it had forgotten that it needed to be a party that could enjoy itself as well as carry out political business. She described the Labour Club where her parents and their friends had socialized in Yorkshire when she was a child. It had held dances on Saturday nights; it was the place for drinking with friends and meeting local people; it was where you went with your housing problems or difficulties with the council. The regional party held regular debating and drama competitions. 'The Club was where the Party recruited young people, got them doing things which weren't necessarily political. They had a good time. In the North, there are still places like that. They're more boozing clubs nowadays, but at least they are there.'

Afro-Caribbean and Asian women had to deal with a double layer of alienation. At one level, they were patronized much as white women were. Sylvette Collins told us: 'I've been to a Labour Party meeting where they actually said, "Ladies, I know you've been waiting for ages, but you'll have to wait a bit longer while we pass the next motion – can you go and make the tea?" It wasn't that long ago, either!' In addition, there was strong resentment at the Labour Party's refusal to allow separate space for ethnic minorities. Diane Abbott, MP for Hackney North and Stoke Newington, saw it like this: 'How black women empower themselves in the Labour Party is part of how black people empower themselves, which, I believe, is through caucusing. Nobody in the United States thinks it peculiar that black people want to caucus. The black section debate is just part of the manifestation of racism in the party.' What infuriated many black women was that the Labour leadership was attempting to subsume black people within its own certainties about the nature of socialism and the needs of the black community. Cynthia Alexander of the Southall Black Women's Centre remarked that she'd rather 'have no black people involved in the Labour Party than have a dozen sitting there agreeing with all the white people'.

All in all, the party of egalitarianism seemed to operate in a manner that was the *reverse* of the way women would choose to organize if left to their own devices. It was formal and hierarchical; it was bound by habit and ritual; it was competitive rather than co-operative in spirit; it had little connection with ordinary women's lives, and less inclination to prioritize their needs; it was unadventurous about change and fearful of radicalism; and it was the last place you'd go for a 'good laugh'. No wonder women had difficulty feeling at home in the Labour Party.

One way in which women sought to overcome these difficulties was to organize separately, through the Party's women's organization. Women's sections, councils and committees met independently, discussed their own agendas and elected their own delegates to represent their views at the general meetings held at each level of the Party, from the ward to the region, and finally to the National Labour Women's Committee, whose thirty-two members were elected by the women's regional conferences. But when it came to the top of the power pyramid, something else happened. Five places were reserved for women on the National Executive Committee, the Party's highest decision-making body. These women were elected not by the national conference of Labour women, at which each delegate had a single vote, but by the annual conference of the whole Party, where the block-voting system operated. Thus, the five women's places on the NEC were effectively in the hands of the unions, to be filled not by the best representatives of the women's cause, but by candidates acceptable to the most powerful sector of the Party.

Women's sections were first formed from the branches of the Women's Labour League (the women's arm of the Independent Labour Party) when it merged with the Party in 1918. Marion Phillips, Labour's first Chief Woman Officer, welcomed them as a useful channel for women 'so newly come into political life that their development will be hindered ... if the whole of their work is conducted in organisations of both sexes'.[7] (That view, interestingly enough, was still widely held by Labour women at the time of writing.)

It was Arthur Henderson, leader of the Labour Party at the time, who dealt the critical blow. He disliked the idea of a separate organization for women, which he believed contributed to the 'unhappy sex antagonism' wrought by the battle for the franchise. What he did want, however, was to strengthen the power of the unions and to weaken the Left (which supported women's rights). Both purposes were served by introducing the block-voting system, and by reserving five seats for women on the National Executive, to be elected via the block vote. This helped shift the balance of power away from the constituencies and towards the unions at a time of high female unemployment, when women's position in the unions was weak. Women had a recognized status within the Party, but where power really mattered, they had none to call their own.[8]

The women's organization was to have a chequered history. In the 1920s, Labour women, among them Dora Russell and the Lancashire campaigner Selina Cooper, looked to their Party to support the provision of birth-control. The national women's conference would pass a resolution overwhelmingly in favour of the availability of birth control measures; but this mattered little because the men – at the party's annual conference – would just as surely reject it. Independent voices from the women's organization were gradually subdued; independent activity was frowned upon. It became hard for women's sections to make any mark, and they drifted into the only role that seemed available to them – the tea-makers and the supporters of the men who made the policy.

Most women's sections were quiescent, or moribund, until the 1970s when things began to liven up again. Feminists who joined the Party in that decade brought with them a positive experience of separate organization. They envisaged a new role for the women's sections: no longer would they function as a cosy, social side-show; instead they would become a real power base, where women could build solidarity, develop policy and prepare strategies for scaling the heights of the Party. 'Policy-making, not tea-making' was the slogan.

Skills learnt in the women's movement were put to good use. Women's sections became a forum for women to learn from each other about politics and political methods. They also attempted to make women's issues a central concern of the Party. Angela Trikic from Manchester echoed the views of Marion Phillips in 1918 when she said: 'The women's section provides the possibility for women to meet together, to provide support and confidence and to intervene in the mixed sections.' She recalled her experience of a women's section in Stockport, which had enabled women to draw the constituency's attention to subjects such as abortion. 'It is not an easy issue – you have to rehearse the arguments. It's hard if you stand up cold to assume that the support is there. But by discussing that sort of issue in the women's section, we could take it to the wards and to the constituency more easily. You knew you weren't the only one who could and would speak out.'

Some women's sections made a serious attempt, not just to create an unintimidating political environment, but also to be a campaigning, bridge-building and empowering organization for women, both inside and outside the party. But they were not ubiquitous, and some continued in the old vein. Anne Suddick, who played a major role in organizing Women Against Pit Closures, found what she called a lack of awareness in her Durham women's section. 'They tend to make tea and things like that. And I don't think that we got £20 from them for the miners' strike in the whole year.' In 1986, there were 829 women's sections and 159 women's councils. More than a hundred constituencies had no women's organization at all.

The resurgence of the women's sections was significant enough to arouse some suspicion and hostility in Labour's ranks. Traditional attitudes died hard. Janice Rose, a Women's Aid worker in Sheffield, remembered a discussion at her local Labour Party meeting on whether to set up a women's section. 'This bloke stood up and said, "My wife's not here at the moment but I know that she fully agrees with me and she's totally against them because they're so cliquey." I said, "What's she doing at home?" He said, "Well, we have got a family you know."'

'Constituency man' could not stop the sections spreading (from 1983 women were able to set them up without permission from the constituencies), but that did not prevent him from some-times displaying unease. One Party official in the North-East, on learning that a local women's section was being set up, was heard to say: 'What do you want to do that for? To discuss Lenin's views on lingerie?' On a more serious level, there were men – and women – who argued that separate sections would become a 'ghetto' and would not help women to become more powerful, or that they would be divisive and weaken the Party as a whole.

The revived women's sections began to take an interest in such areas as child care and sexuality which were not part of Labour's traditional agenda – indeed, they had generally not been seen as 'political' issues at all. The sections also made alliances with groups *outside* the Labour Party – with campaigns for Nicaragua, with anti-apartheid groups or, closer to home, with Greenham women, Women Against Pit Closures and a range of community-based activities. Like the women who set up Links after the miners' strike, they weren't tied by traditional notions about what should – or should not – be their proper political concerns, and they believed such alliances were both logical and empowering.

In some areas, the women's sections seemed to be the only element of the Party that offered political education to members. They held reading groups and socials, and set up stalls at fairs and shopping centres; they organized educational meetings and day workshops. Val Manchee of Newcastle observed that women's sections had the best political discussions in the Party. 'Some men are getting jealous and want to come along. They feel they are missing out on something.'[9] Perhaps women's sections appeared to have closer connections with 'real' life than the usual run of Party business; and they seemed to have imported, from the extra-parliamentary tradition of women's politics, a subversive tendency to have a good time.

Some of the stronger women's sections claimed that they could – and did – put women's issues back into the centre of Party debate. Leslie Thorne belonged to the women's section in the market town of Chorley, near Preston. She was brought up in a Liberal home, then joined a trade union as a young nurse and the Labour Party when she and her husband lived in Salford. She believed that the women's section had made an impact in the mainstream. 'We can bring up issues, we've got delegates on to different committees, we have a say as women. We've put lots of very important issues up as resolutions – about things that men perhaps don't understand. Our little section has really turned the tables. It's made them take note of us.'

Whatever the Labour Party women's organization initiated, however active and politically dynamic it became, it remained, by its nature, marginal. It could encourage and prepare women for power but it was not itself part of the power structure of the Party. Even the national conference of Labour women was only advisory – it could pass as many resolutions as it liked, but each and every one could be ignored. Frances Morrell, former leader of the Inner London Education Authority, commented: 'Leading male figures in the Party frequently say to me: "My goodness, what a tremendously radical conference it is, very influential." And I keep on snarling: "We don't want to be influential." That is the name of the game – either you have power or you don't; but being influential is the same as not having power.'[10]

Frances Morrell became one of the key figures in the Women's Action Committee (WAC), set up in 1981 to campaign for changes in the constitution of the Labour Party that would enhance the power of women. Ann Pettifor, a prominent feminist activist who became WAC's national organizer, declared that it was designed to 'achieve for women what the democratic reforms had achieved for the rank and file'.[11] The WAC wanted to make women the subjects and not the objects of party policy and to ensure that the women in positions of power truly represented the women's organization of the Party. To do this, power had to be taken away from men and given to women, through positive action where necessary. The WAC had five demands: the election of the National Labour Women's Committee by the national conference of Labour women; the election of the five reserved seats on the NEC by the women's conference; the right for the women's conference to table five resolutions on the agenda of the party's annual conference, to be debated as of right; a rules conference for women to draw up new rules for women's organizations; and one woman on every parliamentary selection shortlist.

This last demand was agreed by Labour's national conference in 1986. By the end of the 1980s, it was the only one to have been met – although by that time every constituency had to elect a women's officer with a vote on its general management committee, and a further reform had facilitated the election of at least three women to the shadow cabinet. Cath Potter helped set up a Women's Action Committee group in Manchester. 'We fought for the five demands to be adopted by Manchester constituencies and they all voted for it – at least on paper,' she told us. 'But when it came to the crunch, only one constituency took a resolution for the demands to conference.' There was, nevertheless, a substantial increase in the number of resolutions concerning the women's organization taken to the annual conference – from a total of six between 1974 and 1981 to seventy-four between 1981 and 1985.

The vigorous procedural campaign of the Women's Action Committee made plenty of waves in the Party, even though it scored few immediate successes. Its methods attracted criticism, even from some feminists – for WAC was not averse to a bit of old-fashioned, male-style politicking. Sarah Perrigo observed that feminists tended 'to resist organizing "behind the scenes" or indulging in "fixing" things in the bar. At the same time we are constantly surprised when we are out-manoeuvred by others who are clearly prepared to be utterly ruthless in pursuit of their aims.'[12] Feminist practice was often the subject of self-criticism and hesitancy, qualities not normally associated with political power struggles.

The WAC's preoccupation with the internal workings of the party was seen by others as a symptom of Labour's remoteness from its working-class rank and file. There was a belief among some trade-union women that the women's sections were being hijacked by graduates in dungarees with posh accents and dangling earrings – and nowhere was this feeling stronger than in London and the South-East, where the trend was seen as part of a general malaise. 'I think there's a gentrification exercise going on in the Labour Party,' was how one member of the public employees' union, NUPE, put it.

> In my GC, for example, there are only about five people who don't have university degrees, and I'm one of them. I think it is a disastrous situation for Labour. You see all those women speaking and they don't really know what problems our members have on the ground, what it's like to be an ordinary low-paid worker in a hospital. Well-intentioned as they are, they just do not understand what problems the average woman faces.

The traditional opposition of the trade unions to women's autonomy in the party exacerbated relations between the two groups – which boiled up into a bitter public row at the 1986 national conference of Labour women on the Scottish island of Bute. The crux of the matter was the balance of power between the unions and the Constituency Labour Parties (CLPs). Women who attended the conference as trade-union delegates, representing large numbers of union members, simply had one vote each, as did women from the CLPs, who represented far smaller numbers. The union women had refused to support the WAC campaign for direct elections from the women's conference to the NEC, because they felt their own votes carried insufficient weight, and feared it would give unwarranted power to what they saw as an unrepresentative minority. The row had been brewing for some time.

At the Bute conference, a compromise resolution from NUPE was defeated as a result of lobbying by WAC, while a shadow election, organized by WAC, for women's seats on the NEC was boycotted by most of the union delegates. Unseemly insults were exchanged, and in the weeks that followed some of the unions threatened to withdraw from future women's conferences. At Labour's London headquarters, consultations were set up and compromises sought. One solution that was mooted was for the women's conference to have its own block vote for union delegates, based on the size of each union's *female* membership. This would give the women's conference more clout and strengthen the case for direct elections; it would also lend weight to the heretical notion that there were distinctive male and female interests within the organized working class. Such a reform could not, of course, be introduced without the support of Labour's annual conference – a hurdle yet to be reached at the time of writing.

From a different perspective, Afro-Caribbean and Asian women had their own difficulties with participating in the Labour Party women's organization. White feminists were slow to acknowledge that they had been trying to incorporate black women within their own white framework of feminism and female experience. Monica Johnson of Lewisham Council's Women's Unit commented: 'There I was, the lone black woman in my local women's section of the Labour Party, surrounded by well-meaning white women but not actually being able to communicate. I don't want to sound pessimistic because I think there have been improvements, but it has been a slow process.'[13]

Like other parts of the Labour Party, the women's organization was not immune, for most of the 1980s, to the impact of the Militant Tendency. Militant rejected any notion that women's oppression had a different base from class oppression, and had no scruples about muscling in on women's sections. In some places, this had a severely debilitating effect on morale. Angela Trikic talked about her Manchester experience: 'Our women's section has been heavily dominated by Militant. They take quite a fundamental position in being against positive action, so they'll use the section quite cynically to propose men for posts. They also tend to make women's politics sterile by calling for completely abstract resolutions and by personalizing their attacks.'

In spite of all the difficulties, women did become more influential in the party during the late 1980s, and that influence appeared to count for something. For the 1987 general election, Labour put together a package of policies that was noticed and liked by women, especially younger women. The Party committed itself, for the first time, to a Ministry for Women, with cabinet status for the Minister. It even conducted a special campaign to woo women's votes – a sign that it had come round to the idea that there was a distinctive female constituency that was worth winning. Labour's 'Policy Review', published in 1989, seemed to exhibit a genuine commitment to the particular needs of women. They were dealt with explicitly, not in a brief addendum as had been the practice, but as an integral – even prominent – part of the main text. Labour was still the most likely place for women who wanted to fight in the political mainstream to shift the traditional balance of power between women and men. But men still dominated the party, holding all the key positions. As Frances Morrell pointed out, influence was all very well, but what women needed most was power.

CHAPTER 12

At Home with the Tories

The face of women's subordination wore a very different expression in the Conservative Party – helpful, hard-working and only occasionally riled. (We are necessarily ignoring Mrs Thatcher at this point, for reasons we shall explain later.) For the great majority of Tory women, the Party provided a role which corresponded to their life at home: they were put in charge of domestic organization. This was an expression of Conservative ideology about women's role in life generally, which set them down squarely at the heart of the family, inhabiting a separate sphere from men, complementing rather than competing with them.

Within their domestic world, women were regarded as the chief defenders of moral, social and sexual mores, central to a political philosophy which idealized 'traditional' family life and regarded the family as the fount of essential political virtues: individual freedom, self-help and enterprise. Women stood guard against external dangers that lurked in the public (and usually male) world beyond. Their job was to fend off the spectres of excessive state power, of strikes, of juvenile delinquency, violence, crime and sexual freedoms. All these things posed a threat to Conservative ideology. Ian Gilmour, a Conservative 'wet' and ex-member of Mrs Thatcher's cabinet, wrote in his book *Inside Right :* 'In their defence of the individual against socialism and excessive state power, Conservatives rely chiefly upon the family and private property. ... Man is a member of the family before he is a member of anything else. The family is the centre of his affections and the transmitter of traditions.'[1]

Thus women as wives and mothers had a special place in the Conservative Party as defenders and upholders of the essence of Conservatism. It helped them feel at home in the Party. They were the housekeepers of political morality – a powerful and attractive image to some.

There was room within this definition for various shades of Toryism; it could accommodate the traditional lady who learnt her philanthropy at her mother's knee and who embraced the more 'caring' face of the Conservative Party, as well as the harder-edged Tory of the authoritarian school. The Conservative Party was a wide beach and had a broad harbour. It was easy to dock there because Conservatives did not, on the whole, like to articulate differences – for to do so would suggest the existence of special groups with special needs. This perspective helped to conceal the traditional Tory vices of élitism and snobbery, as well as sexism and racism.

To find a home in the Party, a woman would need only to be herself – so long as her identity was rooted in her experience as wife and mother. The skills and preoccupations of her daily life would be put to use. Not only were her gifts appreciated, but the Tory woman could make sense of her own world in the politics of her Party. A Conservative booklet entitled *Going Places, Women in the Conservative Party* declared that former Prime Minister Edward Heath got right to the heart of things when he said: 'It is through the women of the Party that we can help to sustain and protect, and where necessary adapt, all that is best in the life of the family and of the nation as a whole.'[2] That specific endorsement of their traditional domestic role enabled Conservative women to seek – and find – a sense of belonging. There was no equivalent message for women in the Labour Party.

Audrey Berry was a working-class Tory who had been both a district councillor and county councillor. She lived with her husband in a smartly-furnished semi in the small Lancashire town of Raynford, with a view across fields of corn and cabbage to St Helen's. 'Both my parents were Tories and I've been active in politics for more than twenty years,' she told us. 'Like my parents, I'm not one of the posh Tories.' She did not talk of service or duty to the community, but she represented a pugnacious Toryism that had a particular resonance in the late 1980s. She distinguished her own record of hard work for the Party from the more leisurely approach of middle-class, county Tory ladies.

'The mother is the home, the centre, the homemaker,' she said. 'Perhaps it's old-fashioned, but it's what I believe.' The mother at home was what was right; the mother anywhere else was responsible for what went wrong. 'When they say, it's the environment that causes crime or unemployment, it's eyewash. I blame the lack of parental control and Mums going out to work. When children get murdered, you have to ask, where were the parents?' She declared approvingly that 'Mrs Thatcher is all for the family.' The awkward fact that her party leader went out to work when her own twins were still in their infancy did not appear to dent that certainty.

Conservatives held women responsible for safeguarding social mores, and at the same time blamed them for many of society's ills. Meanwhile, women were often the ones who suffered most when things went wrong – for instance, by living in fear of violence. Yet Conservatism did not offer women the power to control or change their condition. Their only weapon was revenge, and so was born that Tory stereotype: the ardent supporter of capital punishment, long prison sentences and the panoply of repressive treatments for offenders. Moretta Hutchinson, a cheerful and thoughtful retired nurse from Burnley, had a traditional 'tough' attitude to crime. She described her views on 'law and order' as the political response of a mother concerned for her children.

> Women look on things as to how politics affects the family and children. It's a natural part of their make-up. I'm surprised that women in the other parties haven't been in support of stronger punishments for crime, especially where children are concerned. I would be very much in favour of, if necessary, the extreme punishment. Women feel very strongly about that because they bear the child.

The Conservative women, who had their moment in law-and-order debates at the annual conference, endured a climate of fear and loathing, induced by crime and the criminal. 'Conservatism seemed to assimilate women's fear,' wrote Beatrix Campbell in *Iron Ladies*, 'not because its ideology contained any critique which produced it, nor because it contained any programme for its solution, but because moral panic *is* its politics. The politics of fear is central to the Conservative Party's "authoritarian populism"'.[3]

Shreela Flather had good reason to be fearful – she'd had iron bars thrown through the windows of her home and racist slogans scrawled on the walls. She experienced the Tory Party at its most collectively racist when she attended the debate on race at the 1979 conference after the election victory. 'That debate was appalling. There, at the conference, was the first time I'd felt insecure in this country. The hall was so full of hate, it was almost tangible.' But Mrs Flather, who came to Britain from Lahore in 1952 to study law, like her father and grandfather before her, was a Conservative, a councillor for Maidenhead, and in 1986 she became Britain's first Asian woman mayor. 'My whole background is against socialism. I subscribe to old-fashioned, middle-of-the-road Toryism. But staying as a Tory is to feel very exposed. The black community doesn't see Toryism as legitimate. And even though a large section of the party subscribes to racist feelings, I feel I have an obligation to stay and fight and appeal to the others.'[4] The brand of Conservatism which embraced the triumph of individualism – encouraging people to take responsibility for their own life – could, other things being equal, have been attractive to first-generation immigrant communities. It was an article of faith in self-improvement to emigrate from a poor developing country to a new land. But the Conservatives were seen to embrace the racist strands in working-class populism, and Tory politicians found themselves picking up votes by being the party that opposed Black immigration.

While the Tories claimed a monopoly of the support of the 'concerned' mother, Conservative womanhood was also fashioned around those notions of femininity associated with the thrifty housewife, the sober shopper. As *Going Places* put it:

Women must act as the voice of realism. The Women's Organisation can help explain what every housewife knows; that we cannot spend money that we have not got. ... Success in driving this crucial message home affects not only prices – but also our schools, hospitals, the care of the elderly and our ability to do more for those in real need.[5]

This 'voice of realism' endorsed a make-do-and-mend ideology which allowed the Conservatives to see themselves as the 'common-sense' party.

For Maggie Smyth that was what made the Conservative Party attractive. She did not talk about the evils of mothers going out to work or about the sanctity of the family; for a start she had two children outside marriage and, secondly, she was a working-class woman who expected to have to go out to work to survive. She came to London from a Lancashire village where it was 'an unwritten law' to vote Labour. 'You didn't think about politics, you just voted Labour.' In London, she moved into the borough of Brent and what she saw happening there she didn't like. 'I've switched to the Tories because I see they'll allow me a choice where Labour will dictate to you. I also see the Conservatives as a common-sense party. If there's going to be any sanity, women must be there.' She saw the Conservative Party as reinforcing her own belief that women were the cornerstone of home life and the repository of good sense and economic sobriety. Maggie Smyth echoed Mrs Thatcher's reference to living within your means when she equated running the country with running a home. 'A normal woman gets the housekeeping and must make it last. You can't keep running to the IMF and say give us a few more millions.' Conservative women could link the triumph of Conservatism in the 1980s to the 'sensible' politics associated with the 'sensible' sex.

The values of traditional female culture were effortlessly harnessed to Conservatism and helped pull the Tory wagon, but that did not make women powerful within the Party. Conservative women did not operate as activating agents with their own programme for change. They might recline in political contentment, but they were not responsible for their state of grace.

Unlike the women's organization in the Labour Party, the Conservative women's committees at constituency level remained overwhelmingly compliant and supportive, unruffled by dissent.

Seizing our Opportunities, a publication from the European Union for Women, a now defunct arm of the Conservative Party that encouraged women to participate in public life, made its own startling admission of the limitations of the role of the women's organization. It described it as a 'cosy, sympathetic world' remote from the 'real world' of the constituency where women competed against men for the real rewards of elected office.[6]

The basic unit of the Conservative women's organization was the ward or constituency women's committee. (In some constituencies, the chairman of the women's committee was automatically vice-chairman of the constituency.) The women's committees were mainly social, fund-raising bodies in which politics was seen more as an intrusion than as a necessity. In general, the Tory woman did the sort of work that was described by others who had more important things to do as 'invaluable'. She was an integral part of the political machinery because she ran the coffee mornings and the sherry parties, the canvassing and the membership drives, and the money that she raised made it possible for the constituency to flourish; her activity was essential because it enabled others to be powerful. Beatrix Campbell observed:

> Women's role in the party is associated with the self-denying qualities of femininity which support the power of others. That's one way that the women are able to veil the realities of the power structure, because they *confer* power upon the men. And because the men's power appears to be *given* by the women, they consent to it. That makes women *necessary*. But it makes power-sharing unnecessary.[7]

Audrey Berry, once Councillor Berry of Merseyside County Council, was taking things a little easier when we met her, but she was still chairman of the St Helen's North women's committee and was very clear about the hard work she put in and its impact on the constituency: 'I think the women's committee has a very vital role to play because we're workers with backbone; we raise more money and we contribute to political comment.' She was worried that so few young women were getting involved, but believed that the way to encourage them was not to scare them away by talking about politics. The important thing for Mrs Berry was that the women enjoyed themselves – a desire shared by women across party boundaries. 'At first, I don't mention politics as such. Then, if they come, I try to make politics fun and make them aware. Perhaps women see the Conservative Party as élitist, but at the same time,' she said, knowingly, 'they think it's *nice* to be associated with the Tories.' Mrs Berry was proud of the twice-yearly social events that she and the other Tory ladies laid on for the Party. 'Our paté and plonk do in the summer is very popular – we raise £500. The local Tories say that it's through Audrey Berry that we get things done, she works three times as hard as anyone else.'

The role of Tory women as efficient providers and organizers rankled with some younger Tory activists, but it was not a matter for political action. 'The Tory Party has always regarded women as fund-raisers and with a few exceptions they remain the tea-makers. Men are always regarded as superior beings,' said Sarah Bardswell, a graduate of Sussex University, a mother of four children and a leading Party worker in Richmond (a marginal suburban constituency in London). She believed that the women's organization of the Party at constituency level didn't offer much, except as fulfilling a social need for older women whose involvement made them feel wanted.

Sarah Bardswell's response to the inertia of her women's organization had been to set up a Young Wives Group. 'I thought that there was something to be said for having a simple little ploughman's lunch to which mothers could come and bring their children. We had a speaker – usually someone political or from a public body.' Sarah Bardswell was the sort of efficient middle-class woman who could organize a lunch with the minimum of effort to the greatest effect. When she was running the group, she said, it was unusually politically effective in that it spawned future constituency party officers and councillors. 'Now it's completely changed. They have a rather smart lunch with coronation chicken and meringues and they haven't had a political speaker for yonks.' The style and content of such a committee depended on its personalities; because it had no particular strategy or political target its effect was random and its life short. Women like

Sarah Bardswell were conscious of the impasse but powerless to change it – and disinclined to fight for the power they lacked.

Maggie Smyth was not interested in the activities of 'the blue rinse brigade' in the women's committees and had no time for what she called 'sectarianism'. 'There's no difference between men and women except that men have balls. Everyone should muck in and get on with it. Women are just going to have to pick themselves up.' The Labour Party women's sections offered her no example: 'Have you seen them? They're either butch lesbians or they're on about what should be done about one-parent families. They should get on with it – I did.' Conservative women seemed to know how to 'get on with it' only as one individual against another. They were not expected to solve such problems collectively, as women, because to define, for example, one-parent families as a group would create the potential for adopting a sociological approach, a most un-Tory practice; it would open the way to seeing society as a set of structures and systems.

Tory women's organizations were not political nurseries or energizing power bases for ambitious young women. Labour women might complain about the lack of power within their organization, but they did not desert it and, by and large, they did not regard it as a waste of time. To do so would also be seen as anti-women. Conservative women had no such scruples. Many high-fliers would not be seen alive or dead associating with all-women political groupings. Harriet Crawley, former Conservative candidate for Brent East, told us that she refused to attend such all-women events as the Tory women's conference. Her thinking illustrated the way in which the Conservative male's attitude to women was transferred to women themselves – the message being that women were weak and powerless and anyone who associated with them was somehow contaminated by that condition. 'I think it's admitting failure to go to something that's all women. You have to go to where there are men in order to change their minds. I don't believe that there are women's issues which you should segregate from men's. Women get more confidence if it's a mixed occasion. The best feminist argument is to fight in the male domain.'

It was not just young, upper-middle-class Tories from a background of power and privilege, like Harriet Crawley, who perceived the limitations of the women's conference. Even a traditionalist like Audrey Berry recognized that. It might have lost its old image as a sea of ladies in hats, but no one would consider it an empowering or invigorating occasion. 'If you want to get on in the party, it's a way of getting to the rostrum and getting noticed but it's very stage-managed and not much of a forum for political debate,' said Audrey Berry. 'For the rest of the time, you go there to listen to ministers and have a nice trip to London.' Labour women's annual conference might be similarly powerless, but it had a political impetus that could not be found in its Tory equivalent.

Tory women, like their counterparts in the Labour Party, felt a sense of exclusion from aspects of Conservative Party life. Maggie Smyth called the Party 'a male bastion'. The first time she went to her local Conservative Club for a meeting, she wandered into the bar and after finding out in which room the meeting was to be held, she asked for a drink. 'A deathly hush descended on the place as I walked in,' she recalled. '"You can't do that in here," said the man behind the bar, "you're a woman." "I know that," I said. But I was stunned. I mean it's 1987, not 1887. I work, my money spends good but I couldn't choose what to do with it there.' Maggie Smyth was later informed that women could only be admitted to the bar on Saturdays and Sundays, and then only if they were escorted by a man.

This anecdote points to a fundamental difference between the women of the two main parties. Labour women, confronted with such an experience, would probably express their solidarity by passing a resolution or holding a demonstration. The political machinery would be used to challenge male power. That was what happened in the market town of Chorley, near Preston, when the women's section opposed holding constituency meetings in the Labour Club because it didn't give full membership rights to women; pressure was put on the club to change its policy. Tory women did not practise that sort of politics, so their anger had nowhere to go – except, in some cases, to fuel personal ambition.

'I don't think the Tory Party offers women that much,' claimed Sarah Bardswell. Her particular concern was for those at home or in part-time employment, whom she believed were not seen as important. She was 'very disappointed', she told us, when she heard that the Conservative government planned to subject Child Benefit to a means test. Before her children grew up, it was the only money she had for herself. 'It was really vital and I did not have to account for it. It's also a vital support for the family.' Sarah Bardswell had a firm commitment to the family and she didn't see her party practise what it preached. Tory policies left much to be desired: 'It's cheaper if you live in sin'; she also took a dim view of the way some prominent Tories pursued a private sexual morality that was at odds with their public pronouncements. For many Tory women that contradiction cast an uneasy shadow.

A more fundamental contradiction, however, was the Conservative Party's refusal to identify – in policy terms – women as a special group with special needs. Emma Nicholson, the Conservative MP, saw this refusal as a 'subconscious, strong steel thread,' but believed it might be changing.

> We never have any such things as a Conservative policy for women. The Conservative Party has policies which affect women and don't affect men, but it's difficult for it to admit that. I think that it's a paternalistic hang-over that they think they'll do the right thing by the women anyhow. At least, I think that is what it is – the view that perhaps these things aren't frightfully important because the men earn, don't they? And the woman is at home, so it's all going to be all right.

This deeply old-fashioned and anachronistic view sat uncomfortably on the wide-padded shoulders of the Tory high-fliers whose parliamentary ambitions we earlier saw being coached and goaded by Emma Nicholson. Often successful professional women, the high-fliers were impatient with that dishonest 'chivalry' which 'protected' them from positions of power. They wanted to achieve, they demanded equality. They espoused some of the language of feminism, but, politically, they were unwilling to use the tools of the women's movement to activate women's power. Harriet Crawley recognized that men kept women down, but that didn't matter to her because she could win the fight and had the confidence to outwit male chauvinism. The prevailing argument was that political success was a question of having the right attitudes, playing the right cards and, finally, winning the tricks. The prime exponent of that credo was Margaret Thatcher.

It was a curious feature of Toryism that the party which effortlessly patronized women should be led by a woman. Conservative women were immensely proud of Mrs Thatcher. First, her achievement was unique. 'The thing is she's broken the mould, she's created the earthquake, the seismic shock has happened. Nothing will ever be the same again,' said Emma Nicholson. Secondly, it was clear that she hadn't made a mess of her achievement – indeed, quite the reverse: she had consolidated her position and her power. 'Some people think that only men can get to the very top, but she has proved herself and we admire her for that,' was Audrey Berry's verdict. And thirdly, by electing a woman to the leadership the Conservatives instantly acquired a modern feel – the dull dogs were transformed into something rather innovative. They could claim to have given a woman her chance, to have made the historic breakthrough.

After three election victories, Margaret Thatcher's prestige was immense. No other woman – except for the Queen – could match her charisma. There was no one – man or woman – remotely resembling her in the Labour Party. Moretta Hutchinson's account of her meeting with Mrs Thatcher had the magical note of one who had met royalty:

She's most charming and if you had had some doubts before, you'd be her slave after meeting her. She shakes your hand and gazes into your eyes and you feel that you're the only person in the room who matters to her for that moment. She probably forgets she's ever met you afterwards, mind you. But it's quite an experience. She really does have an aura.

What was being a woman all about for Mrs Thatcher? Emma Nicholson, who as vice-chairman of the Party in charge of women worked closely with Mrs Thatcher for some time, told us: 'She sees it as being a mother. She loves her children very deeply. She sees it as being happily married – and she has a very solid, happy marriage, there's no doubt about that at all. And she sees it as having major opportunities outside the home and not being inhibited by having children and a husband.' The difficulties of being a working mother were overcome by buying high-class child care – the problems were practical and were to be solved by each and every determined woman as an individual. The paths to glory were smoothed by individual achievement. Child care, for Margaret Thatcher, was not an ideological problem.

She made light of the fact that she was a woman, and therefore made light of every other woman's difficulties, contradictions and struggles. This was where the admiration of the Conservative women for their leader became a little muted. 'Women who are very successful are often very intolerant of other women and Mrs Thatcher doesn't tolerate fools gladly – I think, ironically, that Heath did more to help women than any other prime minister,' commented Sarah Bardswell. Audrey Berry observed: 'Perhaps she hasn't done as much for women as one would have thought. Perhaps because she is top dog she keeps the women on a lower tier.'

Some women didn't think that this mattered. 'In her position, she doesn't need to appeal to the electorate as a woman,' said Moretta Hutchinson. 'She needs to show herself as a leader. She has shown that women can be leaders – and world leaders.' Emma Nicholson also rejected the importance of Mrs Thatcher's role-as-woman. 'In my view it doesn't matter a scrap what policies Mrs Thatcher has or hasn't put forward for women. Tory women tend to see her as different from them.' While Mrs Thatcher continued to praise women for their hard work and loyalty, she did not exhort them to join her. She remained supreme. Her triumph did not disturb the traditionally 'cosy' relationship between the Party and the women.

CHAPTER 13

The Centre and the Greens

Before the merger of the Liberals and the Social Democrats into the Social and Liberal Democratic Party in 1988, the women of the two centre parties came together to produce a policy proposal document for the 1987 general election. Entitled *Freedom and Choice*, the booklet pointed out how the Alliance was distinct from the other main parties and why this was important for women.

> A fundamental element in the Alliance's approach to politics is the will to challenge established centres of power and privilege and to give people the power to control their own lives, exercise choice and play their full part in the community. This approach is especially important for women who have been too long oppressed by right-wing respect for tradition and hierarchy, on the one hand, and by socialist centralisation of power in the hands of the state, on the other.[1]

The emphasis on the attraction of the centre parties to women was about both style and content. The Alliance could claim that both its parties contained elements of a non-combative approach to politics. From the Liberal Party came a co-operative, pacifist, grass-roots tradition, while the Social Democratic Party offered a 'new broom' to sweep away the rotten old adversarial style of politics.

By staking out the middle ground, centre-party supporters claimed another point of political distinction. Unlike the Conservatives, who were traditionally associated with business and management, and the Labour Party, inextricably linked to industry and workers, the centre parties did not define people according to their economic role. This, they argued, was attractive to women for whom an economic identity was either irrelevant or indistinct. The centre parties could boast that they were not fettered by class-based politics (although the SDP quickly became associated with the middle classes), nor did they have an historic or organic relationship with the trade unions. For politically un-attached women voters, the Liberal/SDP Alliance seemed to hold out new promise.

There was little time, however, to adjust to the Alliance before the two parties merged. How would women fare in the new order? It was too early to be sure at the time of writing, but the Social and Liberal Democratic Party (the Liberal Democrats) was, if nothing else, the sum of its parts – and the best indications could be gained from examining the role of women in both the long-established Liberal Party and in that child of the eighties, the Social Democratic Party.

In the days of its greatest power, the Liberal Party was notori-ous for refusing to give women the vote. Successive Liberal governments had managed to ignore the growing clamourings from suffragists, who included significant numbers of women Liberals. Then, over the long years of decline, after the vote was won, the Liberal Party defiantly held on to its position as the third party in British politics with a small band of MPs preach-ing a fundamental belief in the protection and promotion of indi-vidual freedom against the power of any corporate body – business, unions or the state. The idea of freedom was fused with a commitment to equality, as this statement from Liberal women explained: 'Liberals are committed to the freedom of the individual and to equality of opportunity and the Women's Liberal Federation works to translate these values into the poli-cies and actions needed to bring full equality to women.'[2]

Liberal emphasis on the individual found a new kind of expres-sion during the 1960s when the Liberals gained some public sup-port through their development of grass-roots political activity. To Frances Thirlway, a Young Liberal who was vice-president of the Oxford Students' Union, this was one of the elements that made the Party attractive to women. It made local – personal – issues relevant and political. 'The Liberal Party doesn't have this view that politics is solely about macro-economic policy, defence, all the so-called "big issues". It's much more aware that things like defending your local school or hospital is "politics", just as much as all this stuff about the next five years in the economy.' Ollie Grender, another Young Liberal who worked as a researcher for Liberal MP Matthew Taylor, recognized that her party got lumbered with a particular image as 'the ones who go on about cracked pavements and dog shit'. But, she argued, those issues really did affect people. 'Dog faeces are a good example. A lot of women want to take children to play in parks; dogs foul parks. It's political if you can't take your child to the park because there's too much dog shit.'

The Young Liberals who made that sort of connection were taking ideas from the women's movement about recognizing the political content of women's needs. Other feminist concepts, too, were defined as being within the traditions of Liberalism. This, according to Christina Baron, president of the Women's Liberal Federation and former parliamentary candidate, was particularly true of the way in which Liberals approached conflict. 'I see female ways of working as resolving conflict without killing anyone, defusing conflict and getting people to co-operate. Some Liberals also do that, although it tends to get subsumed by the time people get to the top.' To illustrate this approach, she mentioned the Liberal practice of determining resolutions at the Party conference. 'Before the conference starts, there are day-long, mildly anarchic, free-ranging discussions. It's a typical Liberal way of doing things and it works best when people don't come with prepared positions – it's a meeting of minds and open discussion.' Rosie Dodds, a Young Liberal from North London, described the Liberal approach to debate. 'We take the view that I may think one thing and some other woman might think completely differently about, say, how politics ought to work, and I can't say I'm right and she's wrong. It may mean we get less things done; what matters is that we all participate and join in, get something out of it.'

Another way in which feminism and radical Liberalism found common cause was the emphasis on a grass-roots consultative process and a recognition of individual needs. As Frances Thirlway explained: 'A lot of people think that campaigning and per-

sonal involvement in demonstrations is just a preliminary to the
"real thing" and the real thing is producing the documents, the
evidence, discussing it in parliament.' The 'preliminaries', in her
view, were just as important, if not more so.

Some Young Liberals were also trying to introduce a different
style of politics into the practice of Liberalism. Once again, this
was much informed by feminism. They told us about the way
they organized a conference to be 'more participatory, more flexible' in an attempt to 'feminize' the party. 'We didn't have a
platform and rows of seats,' explained Carina Trimingham, a
Brighton Young Liberal who worked as public relations officer
for the one-parent organization, Gingerbread.

> We grouped the seats in a semi-circle and we had a lot of
> microphones dotted around for people to use. They didn't
> have to put in a speaker's card, then tramp to the front, then
> rant, rant, rant – they could just put up their hand and make
> a point, even if it was just a sentence, at the nearest micro-
> phone. As a result, there were many speakers who contributed
> for the first time.

For the Liberal women we met, there was much about their Party
that seemed especially well suited to the needs and experiences
of women, and they had found feminism to be a useful tool
in refining Party philosophy to increase women's participation
within the Party. Women represented around half of the total
membership. In the 1980s, there was a marked increase in the
numbers of women chairing constituency associations; Young
Liberal feminists were making their mark, and Nancy Seear
became Liberal leader in the House of Lords. Yet for all that,
there was a widespread feeling that the party of equal opportunities and individual freedom was in some ways failing women.
Until Ray Michie won Argyll and Bute for the Liberals in 1987,
only five Liberal women had become MPs – a poor track record
not altogether excused by the decline of the Liberal Party in
general.

Christina Baron detected a 'covert chauvinism' in the Party.

> There's always a group of people in any organization that

spends a lot of time together 'fixing'. In the Liberals, it has always been a group of young, rather chauvinist, males. That is definitely a sexist set-up. Our party is not really an equal opportunities party – the ultimate expression of this was in the 1983 election when senior Liberal women went to see David Steel to ask whether he had noticed that there were no women on the election committee. His response was: 'Unfortunately, I don't know any women.' That was absolutely typical.

A key problem for the Liberals had inevitably been that of reconciling the concepts of individual freedom and equality in a society where male power and privilege were firmly entrenched. If individual freedom was *the* guiding principle, as it clearly was for the Liberals; if the quest for equality demanded social change, as it surely did; and if social change implied an infringement of the freedom of the privileged to continue enjoying their political advantage, as it must – then the pursuit of equality was bound to be less than wholehearted. That is, unless women could assert enough power in the Party to insist on a shift in priorities to favour the freedom of the weak over the freedom of the strong. But that suggested the need for a distinctive women's lobby, and there had been a marked reluctance among women in the Liberal Party to embrace the notion of separate organization.

The Women's Liberal Federation, which celebrated its centenary in 1987, became a victim of that uncertainty. Formed to promote the political interests and activities of women, it had campaigned for votes for women, defying the Liberal orthodoxy on women's suffrage. Constitutionally, it was affiliated to the Liberal Party and elected six members to sit on the Party council. But some women Liberals refused to have anything to do with it (Nancy Seear was one), preferring to work within the main body of Liberalism. The argument was a familiar one: if women were to be equal with men, they should not seek preferential treatment.

Thus the WLF had found itself marginalized, providing rather a cosy, elderly view of women's role, and by-passed by ambitious high-flyers as well as by some of the Liberal feminists. Christina Baron, who took over the WLF presidency in 1986, thought the tide was turning. She herself believed strongly in the need for a separate organization for women.

> It would be nice if we didn't need separate organizations but, in practice, we haven't got very far by trying to behave like men. We find we need to support each other because we have discovered the force of male networking. Women thought they could join them, but they can't. I'm not unhappy if women start in the WLF and then go on to success in the party, providing they don't say that the WLF should be wound up when they've moved on.

Susan Thomas, who was beaten in the election for the presidency of the Liberal Party in 1987, felt that the way forward for women was 'consciously to create a mutual help mechanism if responsibility, status and influence are ever to be equally shared'. This, she said, was a necessary response to the old-boy network where power went to the 'right' people who, 'Surprise, surprise! ... usually turn out to be men'.[3] The stirrings towards mutual support among Liberal women were helpful in pushing women into positions of power within the Party. Christina Baron noticed this during the Ryedale by-election campaign. 'Women wanted to get a woman elected and they poured in to help. There was a marvellous feeling of comradeship with all sorts of women mucking in and working together. The whole campaign had a strong feminist bias.'

Liberal women succeeded in getting sexist language deleted from the party constitution at the Liberal conference in Dundee in 1985. At the same time, a policy resolution on the status of women, which had been carried over amidst some acrimony from the previous year's conference, was won. Jil Hayes of 'Women's Link', a collectively-run newsletter for Liberals, commented on the conference:

> One of the first things I noticed was the number of women chairing debates. Many of them were chairing for the first time. ... The Status of Women debate was well attended; even David Steel appeared on stage for part of the debate. ... I left the debate after the motion had been passed

overwhelmingly feeling that here was a start, something that we could build on.[4]

The policy resolution also included a commitment to one woman on every shortlist, a measure won by women in the new Social Democratic Party in 1981.

'The advantage of a new party is that you don't have to change a massive amount of history,' said Sue Slipman, who stood as a candidate for the Social Democratic Party in the 1987 election. 'I think the SDP is positively facilitating women to become active in politics.' When the SDP was born in 1981, women had a unique opportunity to make an impact on its constitution and policies. From its inception, the SDP claimed that in representing a new force in politics – it was called 'breaking the mould' – it offered a non-adversarial, commonsense view of the world and prom-ised to dispense for ever with the ugly old forms of politicking. This – as we've seen – found favour with newcomers to politics, including many women. Some of these were women who had never previously been involved in politics. Others, like Sue Slip-man, formerly a president of the National Union of Students and member of the Communist Party, were seasoned political activists and high-powered professional women. Sue Slipman found the atmosphere refreshing and rational. 'It's very civilized, you see. The first time someone said to me, "Oh, I never thought about that before, you've changed my mind," I nearly fell off my seat. What women have done is interpose feminist ideas, so that they're part and parcel of what now gets taken seriously. It's changed the framework of debate.'

Even so, Social Democratic women had to fight their corner to ensure proper representation for women. 'Right at the start, in 1981,' journalist Polly Toynbee told *Spare Rib* magazine, 'femi-nists like Sue Slipman and I went up to people and said: "What are you going to do about women, then?" And all these men who'd just left the Labour Party said, "Oh my god, haven't we got away from all that minority crap?" But we won through with our constitutional changes which have made all the differ-ence.'[5] Of the eight elected places on the National Committee, which governed the day-to-day running of the Party, four were reserved for women and four for men. Sue Slipman, herself an elected member of the National Committee, pointed out that the stipulation that women should have 50 per cent of the seats on the Council for Social Democracy, the Party's policy-making body, was lost by just one vote. 'It was,' she said, 'a crucial vote to lose. Nevertheless, women comprise about 40 per cent of the National Council for Social Democracy.'

Not all women, however, supported positive action for women. Rabbi Julia Neuberger, who was also an elected member of the National Committee, observed that the opposition to special representation did not come just from men. 'One of the things that I find quite depressing about this is that quite often it's women who will object on the basis that women should do things on their own merit.' But opinion was shifting, she said, in favour of positive action. 'You can see that people feel it's worked. The party attracted more women, and women felt that they could take part in the political process without feeling like freaks.'

The Social Democrats were the first to adopt another crucial constitutional provision for women: the requirement of one woman on every parliamentary shortlist and two if the list contained more than six people. This caused initial problems because relatively few women came forward, but it was an effective means of bringing women into national politics, some of whom had had little previous experience. Under the Alliance umbrella, the SDP had fifty-eight women candidates in the 1987 election, compared with forty-seven for the Liberals.

Social Democrat women, conscious of their separate strength, worked to ensure that they were included at the heart of the new Party, combining the skills of dinner-party diplomacy with the political expertise they had gained as professional, middle-class women. Polly Toynbee, one of the SDP's inner circle, remarked: 'When we run a campaign we tend to win it. . . . We quite scare people because we're screaming insiders, not screaming outsiders.'[6] While it was clear that women played a major role in the mainstream of the Party, the existence of the Women for Social Democracy, an affiliated group but without any official representation, suggested an ambivalence on the part of women themselves about their position within the Party. Were the special provisions for women enough to ensure their central position, or did women require a separate sphere for support and empowerment? Julia Neuberger observed of Women for Social Democracy: 'It hasn't got that large a membership – I think women don't belong because they don't feel the need. That's wrong, because you need to keep up the pressure.'

As the Liberals and Social Democrats moved towards merger, it became clear that tensions existed between the women of the two parties. The Social Democrats claimed that the Liberals had a poor track record on women. Sue Slipman noted that when the two parties discussed the policy document 'Partnership for Progress', the SDP team consisted of two men and three women, while the Liberals had no women. 'It wasn't conscious and deliberate. The fact was that the SDP women were there in the first place. They're competent and are therefore picked to do things. That's been the case with every SDP committee set up.' Those SDP women who opposed the merger used the position of women in the Liberal Party to attack the proposals. In a letter to the *Guardian*, on the eve of the conferences which sanctioned the merger, Sue Stapely of Women for Social Democracy wrote: 'The Liberal Party has been notoriously unsupportive of its women members, and has made no real progress on any issues of importance to women over the years.'[7] She also claimed that the majority of 'strong and effective' women would be staying with the SDP to work towards the 50 per cent representation of women throughout the SDP and its external bodies – a target, she said, that was supported by David Owen, the SDP's tenacious leader.

Pro-merger SDP members like Julia Neuberger did not believe that women would suffer in the new party.

> The anti-merger women keep on saying that the new party won't be good for women because the Liberals haven't got any tradition of it. But having said that, they have Nancy Seear as Liberal leader in the Lords, they are pushing some women forward and we'll just have to work on it. I think the SDP women are much tougher than the Liberal women so it's not a problem dealing with that.

Certainly, the constitution of the new, merged Party incorporated a greater degree of positive action for women. On the
Federal Executive Committee, the Party's ruling body, at least
four out of the fourteen members elected annually by the Party
conference had to be women. And of the thirteen members of
the Federal Policy Committee, at least four had to be women.
At the annual federal conference, local associations had to
include one woman if they were large enough to have three
representatives. And the final provision for women was for the
parliamentary candidates' shortlist, where there had to be one
woman if there was a list of four, and two if the list was longer.

There was no resolution of the problem which had beset the
Liberals – how to reconcile an overriding commitment to individual freedom with the goal of equality. But policy documents
produced by the Social and Liberal Democrats suggested that
on issues such as positive action for women, the interventionist
tendencies of the SDP had won the day.[8] The constitutional
reforms achieved by women of the two parties paved the way
for increased representation of women. But what kind of women
were they? The high-profile, middle-class women of the SDP
had forged a path for themselves through to the centre, but had
it helped other women to find a way into politics? Christina
Baron of the WLF saw the sister organization, Women for Social
Democracy, as a metropolitan, professional grouping based
around the South-East. 'My impression is that they haven't sold
the WSD to women at home with children. We have tried to
make the WLF relevant to groups of women who found that
the Liberal Party as a whole had little to offer them. Women
who have male-type career profiles have fewer specific needs.'

The Liberal Party, with its broader social base, its emphasis
on grass-roots politics, consultation and discussion, had fallen
well short of delivering equal opportunities to its women. In
contrast, it seemed that the Social Democrats had won women
a central role in the party but had retained a narrow class position. 'We did not attract working-class women – or men,' said
Julia Neuberger. 'It certainly felt very middle class.' But for Sue
Slipman, the nose-to-nose-Volvos image of the party was more
than a social fact; it was a political necessity. 'The whole history

of British representational politics is that people are represented by reformers, and in Britain, reformers have always been middle-class people. That's the reality.'

It was not until the summer of 1989 that the Green Party was thrust – even to its own surprise – towards the centre of the political stage, with a remarkable showing in the European elections. The Greens attracted 14.93 per cent of the national vote, coming third after Labour (40 per cent) and the Conservatives (34.71 per cent) and far outstripping the SLD (6.15 per cent). It was part of an international political trend, as voters in more affluent countries became increasingly concerned with what have been described as 'post-materialist' values: the things that matter more when you have secured the basic necessities – notably the quality of life, the condition of the environment and the ecological well-being of the planet.

The Greens had their roots in the 'alternative' politics of the late 1960s and in the peace movement of the 1970s. They had a strong appeal to women who, according to opinion surveys in the mid and late 1980s, were more firmly committed than men to nuclear disarmament and to issues concerning the environment. In general, women appeared to be shifting faster than men towards 'post-materialist' values, putting the 'quality of life' before narrower economic concerns such as jobs and wages. This was perhaps a consequence of their lives being focused more broadly than men's, on the home and the community rather than on the workplace.

The women's movement had been influential, too. Like the Liberals, the Greens favoured a participatory, non-hierarchical style of operation and banned sexist language from its publications. It managed to create, from the early 1980s onwards, a political culture that was *not* predominantly masculine, and – unlike the Liberals – it succeeded in organizing itself *without* a male-dominated élite. In 1989, nine members of the twenty-five strong National Council were women and all three co-chairs of the Party were women. Of the six 'speakers' elected to represent the Greens to the public and the media, three were women, and most of the Party's policy committees were convened by women. 'All three co-chairs have been women ever since 1986,' explained Jean Lambert, a former co-chair and one of the speakers. 'These posts are elected annually and you can only hold office for three years.'

Yet the Party had no special strategies for promoting women, no reserved places or positive-action programmes. In the early 1980s, according to Jean Lambert, there was a growing concern among members that the Party was becoming male-dominated.

> The vast majority on the National Council was male. We had a chair and vice-chair in those days and both were men. There was a general feeling that this wasn't what we wanted to be. Various papers were put to conference and we had a debate about reserved places for women – but we voted against them. The feeling was that if you were going to be elected it should be because people wanted *you*, not because you belonged to some special category. But the whole business of opening it up for debate seems to have been a turning point. It's certainly true now that if you stand as a candidate for the National Council your chances are better if you are a woman.

Anyone who turned up at a Green conference and inadvertently deployed sexist language (for instance, using the masculine pro-noun when referring to men and/or women) would be taken to task by the mass of delegates, Jean Lambert told us. 'There's a very strong consciousness about that. It's one of the things I notice most when I go to meetings of other organizations. It's always "he, he, he", and it really begins to jar because you're not used to hearing it.'

The feminism that influenced Green Party policy-making was not, said Jean Lambert, the kind that sought to promote women to the ranks of men. It was no less important to change men's lives and challenge male stereotypes. 'Men are always seen as the wage-earners, the politicians. Our policies should allow men to be home-makers and look after the children.' The Greens favoured a basic income for all, which would, they believed, go some way towards recognizing the value of unpaid work, as well as establishing a degree of economic independence for women, and beginning to create conditions for 'sharing out the work that needed to be done among those who wanted to do it'.

At least until their electoral breakthrough in 1989, the Greens enjoyed a certain luxury as political outsiders. Feeling they were still a long way from power, they were able to sustain an idealistic purity – strong on principle, short on detail. They had well-developed ideas on the environment, disarmament and some aspects of economic policy, but in many areas affecting women, including child care, housing and crime prevention, they hadn't got much to say. Jean Lambert admitted they'd been caught on the hop by their sudden success in the European elections. She was also aware that it was easier for women to become influential in a party deemed to be in the margins of power. 'It will be interesting to see what happens once we begin to look more like a "career party" as it were, electable. It wouldn't surprise me if more men tried to muscle in.'

It was, however, a lot less likely than it had been a decade earlier that men would be seen as more naturally suited to political leadership. After all, by 1990 a large part of the British electorate had all but forgotten what it was like to have a man running the country. Margaret Thatcher marched on at the head of the Conservative government. She, rather more than the Social Democrats, had 'broken the mould' in British politics, and had disturbed the popular consensus about a woman's role.

But was it just *a* woman – that one exceptional figure – or women in general whose role had changed? Women's representation in the political parties had increased, and their status had improved; some efforts had been made by all the parties to encourage more women to become actively involved; and some account had been taken of women's special needs and experience. But progress had been painfully slow, and gains were marginal. The presence of Mrs Thatcher at Downing Street had not noticeably diminished the difficulties encountered by other women in party politics. She herself had not beckoned women in her own party to congregate around her, evidently preferring to be the queen bee in a cabinet of drones.

Any advances made by women were gained through their

own endeavours. Unlike Mrs Thatcher, they could scarcely hope to be sitting on the platform when it came to conference time, at the centre of attention and power. More likely, they would be sitting towards the back of the hall (if not hidden behind a pillar) or busying themselves on the edges of the political arena with children, administration or teas. They would be less likely to speak at meetings than the men and less likely to hold official positions within their party. They usually felt they had to be *better* than the average man if they were going to make an impact. If they gained any power, their achievement would usually be in spite of their womanhood, not because of it. If their success derived from their sex, this tended to weaken their position – their role being identified as 'special', their achievement token. Sometimes, women would collectively make forays into the power structures of their party, but this would not necessarily bear fruit because the demands of 'minority' interests were given only partial and occasional consideration.

The exclusion of women from power was an extension, as we have seen, of a more general sense of alienation from politics. The conditions of women's lives cast long shadows across the parties: poverty, class and race also conspired against full political engagement. Yet women's needs seemed to be given only limited space – whether they concerned the times when meetings were held, the provision of child-care facilities at party conferences, or even the simple need to get some pleasure out of politics.

The Conservatives alone had allocated women a special place within the Party. Tory women could feel the warmth of the fireside, although they were discouraged from stoking the fire. Labour could not provide women with that sense of belonging – the concept of working-class solidarity seemed remote to those who lived outside the culture of 'men's work' and trade unions. However, Labour's egalitarian ideology encouraged some women to retain a faith in that party as a place where the powerless could collectively organize to empower themselves. The centre parties' appeal lay, to some extent, in the fact that they did not include the worst features of the other two; but the Liberals had preserved the tradition of male dominance and, while they and the Social Democrats pronounced themselves 'good' for all women, they had nothing distinctive to offer working-class women. The Green Party, as it edged towards the mainstream of British politics, provided a fascinating example of a party in which women had, it anything, more power than men, but it had, at the time of writing, no track record on women's issues for us to evaluate.

Feminism was a vital ingredient in shaping many of the women's initiatives in all the parties. It was particularly important in the Labour Party in fostering women's representation and forcing the party to address women's needs as part of a socialist programme. In a different way, feminism had a strong presence in the Green Party. Feminists had joined the Social Democratic Party and ensured that it made special provision for women in its constitution; the Liberals had dragged behind in their constitutional reform but, by the time the two parties merged, many Liberal women, too, identified themselves as feminists and found in feminism ideas complementary to aspects of Liberalism. The Conservative Party was the least informed by feminism. Strong Conservative women remained wedded to the idea that women were to blame for their subordination and that making a break for power was about beating men at their own game, on men's terms. Not even the Conservatives, however, could deny the influence of feminism and the women's movement in giving women a higher profile and pushing the demand for equal opportunity on to the political agenda.

Each of the major parties had something useful to offer women – which, if combined, could create a more positive political environment than any one of them individually. To fantasize briefly, we could imagine importing from the Tories the affirmation of women's domestic role as valuable and central to human life. From the Liberals, we would lift the concern with issues arising out of everyday life and with building political structures from the community upwards. From the Social Democrats, we would steal the commitment to involve women at every level of decision-making. From Labour, we would take the principle of egalitarianism and the strong, campaigning presence of a separate women's organization. Finally, from the Greens we would import a female political culture and a strong tendency to prefer women as leaders. In the absence of any such ideal combination, we can only look to the parties we've got and search for encouraging signs.

CHAPTER 14

Standing for the Council

When Margaret Brisley first contemplated running for a seat on her local council, it hadn't occurred to her that being a woman might make a difference. Nothing in her job as a secondary school teacher had led her to imagine that she – or anyone like her – suffered any particular discrimination. 'I've got to be honest, I was not the greatest feminist in the world because I hadn't encountered the problems of a lot of women. Then I went on the council and I began to get a little bit more interested, and just by listening I began to think that perhaps women do get a bit of a bad deal.'

Mrs Brisley became a Labour member of Stirling District Council in Central Scotland, representing a ward in the village where she had lived all her life. When we met her, she was the only woman among ten Labour councillors. Middle-aged and from a working-class background, she had been to university as a mature student while her husband helped look after their two children. When the children had grown up and her studies were over, she decided she could take on new commitments. She was well known in the village, and she had the time (just), the energy and the support of her husband for her political ambitions. In 1978 she fought – and lost – an unwinnable seat, but in 1980 she won a tough election in another ward to take her seat on the Labour-controlled council.

But it was not until some time later, when she was invited to give a talk on women and politics to a group of local Labour women, that she paused to examine the position of women in local government. Preparing her speech, she came across facts and figures that amazed her. 'I looked at the numbers of women elected members in Stirling, then at women senior officers employed by the council, and found that the percentages of women were very small. It made me wonder whether it was just Stirling.' She widened her research and found that Stirling was, in fact, quite typical. 'It was a shock to find that women were neither being elected in any great number on to councils, nor getting promoted to senior posts.'

As Margaret Brisley discovered, women were a minority in Britain's town halls both as elected members and as senior-ranking employees. A 1985 survey of all local authorities in Britain[1] showed that only 19.4 per cent of elected members were women, and that they were strikingly absent from leadership roles. Only 5.4 per cent of personnel committees, 2.1 per cent of policy and resources committees and 5.7 per cent of finance committees were chaired by women. Other surveys in the late 1980s showed that only 3.5 per cent of authorities in England and Wales had a woman leading the council, and only three had a woman chief executive.[2]

In the county councils (as distinct from district councils), women accounted for 19.7 per cent of councillors in 1985.[3] There were more women councillors in the South than in the North. The South-East scored highest with 28 per cent, while the lowest representation was in Wales. And while half the county councils increased the numbers of female councillors between 1981 and 1985, more than a third registered a decrease.

Overall, women were better represented in 1985 than in 1969 (when the last comprehensive survey was carried out) – at that time women held only 12 per cent of council seats.[4] Nearly all the big cities showed some sort of increase over that period. Sheffield increased its female representation from 19 to 24 per cent; Bristol from 16 to 24 per cent; Birmingham from 18 to 22 per cent. Norwich, one of the smaller municipal authorities, doubled the number of its women councillors and elected a woman leader.[5] Predictably, the county and shire districts fielded more Conservative women councillors than the metropolitan districts and London boroughs, where Labour women were more visible.

It has always been easier for women to become local councillors than MPS. Even before they won the right to vote in parliamentary elections, they had established a small but significant presence in local government. Between 1870 and 1914, three thousand women were elected to serve on vestries, on school and poor-law boards, and on councils. They went into local government from two main directions. First, there were women from the philanthropic tradition of the conservative middle class whose work on poor-law boards and school boards was, in a way, an extension of their tireless voluntary work. Secondly, there were those from the suffrage movement who believed it was their right to exercise political power at all levels, and hoped that work in local government could help pave the way for political equality on the national stage.

Among the pioneers were Elizabeth Garrett who, in 1870, was the first woman to sit on a London school board; Marion Phillips of Kensington Borough Council who later became a Labour MP; Selina Cooper, the working-class socialist from Nelson in Lancashire; and Mrs Charlotte Despard, the suffragist and poor-law guardian for Lambeth. These and many other women entered the expanding world of local government with a keen sense that women had a vital role to play. As local government began to take on responsibilities for the poor and dispossessed, the sick, the old, the orphaned, the insane, women could argue that in those areas, at least, they were the experts – it was an extension of their domestic skills and duties.

This argument was first used to placate men who were hostile to women's claims to any sort of elected role in local government. But many women used it to underline the importance of women's separate sphere and special needs. They made an issue of the *different* experience of women and men; equal, but not the same – a view that twentieth-century municipal feminists would come to share. Patricia Hollis pointed out in *Ladies Elect*, her study of women in the dawning days of local government:

> In the opening elections to school boards and in the early decades of women's poor law work, women stood as independent candidates. This was not because they saw themselves as free-standing and unaligned individuals, as the men seemed to think; but because they wanted support as representative

women, tacit members of a hidden women's party with its own agenda of family values, individualized care, moral reform, and fair and equal treatment of female clients and staff.[6]

The achievements of women in early local politics were impressive – from investigating infant mortality to introducing free school meals, from the improvement of sewage systems to slum clearance, from provision of play spaces and allotments to fighting for good and caring practices in workhouses and orphanages, hospitals and asylums. 'At their bravest, women were well aware that they were seeking to reshape the priorities of local government, that they were refusing to accept male definitions of what was central and what was marginal, that they were asserting that women's needs counted for as much as men's.'[7]

The long and distinguished history of women's participation in local government contrasted sadly with their showing in the national arena. Why the difference? First, it was easier for a woman to hold family life together as a councillor than as an MP, because the work was local and it was (officially, at least) part-time. Secondly, many women were drawn to council work because they felt that it *could* make a difference, that an individual's contribution counted. Local politics might be stuck with a 'parish pump' image, but it had an immediacy that held a far greater attraction to many women than the no man's land of the backbench MP. Margaret Hodge, leader of Islington Council in North London, pointed out that one of the things she valued about her council work was that she could see what she had contributed to her neighbourhood. 'I can take my children to the local swimming pool and say to myself, "I thought about this eight years ago and now it's happened."' The satisfaction came from effecting change at close quarters, from being able to contribute directly to policy-making and so influence the shape of one's own community.

Women's access to local government was also eased by the relative lack of competition for seats. The everyday tasks of a councillor required selfless dedication – long hours spent at countless meetings and on endless casework of the most mun-

dane, but nevertheless important, nature: council-house lighting, refuse collection, the upkeep of flowerbeds in municipal
parks . . . and all unpaid. It was neither glamorous nor glorious
enough to preoccupy for long a young man whose heart was
set on a *career* in politics.

This is not to say that women suffered no prejudice. Selection
committees had become less mesmerized by the myth that people
wouldn't vote for women, but research suggests that women
tended to be chosen more often for marginal or unwinnable
seats: 'There is some evidence to show that, at both national
and local level, where it is a matter of waving the party standard
rather than a genuine competition for election, women are likely
to be found in greater numbers.'[8] Similarly, parties with little
chance of electoral success have shown a greater willingness
to select women as candidates.

In recent times, nearly all councillors have stood as representatives of a political party – a change from the days when many
stood on independent platforms. Potential candidates first
needed to be approved by the local party association. If more
than one name were put forward, a selection committee or ward
meeting chose between them. It was a system which necessarily
favoured those known to the in-group, who were part of the
local political network and already had a track record in politics.
As we have seen, it was more likely for women to find their
way through this obstacle course if they were middle class. In
the Labour Party, it was not unusual for supporters of a female
candidate to be challenged by others arguing that it was better
to have a working-class man than a middle-class woman.

In all parties it was more difficult for women to win recognition. When we met Maggie Smyth, a Conservative from Brent
East, she was building up her political experience and was keen
to become a councillor. She was enthusiastic and dedicated, but
it wasn't enough.

I want to go into politics and I was all ready to fill in the
forms – they're on the mantelpiece somewhere. Then I heard
this chap wanted to stand in my ward. He's chairman of this
and that; I had heard him speak and he's so patronizing. So

I thought, what am I? I work, I have a couple of O levels and enthusiasm. That sort of undermined my confidence, and I've got to re-evaluate it. I hate all the backbiting and fixing behind the scenes. I want to be there because I'm me – for me and for the people I represent so that I can act in their best interests.

Politics has little time for the diffident or the unsure.

While some factors inhibited women's involvement at all levels of the political process, others were peculiar to the nature of local government. Men and women who entered local politics accepted that it was unpaid work. The attendance allowance of £16 a day before tax was discretionary, and some councils did not pay the full rate. Expenses could be claimed, but these were not generous: travel by public transport to and from council business, and a subsistence allowance when away from home on council business. Some councils had introduced a baby-sitting allowance – Lewisham in South London, for example, was known to pay a small hourly sum. With a minimum of financial reward, councillors would have to continue in paid employment unless they had an independent income, were retired or were financially supported by a spouse. Some councillors fitted their council work around full-time employment, but many women with children and paid employment were unable to consider council work; the 'triple burden' was intolerable. As we have discovered, the weight of domestic responsibilities prevented many women – particularly working-class women – from participating in politics at any level.

Married to the Council?, a fascinating study from Bristol Polytechnic, explored the links between the demands of council work and the personal lives of county councillors. It found that the average time spent weekly on council work was thirty-four hours. Women spent longer than men on council duties, devoting an average of 37.6 hours a week compared with 30.8 hours for men. Labour councillors, male and female, worked longer than Conservatives and marginally longer than Liberals. 'The fact that approximately one third of our sample appeared to spend the equivalent of a forty-hour week on their work suggests

that over the country, a large number of voluntary elected representatives are undertaking the equivalent of a full-time job for
very little reward.'[9]

It was not only the long hours demanded by council work
that made it inaccessible to so many women (and men). It was
when those hours were scheduled. Although most council meetings were held in the evening, other important meetings with
officers took place during the day. Committee chairs would certainly be required to be available during working hours. For those
in full-time employment or at home with small children, there
was an immediate conflict between the demands of council work
and personal commitments.

It is hardly surprising to find that this onerous, time-consuming and responsible job has produced a whole set of pressures
on councillors, some centred around their families and some
around council work itself. The Bristol study found that married
councillors worried about how council work disrupted family
life, and women councillors tended to feel more anxious than
men. *Married to the Council?* commented:

> While both husbands and wives are affected to some extent
> by their spouses' council work, female councillors seem to
> try much harder to minimise the adverse effects on their fami-
> lies. Perhaps women tend to feel that their husbands' tolerance
> is conditional only, and could be withdrawn if they made too
> many demands, or took it too much for granted. . . . Conserva-
> tive women, in particular, were usually very concerned to give
> their family lives and the comfort of their husbands their first
> priority.[10]

Anxieties about fulfilling home responsibilities were exacerbated
for some councillors by the obvious pressures of their municipal
workload. The survey suggested that Labour women, in particular, felt the most pressure, while Conservative men felt the least.
The level of concern was affected by the way the councillors
defined their public role: female councillors expressed more frequently what was called a 'community-centred' view of their
representative duties; they worried about not being able to fulfil
their role and expressed a greater commitment to the 'job'. The

Bristol study declared: 'Female councillors asserted a view of the councillor's role which required a degree of commitment in terms of time, preparation, requisite skills and research which was analogous to that required of someone working in a professional capacity.'[11] At the same time, Labour councillors were particularly preoccupied with casework and policy-making; Conservative councillors were less interested in those areas and more concerned about attendance at council meetings.

The range of barriers to women's participation in local government perpetuated the recruitment of women councillors from a narrow social range. So who was the typical woman councillor? Overwhelmingly, she was not in full-time employment; in 1976 a sample survey found that 91 per cent of women councillors were housewives, retired or in part-time work. And 29 per cent of the sample were over sixty.[12] In search of the typical Conservative, we might find a middle-class woman in her middle years with experience in voluntary work such as running meals-on-wheels or serving as a school governor. She would be married, either with no children or with older children, and living in some financial security with a supportive husband in prosperous rural England. Her Labour counterpart was more likely to represent an urban area, and to have a job in the public sector as a teacher or administrator. She, too, would be middle-class but younger than her Tory equivalent, and either married with a young family or single; and she would have cut her political teeth as an activist in the local party association.

If we now look more closely at the experience of individual women, we can get a clearer picture of the conditions that made it possible for them to enter the world of local politics, as well as the distinctive approaches of women and men, and the differences between women in the two main parties.

Margaret Brisley, as we have seen, waited until her children were grown-up before standing for Stirling Council, and then combined employment with council work. After her first election win, Margaret turned the most marginal seat on the council into the safest, becoming treasurer of the council and chair of the women's committee. 'It's strange some people feel that a woman wouldn't have the same staying power or abilities as a man.

Often it's other women who say that – perhaps it's because their aspirations don't go that way,' she commented. But she herself had one major advantage: her terms of employment as a teacher allowed her to take off two days each week for council work. 'Most days I leave school at ten to four, come into the council to see officers and try to get work cleared up until about six o'clock. Then on Tuesdays and Thursdays I do council work all day and we have group meetings on Tuesday evenings.'

Conservative Audrey Berry waited until her son was at university before she went on the council. But, more typically for a Conservative, she came to council work from the voluntary sector, graduating from one form of unpaid work to another. 'I was secretary of the local NSPCC, treasurer of the WI, on this and that, as one is.' Her husband, like Margaret Brisley's, was happy for her to take on political responsibilities.

Younger women have had to juggle their professional and personal commitments in different ways. Margaret Hodge, leader of London's Labour-controlled Islington Council since 1982, combined mothering and council work. Before her marriage she had worked in international research, but travelling became impossible when she started a family. 'Somebody said to me that I should go on the council because "It'll keep you sane while you're changing nappies". I saw it as a stop-gap while I was tied to the home.' She was first elected to the council in 1973, and three of her four children have been born since then.

Edwina Currie became a Birmingham City councillor at the age of twenty-eight with, as she put it, a five-month-old baby tucked under her arm. Her second child was also born while she was a councillor. Mrs Currie believed in what she called 'maximizing her advantage' and, as a young mother, she chose to go on to the social services committee (which she eventually chaired).

Having a small child was a tremendous advantage. One of the key tasks of a councillor on that committee is to fulfil the statutory obligation to inspect children's homes. There's nothing easier than to put the carrycot in the car and toddle off and do them. Then, when I visited old people's homes, it rapidly became apparent that when I took the baby, they were thrilled to bits. One could use the baby to see the level of stimulus they were getting.'

Marilyn Taylor also combined mothering and council work. Elected to Manchester City Council as a Labour councillor in 1983, when the youngest of her six children was two, she came into local government through community politics – organizing adult literacy schemes, launching a Woodcraft Folk group and getting a children's summer play scheme going. 'I felt that the Labour Party could be the vehicle through which I could get those things done and give local people a voice. When I stood for the council, I was trying to get working people's interests represented in a different way from the Tories' paternalistic approach.'

Inevitably, the more accessible councillors made themselves, the more they raised hopes about what they could achieve, and sometimes they were the focus of demands they could not meet. Merle Amory became leader of Brent Council in 1986 – she was black, female and young, a combination which generated an intolerable burden of expectations. 'As a young person, people looked to me to be accessible. As a woman, they expected me to be maternal – to solve disputes between councillors and things like that ... and naturally [the black voluntary sector] wanted my presence at their meetings, as a symbol of the council's respect for them.'[14]

That socialist concept of giving a voice to the community contrasts with the Conservative emphasis on public service – *helping*, rather than *empowering*. It is one of the ways in which the two main parties differ in their approach to council work. Another difference is that Conservative councillors appear to regard council business more as a worthwhile leisure activity than as *work*. Margaret Brisley noticed that Tory women on Stirling Council had a particular view of their town hall duties. 'I wonder if they look on being a councillor as another aspect of do-gooding. Only two of the eight Tory councillors here work, and four of the five women don't seem to need to work. Perhaps they feel they are just filling in their time.'

That was not true for Audrey Berry. Though in many other ways she was a typical Conservative – albeit working-class – her attitude to council work was more in tune with Labour's Margaret Brisley than with her own colleagues.

In 1974, there were five women out of twenty-four on the Tory group of Merseyside County Council, but I didn't have much in common with the other women. One, for example, had been Mayor of Southport and a headmistress. They were all MBES or JPS, from places like the Wirral. I didn't get the impression they knew how to work, although they were always friendly. Perhaps they regarded it as a hobby being a councillor. To me it was a job and being a housewife was my hobby.

The 'hobby' school of local politics was, in part, a legacy of the middle-class philanthropic tradition. A Conservative women's booklet advocated life in local politics in this way: 'If you are the sort of person who enjoys the satisfaction of getting things done, who believes in service and who is attracted by an outlet that demands commitment, you could be just the candidate your council is wanting.'[13] That approach reinforced the idea of public service through personal contribution. It applauded women's capabilities, urged them to bring those skills to local government, and hinted at some sort of civic recognition. What it did not do was to present local politics as a vehicle for political change in general, or as a platform for representing women's needs. It by-passed the question of whether more women on the council could mean more power for women *as women*. For Conservatives, that was not part of their perception of politics.

In contrast, many Labour women councillors seemed to have more in common with the suffragist tradition, which insisted on women's separate sphere and special interests. Labour women who had taken feminist politics into the party then grasped the opportunity to introduce feminist ideas into local government.

Strong-minded feminists who made their way into council chambers during the late 1970s and 1980s were in for a culture

225

shock. Local politics had bred its own power and prejudice. Britain's provincial cities still boasted gothic town halls, monuments to those stern merchants and industrialists in frock coats and whiskers who had become the 'city fathers'. These were remote and cloistered places, full of tiptoeing clerks and humble supplicants. Civic pride was exemplified by the mayor, his retinue and the chains of office.

Newcomers were outraged to see good money spent on cleaning the town hall chandeliers, or on expensive junketings, while facilities for women – both as council employees and as councillors – remained so poor. Val Stevens, an ex-chair of Manchester's equal opportunities unit, was one of three women councillors who took their children into the council chamber one morning in 1983. They were protesting against the Labour administration's failure to provide child-care facilities at the town hall while planning the conversion of part of the members' lounge as a bar and snack area at a cost of £40,000. 'We refused to leave with our children. Standing orders say members of the public can be asked to leave, and if they won't the police are called. I wouldn't budge, so up came this lurking policeman. It was absurd. Eventually the council meeting was adjourned. We had made our point.'

Many of those involved would say that women tend to have a different way of going about council business – less formal, more accessible and practical than the traditions built up by men. 'It continually shocks me how male working cultures are not about delivery,' said Anna Wyatt, chief executive of Southwark Council in South London. 'They're about status, position, about *being*, not *doing*. Women want to see results, are prepared to be flexible and make changes in themselves.' Southwark was one of the few councils to have a female chief executive *and* leader, Anne Matthews. Women in the borough found that this made a considerable change in their relationship with the council. 'Going to see the council leader used to be like going to see JR in Dallas,' we were told by two workers at the Rotherhithe Community Planning Centre, which is funded by Southwark Council.

But it's not like that any more. The atmosphere has totally changed. There isn't a big drinks cabinet – Anne just makes you a cup of coffee. And she's so accessible. You can phone her up about anything. I got her down to look at a piddling little street improvement. It was important to us, but you would never have got a man interested in something like that. She's brilliant.

Across the River Thames, in Islington, Margaret Hodge recognized the change in atmosphere as more women gained political power. It was wonderful, she said, when the leader, deputy leader and chair of the social services committee of Islington Council were all women.

Women are gentler. All those radical men from 1982 onwards are such bloody chauvinists. They out-shout you. They bully you and their manner of doing business within the constraints of debate is very aggressive. We've just changed from having a woman as chair of the Labour group to a man, and you can really sense the difference – there's much more shouting across the room.

Conservative Audrey Berry from Merseyside, on the other hand, enjoyed being in a minority: 'I think the fewer women there are, the better you do. You get more respect.' Yet even she acknowledged that women had a different point of view that could be an advantage: 'Women can see that if the council puts bollards up, prams won't be able to get through.'

Feminists had been part of an earlier – and wider – process that had changed the priorities and style of local government, particularly in London's Labour-controlled authorities, during the 1970s. In Islington, Margaret Hodge found herself caught up in that process in the early part of that decade. Like thousands of young middle-class people who moved into poor, working-class areas of London during that time, she had grown up in the 1960s, learning her politics through Aldermaston marches and student demonstrations. She and other politicized, middle-class owner-occupiers found themselves living next door to the urban poor in rented slum accommodation. That juxtaposition triggered a new approach to community politics and prepared

227

the ground for Labour supporters like Margaret Hodge to stand for the council themselves.

> I lived in an area that had been subject to early gentrification and massive class division, and that really threw me. I'd come in as a gentrifier while my neighbour was having rats put in her home to winkle her out. I got involved in that and led a number of campaigns from the community to get the council to shift their policy on a number of issues.

A range of groups within the community, with different experience and interests, began to make demands on the council. They didn't simply want to be *provided* with whatever the council thought they needed; they wanted to have a say themselves in what was provided and how. It was a distinctive approach, shared by many of the younger generation of left-wing councillors who became powerful in London and in some provincial towns and cities in the 1970s and 1980s. The new breed of local activist-turned-councillor was predominantly middle-class (professional, university-educated) – more so than the old guard it sought to replace. But it identified strongly with what it perceived to be the interests of the working class.

The new community-oriented politics often involved attempts to introduce more open and participatory forms of democracy. In some areas, like Islington, it meant diminishing the power of the old Tammany Hall 'mafia' where favours were controlled and bestowed by the few in return for the votes of the many. The new Labour leaders were committed to the ideal of genuine representation and accountability. Some succeeded better than others in giving that ideal practical expression. It usually involved forging closer links with groups outside the Labour Party – including women's groups and black groups, as well as tenants' associations, issue-based campaigns and other local pressure groups. Responding to demands from these groups, the 'new Left' councils were not afraid of extending the influence and activities of local authorities, raising rates to improve and augment services. A controversial style of high-spending, interventionist local government developed.

But, by the 1980s, it was on a collision course with the ascendant

Thatcherite philosophy of 'rolling back the state'. The 'new Left' councils were labelled 'Loony Left' by an increasingly strident right-wing press, which lost no opportunity to pillory their more radical initiatives. Some criticism may have been merited, but many well-intentioned moves were misconstrued and widely misunderstood. It helped to clear the way for Mrs Thatcher's government to introduce legal and financial restraints, which curtailed the power of local authorities and restricted their activities.

As we shall see, provision for women's needs, as well as campaigns against sexism and racism, were an important part of the new municipal socialism, and women themselves helped shape the experience, both as councillors and in the community. Women were beneficiaries of 'new Left' policies in local government, and were drawn in towards the centre of the stage. When the going got tough, they found themselves nudged back towards the margins.

CHAPTER 15

Town-Hall Feminism

Pointing out the differences in style and approach between women and men was part of a feminist critique inspired by the Women's Liberation Movement in the 1970s. In the 1980s, it developed into a struggle to shift the balance of power away from men and towards women. (Black communities were involved in a similar initiative.) The idea that women's needs, both as citizens and as council employees, should be considered separately, with funds and personnel earmarked for the purpose of empowering them, was a radical departure for local government. It was one way of trying to distribute goods and services more fairly and getting councils to practise what they preached.

The first tentative steps were taken by Lewisham Council in South London, which set up a women's rights working party in 1978. The only precedent it had to follow was its race relations working party, formed in 1974 in conjunction with the local community relations council. This had been an instructive experience for the Labour-controlled council and it formed a model, both for maximizing the usefulness of the council to particular groups in the community, and for winning the hearts and minds of councillors and officers for anti-discrimination policies.

The level of political will was crucial in the development of anti-racist and anti-sexist policies. In Lewisham, Andy Hawkins was council leader from 1971 to 1984. He was willing not just to listen to the needs of blacks and women in the community, but to put his political power behind practical measures.

During the 1970s, the impact of the women's movement was felt all over the country. Lewisham was no exception. A women's resource centre had been set up in Deptford High Street and a local women's refuge had been opened. Both were funded by the council where women, as councillors, were beginning to voice their demands. This was the background against which the new women's rights working party was set up. It was composed of six representatives from the women's centre working alongside six councillors; not all were women, and two places were allotted to Conservatives. It was chaired – like the race relations working party – by Andy Hawkins. (The women took the view that his presence in the chair would help rather than hinder the development of the working party.) ·

One of their first acts was to set up a women's unit with an officer and administrative assistant to service the working party and to start collecting the information required to build up a picture of women's needs in the borough. The working party took a fairly wide view of its responsibilities. An early item on its agenda concerned objections to offensive advertising hoardings; it also took action against a Deptford night club called 'Cheeks', which had erected an illuminated sign of a woman's bottom.

Lewisham Council's pioneering activities encountered many of the problems that other women's committees would face later. Shortage of funds, hostility from the local press, resistance from some councillors, including some of the older Labour men, stonewalling by unsympathetic council staff, difficult decisions about how best to organize the women's unit – all were lessons that had to be learned. Lewisham made a precious contribution to a slim body of knowledge that became weightier and more widespread as other local authorities took up the challenge.

The first fully fledged women's committee was formed by the Greater London Council in May 1982. When Labour took control of the GLC in 1981, one of its basic objectives was the channelling of 'power, resources and opportunities to the deprived, marginalized and disadvantaged sectors of London's population'.[1] But with only the Lewisham experience to go by, it had little idea of how to implement its policy commitments to women. The task was enormous. There were only nine women out of fifty GLC councillors. But there was by this time a feminist presence – both among councillors and among officers. And that made a difference. Women who had been involved in recent campaigns to democratize the Labour Party saw in the GLC a way to put their ideas and demands for women into practice in mainstream politics. It was the first time women were able to flex any political muscle, the first time they could begin to carve out for themselves a space in the local state.

In the early days of the Labour administration of the GLC, a small women's advisory group was set up by Valerie Wise, then vice-chair of the Industry and Employment Committee. From that sprung the concept of a women's committee. (Unlike a working party, a full council committee had executive power.) It started with a staff of three and a budget of £300,000, but by the time the GLC was abolished in 1986, the women's committee had a budget of some £9 million and its own support unit with a staff of ninety-six. It inspired a host of women's committees in other local authorities and helped to organize the Standing Conference of Women's Committees, set up in January 1985 to monitor and support the development of these committees at a national level.[2]

The GLC Women's Committee hoped to change women's lives on two fronts: both within the council, in terms of employment practices, and outside it by identifying and meeting the needs of women who lived in the Greater London area. It wanted to empower women by helping them to take control of their own lives and by offering them a unique chance to participate in the decision-making process. It also sought to shift the emphasis of its work in favour of women seen to suffer most from discrimination – especially working-class and black women who, in the past, had been largely excluded from the aspirations of the white, middle-class women's movement.

The GLC's women's committee had to start from scratch. It took the view that 'ordinary' people had never before been asked for their opinion and that, by responding to the needs of 'ordinary' people, some injustices could be redressed and discriminatory practices ended.

It was only ten days old when it held the first of many public meetings. More than a hundred people turned up to find out about the committee and to offer ideas as to what it should be doing. 'It was not enough to have sympathetic, feminist women

232

working for us,' said Valerie Wise. 'They can never make up for the women with real-life experiences. It's best to go out and talk to women out there about their views.'[3] Instead of closed, private, formal, distant council meetings, the women of London met in crowded, hectic gatherings, clamouring to hear and be heard. Surrounded by babies, shopping baskets and agenda papers, women of all ages, races, classes and interest groups met to discuss such issues as transport, health, work, planning, immigration. Suddenly London's disparate and booming women's movement had a place in the sun: it was called County Hall. How many could qualify as 'ordinary' women remained an open question.

But it was a wholehearted attempt to fill an enormous void. A profile of the lives of women was being drawn up by one of the most powerful local government bodies in the country. What emerged was a clear picture of services devised *without* women in mind. Transport services paid no heed to women shopping with children, or travelling alone at night via ill-lit stations or lonely bus-stops; the planning department had never considered the implications for women of housing developments, shops, schools or hospitals. Every aspect of women's experience – from images displayed in public to life in prison, from employment to racism, from child care to the needs of women with disabilities – all cried out for attention.

From these open meetings, working groups were set up to pull together ideas, determine priorities and decide how best to deploy the committee's powers. More detailed information was obtained by specially commissioned surveys – into London transport and shopping facilities – which focused for the first time on how women were affected.[4] When the Greater London Development Plan was revised, a chapter on women was introduced, again for the first time. The women's committee made sure that wherever the GLC was, women were taken into account. Other council committees were required to investigate and act upon the needs of women in their own fields.

The women's committee was keen to share power with women in the community. Eight women were elected from the floor of the open meetings for co-option on to the Committee, with full voting rights. Elections were held within different categories: black women, lesbians and the disabled. Two more seats were reserved for co-opted trade-union women. A further twelve women, representing areas such as mental health, planning and transport, also sat on the committee, but without voting rights. Membership of the Labour Party was not a requirement for co-optees, except in the case of the union women. It was a bold move, and one that disturbed the determinedly party-led traditions of Labour local government.

One of the GLC's priorities was to promote equal opportunities for women in the council's employment. Evidence pointed to patterns of institutional sexism and racism, with women and ethnic minority employees concentrated in the worst-paid, low-status jobs. To change this, the GLC's Equal Opportunities Unit (which was separate from but worked closely with the Women's Support Unit) first analysed the employment structure to see where disadvantage lay and then introduced a programme not just to dismantle patterns of discrimination but to provide a policy of positive discrimination. Child care was an essential element, as was training. A huge number of new training programmes was established, to improve women's skills at all levels in all kinds of work, traditional and non-traditional. For the first time, women were encouraged to join the London Fire Brigade; in 1981, there were no women firefighters, but as a result of equal opportunities initiatives, seven women were appointed by 1985 – a small but significant breakthrough in a particularly male-oriented field.[5]

The women's committee developed a strategy of funding voluntary groups as another way of meeting women's needs. Child care, traditionally perceived as being part of women's unpaid labour, was singled out for particular attention. Of the £30 million that the GLC gave to the women of London during its four-year existence, nearly half was for child care. More than two hundred projects – including workplace nurseries, toy libraries, 'latchkey' projects (supervised places for children to attend after school) and mobile crèches – were supported by GLC grants. By 1986, the women's committee was responsible for funding 12 per cent of all full-time provision for under-fives in London.[6]

'We funded the whole range of care, including mother and toddler clubs, so women would get involved in our work from going to those clubs,' explained Valerie Wise, chair of the women's committee. The policy was reinforced by grants to voluntary sector child-care campaigns, by training child-care workers, and by encouraging wide discussion about pre-school care in general. As for the other half of the £30 million, that was devoted to (among other things) sixty-nine health projects, sixty information and resource projects, and thirty-seven women's refuges.[7]

With the abolition of the GLC, the bubble burst. The London boroughs managed to take over some of the work started by the women's committee, but it had made itself irreplaceable. Women, who had more to gain from the GLC's innovations than any other single group, were now the main losers. Nurseries, health projects, refuges and training programmes were starved of funds. Many closed down altogether. But the consciousness-raising effect could not be extinguished. Women had glimpsed what they needed, and the GLC had set an example for other local authorities to follow.

First off the ground were the London boroughs and the metropolitan districts - all under Labour control - but as the word spread, councils from Stirling to Southampton adopted some sort of equal opportunities policy. Nearly all of these policies covered women; others incorporated race, disability and sexual orientation. Many led to the establishment of special committees and units. The nature and the scope of these new organizations varied enormously. Few could match the political will that drove the GLC. None could compare with its size or wealth.

A 1986 survey of all 514 local authorities in Great Britain found that, of the 446 authorities who responded to the survey, just over half had some sort of equal opportunities policy covering sex equality. Of these, 82 authorities – predominantly the metropolitan districts, London boroughs and English county councils – had an equal opportunities committee or working party, and 59 authorities employed an officer. The survey, by the Equal Opportunities Commission, observed that these measures represented 'the most positive and public commitment of resources to the issue of equal opportunities'. Only 15 per cent of Conservative authorities with an equal opportunities policy had a women's committee, compared with 51 per cent of Labour authorities. Labour had set the political trend for equal opportunities, but not all Labour boroughs followed suit: in May 1985, more than a third had no equal opportunities policy at all.[8]

In town halls up and down the country, there were stories of success and failure, support and hostility, as women battled to create their own political space and to initiate and implement policies that addressed women's needs. They adopted a range of different structures and strategies, but the women's committees had certain features in common. First, they were very much a creation of the Labour Party, more specifically of the radical strand of the Labour Party (which explains why only some, and not all, Labour-controlled councils had equal opportunities policies). Secondly, the new priorities prescribed by the radical Labour councils were informed by feminism and it was feminists who provided the political commitment and the skills. Thirdly, the women's committees were a largely middle-class initiative because politics remained – even more so for women – a middle-class activity, in spite of efforts to involve 'ordinary' people. Women's committees were based on the recognition of the needs of working-class women, but it was mainly middle-class feminists who were the decision-makers and power brokers. Finally, women's committees were oppositional in style and content. They were in opposition, first, to traditional male institutions, and secondly, in many cases, to the political establishment, whether Conservative or Labour.

Greenwich was among the first of the London boroughs to follow the GLC and set up its own women's committee. In October 1983, Kathryn Riley was appointed head of the Equality Unit, with responsibilities covering both women in council employment and women in the community. She took the view that there was no point looking for support in the community if one's own house was not in order:

My idea was to talk to women council employees about basic bread-and-butter issues like child care, flexitime, job sharing, health, and to effect change for them so that they began to take control over what was happening to them. Then they would be in a position to begin to work with women in the community and help them articulate their needs.

Kathryn Riley convened a group of women working in the borough's housing department (where the director was sympathetic to her aims). The Women and Housing group, which was made up mainly of women in the lower-paid, lower-status jobs, first looked at their own employment needs. They made suggestions for introducing flexible working hours and medical screenings, which were subsequently taken up by the borough. Next, they undertook a survey of the needs of women as users of the council's housing service. They discovered that women tenants wanted more and better laundries on the estates, more imaginative play areas, better security, more efficient lighting, and countless improvements in the channels of communication between tenants and the council. The group drew up a report, which concluded: 'Women, as the major consumers of the housing service, often have a different perception of the service provided to that of officers and members and they may have different priorities for areas of improvement.'[9] Proposals outlined in the group's report were taken up by the council. Kathryn Riley's strategy was to build on initiatives of this kind, gradually altering the consciousness and practices of the council.

In the great northern city of Manchester, an equal opportunities committee was set up in 1984 when the left wing of the Labour Party took control of the council. It created a women's steering group, open to the public. Here – as in many other authorities – top priority was given to child care. 'Nowhere in the council was child care being addressed in terms of parental need,' explained Val Stevens, ex-chair of the equal opportunities committee. 'We made it our policy that provision should reflect and meet parental need because we knew that child care was at the root of women's emancipation.' Manchester's Equal opportunities committee planned to build thirteen children's centres in conjunction with the education and social services committees. The centres were intended to provide child care through the day, before and after school and in school holidays. They would also have general facilities for the local community.

Two hundred miles north, the Scottish town of Stirling set up its own women's committee in the same year. There too, as we've seen, child care was a priority. A free shoppers' crèche, set up in the new town centre at the committee's instigation, was at first highly controversial but soon highly popular. It was what women wanted – the committee had discovered that from questionnaires, public meetings and fact-finding tours of the rural areas in a special women's bus, where a range of subjects, including transport and health, were discussed with local women. As Marie Kane, Stirling's women's officer, explained:

> There was a lot of emphasis on the lack of provision for chil-dren. The problems that were raised by women focused on the lack of places to feed children, to change them in the town centre, the problems of shopping with children. The crèche won people over – before long it wasn't seen as a madcap scheme but as meeting a real need.

Although Labour women were the driving force behind the women's committees, women from the Conservative and centre parties were also drawn into the act. Some chose to get involved; others were instructed to do so. The Liberals were ambivalent. They supported equal opportunities for council workers, endors-ing crèches, maternity leave, and child-minding expenses for councillors. But, as Christina Baron, president of the Women's Liberal Federation, explained:

> Liberals are not happy with the notion of women's issues being side-tracked. We would see something like child care as part of the whole political agenda and not something that just con-cerned women. In the same way as we oppose the Ministry for Women, we are uneasy about women's committees because it's a way of removing politically inconvenient issues to the sidelines.

Among the Conservatives, some found the experience a positive excursion into feminist territory, while others found the lan-guage, style and political perspectives of left-wing feminism alien and distasteful. Attacks on sexist language in council literature seemed trivial; the emphasis on women's special experience and vociferous demands for a women's perspective on every issue were politically unacceptable. The Tories' own philosophy had no truck with special measures for special groups. When controversies arose over the work of women's committees, they were often used by the Tories as a stick to beat high-spending radical Labour councils.

On Merseyside County Council, all women councillors, from all parties, were drafted on to the women's committee, including Audrey Berry, the Conservative councillor from St Helen's. She told us:

I begged to be taken off it. I dreaded going to those meetings. I didn't think there was a need for it. I deplored the fact that someone was addressed as 'the Chair'! When they talked about smear tests, that was all right, but then they'd go over the top. They went on about a crèche – I believe that if a woman has young children she shouldn't be on the council.

In Aberdeen, Conservative councillor Jill Wiseley became a firm supporter of the council's women's committee. She had been a housewife for twenty years before finding an underpaid and exhausting job as a shop assistant in a high-street boutique. 'That experience reinforced my feelings about the women's committee. There was a total emphasis on child care. A lot of men said the agenda was always the same, but I thought that was a definite plus, to try to further the childcare facilities, which are absolutely appalling in Aberdeen.'[10]

Much of the Conservatives' suspicion of women's committees was related to economics. Low spending, a priority for Tory local government, became a benchmark of sane and successful economic behaviour. The two Tory women brought on to Stirling's women's committee thought it was a bit of a 'frill', according to Labour councillor Margaret Brisley. However, they were positive about some aspects of its work.

We were sent an offensive postard on rape and they supported getting it removed from the shops. They also supported public meetings and going to talk to women in different areas. But whenever we talked about money they opposed it, and each year they have stood up in council and proposed that the women's officer's post be deleted from the budget and that we shouldn't have a women's committee.

In spite of opposition in many quarters, bold and imaginative projects concerning women's employment, health, housing and transport needs were being planned all around the country. But these could only scratch the surface of women's unmet needs. And there were a great many obstacles and pitfalls. The very existence of women's committees depended on male support. The power to bestow and to take away still lay with men. The GLC women's committee was able to flourish as it did because support came from Ken Livingstone, leader of the GLC. As Valerie Wise, chair of the women's committee observed: 'We were lucky having Ken Livingstone as leader. For whatever reasons, it suited Ken's politics to have a thriving women's committee. This meant he always gave me support for demands we made as a committee.' Few other women's committees enjoyed that degree of endorsement from the top.

Isabella Stone, who carried out a survey of equal opportunities for women employees in local authorities, found that support came from very few members and was, for the most part, 'tacit if not tokenistic'.

> In very few of the authorities did officers feel that a commit-
> ment to equal opportunities issues was a major element of
> the ruling party's perspective, and in most the commitment
> was seen as at best reluctant and at worst entirely superficial.
> Thus in several cases a situation appeared to prevail where
> one or two committed women councillors were carrying the
> whole burden of advocating women's issues within their party
> group, with one or two officers fulfilling the same function
> on the officer side.[11]

The extent of support from the ruling council group determined, in most instances, the scale and structure of women's committees and their support units – and that, in turn, determined how

TOWN-HALL FEMINISM

powerful the women were and how much they could achieve. The GLC women's committee was a full council committee with corresponding power and status. It had wide terms of reference and its own budget. A retrospective report commented: 'These three elements – together with sufficient staffing resources – were the key to the Committee's ability to effect real change for women in London; without any one of them, the range and influence of its work would have been much reduced.'[12]

Most women's committees and units suffered from being the smallest and least significant in the council. Even in Greenwich, where there was an established political commitment to equality, the women's unit at its largest could boast only eight full-time workers. 'Women's officers will die young,' said Marie Kane of Stirling, who had been doing the job single-handed since 1985.

> They have so much to do. One person – me – is responsible for developing activities for women in the community, for identifying gaps in council services, for analysing council services and the council as an employer, for putting forward positive action measures for women, and for running campaigns and activities for women in the community.

At the same time she was also aware that nobody within the council seemed to know what a women's officer was supposed to do. 'You're sent in to change this huge institution which has been operating in its own way for centuries. There weren't any precedents in Scotland – people here just thought a women's committee would be a good thing to have.'

The very *nature* of projects undertaken by the women's committees was bound to make their workload almost intolerable: they existed to change the status quo, to shift the traditional balance of power. Almost everything they had to do involved a struggle against vested interests and bureaucratic inertia. 'There was not much thought about how I'd interact with other departments, about how my criticism of departments and the very existence of a women's unit might be uncomfortable,' said Marie Kane. 'There was no recognition that change would be difficult.' Margaret Brisley, the lone Labour woman councillor in Stirling, observed: 'The men were very supportive until the

241

women's committee started demanding resources. This might have meant that their pet schemes had to go.'

Almost inevitably, women's committees wanted to see their ideas implemented by every council department and to see all council services changing to take account of women's lives in the community. Valerie Wise at the GLC set up an equality structure in the planning and transport department. It was not enough, she argued, just to have a women's unit – what was needed was a network of 'mini-units' throughout the council. It became part of the problem for women that they were engaged in a constant policing of council departments and officers – a kind of war on all fronts to ensure that women were not being isolated or ignored.

> For every set of twenty officers, it was part of someone's job to ensure that equality considerations weren't forgotten. We didn't get it all off the ground because of abolition, but we did have this little unit where the women's officer had dual accountability to the head of the transport and planning department and to the head of the women's unit, so that she couldn't be isolated in that department without having support from women.

The smaller the unit, the more limited was its ability to influence what was happening in council departments and in the community. Valerie Wise said that the first lesson she had learned was to think big.

> One of our successes was that we actually had the nerve to ask for a lot. Although our money was still a small bit of the total GLC budget, it was an enormous amount of money for women in London. You have to have the gall to ask, because you're never going to get exactly what you've asked for in the first place.

But the idea of building bigger and bigger separate women's organizations within councils remained controversial, even among feminists. There was more at stake than creating an enormous organization to match the enormous task at hand. Too many people were suspicious of any increase in state power and unwilling to pay higher rates. Kathryn Riley in Greenwich took the view that women might not win hearts and minds if they were seen to be empire building; even if the money and the political will were there to build up a large bureaucracy, she would still favour a smaller, strategic outfit. Val Stevens of Manchester observed that being *seen* to be effective was all-important, and not necessarily related to the size of the organization. 'You could put enormous numbers of people into the unit and still people would say, "What have they done?"'

Large or small, the women's committees were ultimately justified by a belief that women with power inside the council could help to empower women in the community. But which women? How far could the committees really deliver to the poor, the unorganized and the inarticulate? As far as their limited budgets allowed them, they undoubtedly delivered services which these women needed: child care, improved transport, street-lighting schemes, funds for women's refuges, skills training and so forth. But what proved harder to deliver was decision-making power.

Deborah Worsley, who was joint head of the GLC women's committee support unit, commented: 'Of those who attended the early huge meetings, there was a very strong element of the white women's movement, and there's no doubt that they saw the opportunity and the resources as rightfully theirs.'[13] This distinctive but unsurprising situation arose because middle-class feminists were more organized than other women and had the political skills to exploit the new commitment to greater openness and accountability. The strategy of co-opting outsiders on to the GLC's women's committee briefly demonstrated how the new openness could be abused by a determined minority: two co-optees from the notoriously sectarian King's Cross Women's Centre attempted to take control of the Committee and had to be voted down by a wide coalition of members opposed to 'bullying tactics'.

In areas with a strong feminist network, every women's committee had to face the demands of a highly politicized and articulate élite. Margaret Hodge, the leader of Islington Council in North London, suggested that a majority of women might be put off making demands because their concerns were so far

removed from those of some activists. 'Many people feel alien-
ated by their very highly political, radical concerns. I recently
took my child to hospital and stayed there with her. We were
stuck in this little ward with women from all sorts of backgrounds. The interesting thing was that all they talked about
was not coping.' The more sophisticated feminist campaigns
being waged in the neighbourhood dealt with important issues
such as lesbian rights and pornography, but they weren't a priority for the women Margaret Hodge met in hospital. 'Their agenda
was simply coping with the stresses of day-to-day parenting.'
Survival was their key preoccupation and it was fanciful to
imagine they would want to get involved – however accessible
the decision-making machinery contrived to be – if the issues
at stake were marginal to their lives.

The impact of feminism on municipal politics had largely been
an expression of the white women's movement. Black women
had been identified as among the disadvantaged, rather than
as decision-makers in their own right. Judy Watson, a white
woman, was a member of Camden Council's women's unit when
it was staffed exclusively by white women. 'Looking back, there
wasn't a lot of emphasis by the councillors on black women being
appointed. One of the criteria for the job was involvement in
the Women's Liberation Movement and that was a very white
view of the appointment of staff.'[14] Pressure from black women
forced a change and, by 1986, 50 per cent of Camden's women's
unit was black and issues were being redefined to relate more
to the needs and experiences of black women.

There was no straight and narrow path to genuine equality.
Well-intentioned efforts to help one group carried the risk of
offending others. At the GLC, one of the conditions attached
to the women's committee's funding policy was that special
efforts be made by grant-aided organizations to counteract discrimination against disadvantaged groups – including black
women, lesbians and women with disabilities. If, at the outset
of funding, an organization could not comply with the non-
discriminatory conditions, it would be asked to show a willingness to change. What was seen at the GLC as a way of redressing
the balance of power towards more 'marginal' and hitherto ne-

glected elements in society was interpreted by others as over-zealous and alienating. The Birner Women's Centre in Tower Hamlets was mainly used by Asian women and pensioners. 'The GLC just insisted that we make a policy statement about working with lesbians,' said one member of the management committee. 'It seemed to us . . . an example of being out of touch with what was happening.'[15]

What the women's committees needed badly was to be seen to be accessible and on the side of working-class women. What they got instead was a constant barrage of hostile – and often wildly distorted – press reporting. 'Gay day pay for lesbian mothers' was how the *Daily Mirror* headlined its story about child-care expenses offered to mothers attending a lesbian day at Camden Women's Centre. 'Loonies ban sexist Robin Red-breast' was a story in the *Sun*, alleging that Ealing Council had banned the children's book *Robin Redbreast* because the word 'breast' was considered sexist. In fact, no books had been banned and there was no policy forbidding the use of particular titles.[16] The Media Research Group at Goldsmiths' College, which analysed the media coverage of Labour councils in London, com-mented:

> This selective obsession of the press with supposedly marginal or minority causes is incessant and repeatedly plays to racist, sexist and anti-lesbian and gay prejudice. A particular theme is the idea of the majority of ratepayers supporting the activi-ties of marginal and bizarre minorities.[17]

That the recipients of most grants given by women's committees would have raised not an eyebrow among Victorian women in public life was hardly a matter of interest. Tabloid newspapers pounced on the most controversial. A grant to a group called 'Babies against the Bomb', for example, was portrayed as another example of crazed feminists in search of ever more decadent covens to endow with public money. In truth, this small grant (only part of which was taken up) was earmarked for a mother and toddlers' group on a London council estate. The young mothers of the group had been particularly interested in peace issues and, required by the funding rules to give their group a name, they had devised its rather snappy title.[18]

Some councils changed their funding strategy in the face of adverse media attention. After two years of being hounded by the press, Islington Council stopped administering grants through its women's committee and handed the work of funding women's groups in the voluntary sector to other council committees. 'We got egg on our face for one or two controversial grants,' said Margaret Hodge, 'and it was all very time-consuming.' The women's committee had given two grants for self-defence training – one to a lesbian group and one to a group of women in a tenants' association. Inevitably, the grant to lesbians grabbed the headlines in the homophobic press. It was not until early in 1988 that Islington Council again considered the possibility of administering small grants through its women's committee.

In Manchester, the equal opportunities committee had never given more than small start-up grants to voluntary-sector organizations. 'It would be a maximum of £200, to pay for a room, that sort of thing. The idea was to generate grass-roots activities,' explained Val Stevens. 'We gave £200 to a lesbian arts group – they thought it was amazing.' But even these small gestures got the equal opportunities committee pilloried by the press. Meanwhile, the social services committee and the education committee, which gave larger grants to more 'acceptable' women's organizations, escaped political or public criticism.

Kathryn Riley in Greenwich told us she tried to initiate positive press reports on the work of the equality unit, with the help of a newly-appointed press and publicity officer. 'Now we have jolly pictures in the paper of our shoppers' crèche, groups of mums in playgroups and so on. We were also very careful when we did controversial things that nothing sloppy ever appeared on committee reports about our activities.' The women's committee in Stirling enjoyed mainly favourable media coverage, but that did not stop the leadership from worrying about its impact on the reputation of the council. As Marie Kane put it: 'The Labour progressive in this part of the world is a hard man who doesn't believe in artsy-fartsy women's business.'

One effect of media distortion was to widen the comprehension gap between women's committees and the very women who most needed to be empowered by them: the poorest and least powerful in the community. But while some committees were beset by demands from more privileged women, others would have been grateful for any kind of pressure from any section of the community. Most women in Stirling, said Marie Kane, tended to accept the traditional relationship between council and community. 'They don't come clamouring to the women's committee with their demands, but when we do things they approve of, they are quite appreciative. Lots of Conservative groups don't see what the problems are so they don't make demands on us. I would welcome the pressure; it would make me feel less vulnerable.' Without a constituency actively demanding that things be done, she had no clear context in which to work, or from which she could draw affirmation and determine her priorities. In Manchester, council members of the equal opportunities committee were disappointed by the lack of outside interest. As Marilyn Taylor said:

> It would be great if we were pushed, but we're not. The women's steering group is open to all women in Manchester. The meetings are publicized to 300 to 400 women's groups, and at one stage we had a good response from Catholic women and the National Council of Women – I was pleased about that. The potential's there, but in fact we get about ten to twelve people turning up.

'Outreach work' was one way of coping with this problem. It involved sending representatives out to make contact with women in the community, and it helped to identify those – usually the most needy – who never came to official meetings. Valerie Wise explained that this was an important development in the GLC's latter years.

> Near the end of the life of the GLC, we had four outreach workers who divided London into four so that each had a base in a women's centre. They were very much more on the ground and sometimes they would pick things up that we

weren't picking up and get things over differently. I think that's something that we'd have developed more if we'd had more time.

Time was not on the side of the GLC, and by the end of the 1980s there was a distinct chill in the air around London's municipal feminism. In February 1989, pioneering Lewisham abolished its women's unit. The plan was to form a single equality development unit with five sections dealing with pensioners, people with disabilities, lesbians and gay men, women and blacks. The budgets of the women's and race units were to be pooled to fund the new unit, which would have a total of eight officers (the women's unit alone had had nine posts). No extra funds were allocated. The women's committee was moribund as the council tried to decide what to do with it.

Opinions varied as to whether or not this meant the end of effective work for women in the borough. 'The new unit has been set up to fail,' was the view of some who had worked in the old women's unit. 'You need money to develop this kind of work. The money's being spread far too thinly now.' Andy Hawkins, former leader of Lewisham Council but no longer a councillor by this time, saw it as an inevitable result of the almost intolerable squeeze put on council spending by the Tory government:

> If there's a straight choice between looking after children at risk and keeping open old people's homes on the one hand, and equal opportunities for women on the other, it's extremely difficult to make any other decision. But the work already done in this area hasn't been lost. Notions about sex equality are more embedded in council thinking than before.

Brent was another London borough that scrapped its women's unit – and the women's committee too – in 1989. Hackney merged its women's and race units into a single section, and there were rumours of Camden and Lambeth going the same way. It was part of a general move among London authorities to 'rationalize' activities in the face of acute financial difficulties. Outside London, Birmingham had taken similar steps, merging its women's committee into a 'Policy and Community Initiatives Sub-Committee of the Personnel Committee', but retaining a women's unit. Bradford, which fell to the Tories with the casting vote of its mayor, scrapped its unit and committee.

But elsewhere the picture was not so gloomy. The centre of gravity had shifted north. The big growth area for town-hall feminism in the late 1980s was Scotland – increasingly a stronghold of the Labour Party. Atiha Mohamed, co-ordinator of the National Association of Local Government Women's Committees, told us in 1989 that more than a dozen Scottish authorities had women's committees and units, or an equivalent structure. Many were only a year or two old. Aberdeen, which had been the first authority in Britain to scrap its women's committee when Labour lost control of the council in 1986, reinstated it after Labour was voted back into power in May 1988. Aberdeen now had a unit with five officers dealing with women as well as race and disabilities, and what one worker described as 'quite a healthy budget'.

Throughout Britain, there were by 1989 some fifty authorities with a women's committee or something similar, and a unit or officers working on women's issues. Outside Scotland, most were in the North of England and inner London. There was one in Wales, but none to the south and west of Southampton and Bristol. Nor were there any in the South-East, apart from London and new towns such as Basildon and Harlow.

In Manchester, the women's steering group became a formal sub-committee of the equal opportunities committee (regarded as a step forward). By 1989, four of the children's centres it had devised were completed and two more were planned for the following year. Progress had been slower than originally hoped, but it was progress none the less.

The map of feminist activity broadly followed the map of Labour control. The National Association of Local Government Women's Committees (NALGWC) had thriving regional sections in Scotland and the North-East, where 'networking' between authorities encouraged the spread of women's committees and units. NALGWC, which developed from the Standing Conference set up in 1985, acted as a means of support and information exchange through its offices at the Pankhurst Centre in Manchester. It enabled understaffed and underfunded committees to have access to specially prepared and researched material which helped them develop and implement policy, and keep in touch with national developments. It held quarterly meetings where themes such as disability, safety on estates, education, poll tax and housing were on the agenda.

Small though it was, with one co-ordinator, an assistant and part-time researcher, NALGWC's endurance was a sign that seeds sown a decade ago by Lewisham and the Greater London Council had taken root. But the obstacles were still considerable. For one thing, women's committees had a precarious legal status. Unlike other full standing committees, there was no legislative basis for their existence. Local councils' responsibilities under the Sex Discrimination Act 1975 were open to various interpretations, but the Act gave no clear statutory duty to local authorities to promote equality of opportunity for women.

They were therefore all the more vulnerable to the ideological war being waged over local government. On one side were the interventionists, who favoured special measures to empower disadvantaged groups. On the other side were the 'neo-liberals' who believed that the market, not the state, was the best arbiter of fortunes, that individuals should shift for themselves, and that no one should get any special help. Throughout the 1980s, the neo-liberals had the upper hand in the national arena and their high priestess, the prime minister, did all she could to impose their ideology throughout the kingdom. The power of local councils was cut drastically; financial restraints and rate-capping meant that they ceased to be free to raise the funds they needed to implement policies determined by a majority of elected representatives. Some councils, like Brent, gave up the unequal struggle to make equal opportunities a priority; others were all but paralyzed by caution.

But the Tories weren't the only problem. Even where budgets were 'healthy' and political will on the council strong, a constant battle had to be waged against the passive resistance of senior male officers who had no desire to hasten change, especially the kind that sought to diminish the power of men.

The history of women's committees has turned on the energy and presence of women in local politics. But would the number of powerful women continue to grow as it had during the 1970s and 1980s? There was some indication by the late 1980s that changes in the patterns of female employment would diminish the numbers of women potentially available as councillors. Islington leader Margaret Hodge observed that there were more women on Islington Council in the 1970s than there were a decade later. 'When I first had children it wasn't acceptable as a caring mother to go back into full-time work, so you looked for a part-time alternative. Going on the council was the sort of activity that fitted in with that concept of mothering. Now, full-time work is completely acceptable so mothers are not choosing to go into council work.' The Conservative authors of *Seizing Our Opportunities*, a booklet written in 1982, also drew attention to the failure of local government as a growth area for women. The reasons, they said, were two-fold: first, not enough women put themselves forward, and secondly, an increase in female employment and late marriages made a commitment to council work very difficult.[19]

Men, as we've noted, could more often combine council work with a full-time paid job because they had few responsibilities at home. For women, this was almost impossible. The question of 'choosing' whether to pursue a career or take up council work was, of course, a middle-class preoccupation. Working-class women had no option: they needed paid work to survive. So, if the number of middle-class women standing for the council looked like dropping, the number of working-class women (already negligible) would certainly not increase. As the Bristol study, 'Married to the Council?', warned: 'Council work will increasingly become the preserve of an unrepresentative minority (some of whom enjoy particular kinds of privilege) – thus jeopardising one of the principles of a widely-held concept of "democracy", namely equal access to political power.'[20]

PART IV

Power, Prejudice and Positive Action

CHAPTER 16

'I Spy Strangers'

The lobby of the House of Commons was crowded with members waiting to vote on a Bill to abolish the Greater London Council, one of the most controversial measures of Mrs Thatcher's second term of office. Among the MPs was Harriet Harman, the Labour member for Peckham. Nine days earlier, she had given birth to her second son in the maternity unit of St Thomas's Hospital, across the river from the Palace of Westminster. On the day of the vote she had driven to parliament from her home in South London, bringing the baby with her in a carrycot – the abolition of the GLC was a key constitutional issue and the Labour party needed all the support it could muster. She had taken baby Joe to the Whips' Office to be cared for while she voted, but she had been spotted on the way in – and in that place, a mother and baby were a rare sighting. As she filed through to vote, the cry went up 'I Spy Strangers!' – the curious old phrase used if a non-MP is suspected of going through the division lobby. The MP for Peckham was being accused of smuggling her baby, hidden beneath her cardigan, into the inner sanctum.

'I was quite fat after having Joe,' Harriet Harmon told us (by way of explaining how she might have seemed to have had a baby up her jumper).

Somebody told the Chief Whip in a hysterical sort of way that I had carried him through the division lobby. I thought it showed such an unstable approach to this little baby. He was no threat to anyone, yet the very idea of him deeply attacked people's nerve endings. I had come from a cosy home environment, and before that from hospital with all those new babies. To arrive in the Commons and find it full of anti-social, alien

types of men who'd been festering all day before the vote
– it really was a culture shock! And then you have to be
stripped of your baby in order to exercise your right to vote
because that makes you a *real* MP.

We relate the case of the fantasy baby, not to defend the rights
of infants to participate in parliamentary business, but to help
demonstrate that parliament is more than an institution of
ancient mystique and obscure language; it is a place made by
men for men, and still fiercely ruled by them. Women have been
admitted, but their presence is acceptable only if they do not
draw attention to themselves as women and only if they divest
themselves of any uniquely female preoccupation such as motherhood. So there, in the division lobby, at the heart of Britain's
legislative process, where decisions are made on all manner of
policies affecting women's lives – whether they should have
abortions, or claim maternity rights, get Child Benefit, become
bus drivers, work at night, gain equal pay – the merest *thought*
of a woman passing through with a baby in her arms not merely
offended convention, but seemed to threaten the very security
of the institution.

The British parliament, like any other, has its own rules and
ethos, but, perhaps more than most, it has generated a particularly rarefied atmosphere, which is supposed to enhance its prestige, but also throws up a *cordon sanitaire* between itself and the
everyday world. Consider how Anthony Trollope, by no means
a romantic about politics, described in his Palliser novel, *Can
You Forgive Her?*, the triumph of a successful parliamentary candidate.

Ah, my male friend and reader, who earnest thy bread, perhaps, as a country vicar; or sittest, maybe, at some weary
desk in Somerset House; or who, perhaps, rulest the yard
behind the Cheapside counter, has thou never stood there
and longed, – hast thou never confessed, when standing there,
that Fate has been unkind to thee in denying thee the one
thing that thou has wanted? I have done so; and as my slow
steps have led me up that more than royal staircase, to those
passages and halls which require the hallowing breath of cen-

turies to give them the glory in British eyes which they shall one day possess, I have told myself, in anger and grief, that to die and not to have won that right of way, though but for a session – not to have passed by the narrow entrance through those lamps – is to die and not have done that which it most becomes an Englishman to have achieved.[1]

Trollope himself had once aspired to that hallowed 'right of way' as a Liberal candidate, but without success.

So well preserved is the arcane character of Westminster that the scene described by Trollope was still recognizable a century later. Anthony Sampson wrote in his *Anatomy of Britain* that MPs, though 'mostly very ordinary people, assume the heightened manner of a club – the affectation of an older, more confident generation'.[2] The image of that club was both socially and sexually exclusive – frequently compared with a boys' public school. Sampson quoted Mark Bonham-Carter, then a newly-elected MP, who remarked with some relish: 'It's just like being back as a new boy at public school – with its ritual and rules, and also its background of convention, which breeds a sense of anxiety and inferiority in people who don't know the rules.'[3] So the House of Commons has remained a narrow sort of place, comfortably familiar to those who have been to the best schools. It has stripped itself of distasteful associations with the outside world; it is competitive, self-protective, and, above all, effective at distancing itself from the daily experiences of the electorate.

In 1989, sixty years after the first woman took her seat in parliament, there were forty-two women in the House of Commons. It was the largest number ever – and represented an increase of 78 per cent since the general election of 1983, when twenty-three women were returned. Yet women still accounted for only 6.3 per cent of the total number of MPs.

One reason why there have not been more women in parliament is that ordinary women have had that familiar set of 'difficulties' to overcome – time, money, family commitments and day-to-day experience – not shared by the established political élite. We have seen how these presented problems for women participating in politics at other levels; in the national arena they became even more acute. As a result, women still did not come forward in large enough numbers as candidates.

At the same time, the parties' selection committees (whose job it is to select candidates) were evidently still reluctant to choose women. The reasons why were a matter for debate. It might have been because the committees were generally prejudiced against women, or because women were perceived as an electoral risk – or a combination of these. And sometimes it was because women chose to boycott the proceedings – not out of diffidence, but because they felt an aversion to it. We have seen this operating in other areas of political activity – a peculiarly female response to a political system designed and constructed by men.

The pathway to Westminster would begin for many with the party 'lists'. To be approved of by your party, and thus get your name on the list of potential candidates, was a relatively minor hurdle. Yet when Emma Nicholson, now an MP, was first put on the Conservative Party list, she was told that out of the 700 names, hers was only the eighth belonging to a woman. 'There were not nearly enough women putting their names forward. You can't blame discrimination and the selection committees unless you have much nearer equal numbers.' As vice-president of the Conservative Party with special responsibility for women, Emma Nicholson made a concerted effort to bring more women on to the lists in the early 1980s. She was looking for what she called the 'right' women – preferably over twenty-five and under fifty, with experience, qualifications and talent. And they had to be competitive with the men. 'The only way a non-working woman can conceivably have the right qualifications is by becoming a councillor, because that brings her into the world of work,' said Emma Nicholson. 'It's always said that a housewife has all the skills of a business person, and in a sense that's true, but on such a microscopic scale, it frankly doesn't help. The women have to stand up on paper against the men.'

In the Labour Party, after decades of inactivity, by the mid-1980s some efforts were being made to encourage female candidates. Nevertheless, in 1989, Labour's List A (made up of union-sponsored hopefuls) had seven women out of a total of ninety-seven; List B (interested individuals, including those put forward by women's sections and the Young Socialists) had ninety-nine women out of 511, and List C (sponsored by the co-operatives) had fourteen women out of eighty-nine.[4] There is nothing here to suggest that a working-class woman might gain her opportunity to enter parliament through her links with a trade union. The figures for List A confirm our impressions, outlined earlier, that women remained marginalized in the trade-union movement.

The business of entering national politics has been widely perceived as a profession and a 'career'. It demanded qualifications, expertise, achievement and so acquired status and middle-class values. When Mary Kaldor stood as a Labour candidate in the 1983 election, she remarked that people would say to her: 'I hear you're going into politics.' She found this strange since she believed that she had been 'in politics' all her life. 'What they meant, of course, was that I was going into a well-paid job, with a career structure, a job that is called "politics".'[5] To pursue a career was something men were educated and trained for in a way that women were not. And whether you were male or female, it helped to be middle-class, if not by birth at least by experience.

For women, even the most impressive array of qualifications was not sufficient to ensure a smooth path to parliament. Emma Nicholson had wide experience in the computer industry and in charity work, where she controlled a £1.5 million budget and a staff of ninety-five. She was also from a classic Tory mould – daughter of an upper-class political dynasty which had presided over rolling acres for generations. Yet her search for a seat took her to forty-two constituencies. Many other women with glowing credentials had equally lengthy battles to get selected – among them, Conservative Edwina Currie, a former Birmingham City councillor, and the Labour MP Joan Ruddock who had a distinguished career at Shelter, the Citizens' Advice Bureau and the Campaign for Nuclear Disarmament. There have been some exceptions. Harriet Harman was adopted by Peckham (a Labour stronghold) on only her second attempt to find a seat. It was 1982, and a time when women in the Labour Party were beginning to push for the selection of feminists; thus Harriet Harman found herself in the right place at the right time.

Parliamentary hopefuls needed to devote themselves to an assiduous courtship of potential constituencies. Jo Richardson, Labour MP for Barking, explained:

> Men who are keen to get into parliament spend hours and hours going round the country, attending selection meetings, keeping themselves well informed. Usually, they have someone at home who makes sure they've got an overnight case and a clean shirt. Poor woman, if she's the one who's seeking a seat, she's got to find a childminder while she belts off! It's just an impossible task unless you're very dedicated and have some money.

One essential quality for the aspiring candidate was what Edwina Currie called 'zeal', another was economic well-being.

The need to spend money didn't let up with selection – as Margaret Joachim discovered when she stood as a Liberal candidate; the costs of nursing a constituency were considerable.

> There are the travel costs, by car or train, because they would be mortally offended if you didn't turn up to everything. If it's a social event you can't get away without buying raffle tickets. And they'd be terribly upset if you weren't reasonably presented. The average bloke can get away with two or three suits, but if I turned up for a month wearing the same three sets of clothes, people would start wondering. Then there are phone bills, baby-sitters, paper, magazines, subscriptions for this and that.

If you couldn't pay, you couldn't stay the course.

Edwina Currie entered parliament in the 1983 election, won notoriety for her provocative and brash style, and was promoted to the front bench during Mrs Thatcher's second term. She was Minister of Health until her fall from grace during the salmonella scandal in 1988. Keen on encouraging more women to go into parliament, she stressed the importance of presentation – good clothes, smart hair, confidence, authority.

It takes a bit of self-discipline, but if you're going to look after

82,000 people and work a ninety-hour week, in two places,
you have got to be self-disciplined anyhow. And if you can't
sort our your personal life, how the hell are you going to sort
out anyone else's personal life? If you go to a selection committee that wants you to look after their problems, it's no good
going as if *you've* got problems. You don't have to be exceptional and there are plenty of plain women in parliament, you
don't have to wow them with sex appeal. But you have to
feel authoritative and confident and you have to *look* authoritative and confident. If you don't you won't get it. It's as simple
as that.

According to the Currie school of thought, the best remedy for
a woman who had trouble getting selected seemed to be a spell
at a health farm and a course in confidence-boosting. It might
help some, but it hardly amounted up to a comprehensive solution to what was clearly a complex and intractable set of problems.

Selection committees, up and down the country, were responsible for making their own choice of candidate. In the Conservative Party, the committee was usually made up of senior
members of the constituency, while in the Labour Party the
choice was based on a vote among all constituency members
and affiliated unions. Naturally, selectors wished to choose a
potential winner. There was some evidence to suggest that selection committees believed women were 'risk' candidates. Yet
there was also evidence that, except under peculiar circumstances, such as a highly-publicized by-election, candidates
would pick up – or lose – fewer than 500 votes on the strength
of their personal attributes; most candidates would be swept
along with the political mood of the moment. A survey com-
paring the success of male and female candidates of both Labour
and Conservative Parties suggested that gender made only a
very small difference to voters. 'Up to the 1974 election, the
gender of a candidate had only a very marginal impact on electoral outcome. It seems that if parties exclude women from fighting elections in favourable seats, on the basis of "risk", they
do so irrationally.'[6]

Between 1970 and 1979, only three non-sitting women (all Labour) were adopted in safe seats. By 1987, this had increased to fifteen (eleven in the Labour Party and four for the Conservatives). Yet in that election – historic for the increased number of women elected – the great majority of women candidates remained in unwinnable seats. Out of Labour's ninety-two women candidates, nearly three-quarters were in hopeless seats, and out of the Conservatives' forty-six candidates, half were in that situation. The Alliance – who fielded the most women candidates – had, anyhow, little chance of success.[7]

Conservative women MPs have been inclined not to blame the selectorate, as such, for the paucity of women chosen for winnable seats. According to Emma Nicholson, the selection committees absorbed the culture of their parties. 'People blame them but actually they are just the tail end of the whole party mechanism.' Edwina Currie took the view that blaming the selection committees was 'a powerful and effective myth'.

To counter the lack of women being considered for seats, the Labour Party, the SDP and the Social and Liberal Democrats introduced a rule that there must be one woman on every short list. The Conservative Party, characteristically, steered clear of any such measure. Emma Nicholson explained: 'There's a very ingrained feeling in the Party against it, although I have discussed it at the top end and obviously I wouldn't say no to anything that would get more women into parliament. My own view is that we've got to get everybody up to the starting line equally and it's up to them who wins the race.'

Even among Conservatives who chose not to see discrimination looming at every corner, there were those who felt its influence at selection committees. Doreen Miller, chair of the 300 Group, which campaigns to increase women's representation in parliament and public life, had put herself up for selection to ninety Conservative associations. She had been interviewed nine times and had twice been runner-up. Her view was that women were asked questions that would not be put to a man.

I was asked: 'If your children were ill and rushed to hospital and we needed you in the association, where would you be?'

I said I would be in the hospital. There were three men in front of me and I said, 'Did you ask the men the same question?' They said, 'Of course not, it's not relevant.' I said, 'Why not? A man who can't put his sick child before his constituency isn't going to be any good anyway'.

She added that questions like these were often put by female committee members. 'The ones who haven't been out to work themselves are very hard on other women.' Doreen Miller's tale was one of many accounts we heard from women in different parties, all indicating that selection committees were unwilling to believe in women as 'suitable' material for parliament. Shirley Williams, former Labour Minister of Education and co-founder of the Social Democrats, said she had seen many women who could 'do so well for the country, the House of Commons and their constituents, who just have the door shut in their face'.

The remedy, according to the 300 Group, was to 'train women for the fight'. To encourage them to be more confident it organized all-party programmes of debating, informing, practice at chairing meetings and improving appearance. As one commentator explained, 'What the 300 Group is trying to do is to identify and work at the most obvious institutional or psychological barriers which women face and by giving them the experience of performing competently increase their self-assurance and hence their performance.'[8] This was an advance on the Currie formula, and it was similar to the approach adopted by the Conservative high-fliers' group, first nurtured by Emma Nicholson. But it was a view contested by some feminists in the Labour Party. The problem as they saw it was not women's ability to compete, but the nature of the contest itself. It wasn't women who needed changing, but the values, culture and mechanisms of the parliamentary system. 'You need a rather blinkered approach to slot easily in to the procedures,' argued Harriet Harman.

I'm not sure that organizing courses in assertiveness training is really where it's at. I think men have a lot of the wrong sort of confidence. The wider your perceptions are the less you feel it's your automatic right to plant yourself forward and, say, I'm going to be the be-all and end-all for these 70,000 people – because you are aware of the fragmentation and diversity of the situation. What's more, the system awards merit points for turning your back on your children – and that's where women score low.

Margaret Hodge, Labour leader at Islington Council, had been courted persistently by her party to go into parliament – a temptation she resisted for some time. 'My family and a life at Westminster are completely incompatible,' she explained to us. 'Your whole life as an MP would have to be committed to the party and I'm not prepared to do that. It's the single-mindedness that I don't like.' Margaret Hodge saw parliament as an institution where people were removed from the real world: 'When you're there, you forget the values and principles that brought you there. You become entirely institutionalized and start playing their games which are all about winning debating points. There's an utter self-obsession and selfishness and I don't want anything to do with that.'

Edwina Currie argued that women failed to reach parliament because they did not adopt a 'long-term plan', a strategic approach to a political career. Mrs Currie laid her own parliamentary plans while she was in Birmingham's council chamber. 'Most women don't think like that when they're young enough so that by the time they begin to wield power, they are fifty and heading to be Lord Mayor. They are thoroughly enjoying themselves and see no reason to come here.' (She might have added that at fifty many women would be thought too old to enter parliament.)

For those who were willing and able, who felt neither excluded nor undermined, there were further hurdles to negotiate. Such women would need to juggle their personal life with their political life, they would need sufficient quantities of cash, status and verve, and, finally, they would have to convince the selectorate in a winnable seat (where few unorthodoxies would be tolerated) that their political and personal profiles were appropriate to put them on course for victory. It was a fine filter through which only a tiny number could pass. And of that group, inevitably, an even smaller fraction would eventually emerge as MPs.

What did it feel like to belong to that small band of political achievers at the 'pinnacle' of the electoral system? Did the constraints that women suffered on the way to Westminster continue to plague them once they'd arrived? And how far did women exercise power *as women* in the House of Commons?

'I find,' said the young Winston Churchill in 1919, 'a woman's intrusion into the House of Commons as embarrassing as if she burst into my bathroom when I had nothing with which to defend myself, not even a sponge.'[9] Such was the welcome that greeted Lady Astor, the first elected woman MP to take her seat, when she arrived in parliament in 1919 as the new member for Plymouth, Sutton. Churchill was not alone in his discomfort. As Lady Astor recorded: 'Men whom I had known for years would not speak to me if they passed me in the corridor.'[10]

Seventy years later, when Britain had had ten years' experience of a woman prime minister, that sense of exclusion remained. Joan Ruddock, MP for Lewisham, Deptford, and a seasoned political campaigner, wrote in parliament's own weekly organ, *The House Magazine*, that the Commons was the 'least friendly place I have ever worked'.[11] Harriet Harman agreed. It was, she said, 'very inhospitable and alienating. I just don't find it a conducive place to work. Perhaps it's not really just attributable to being female, but because I am a mother, I feel that I've got a different agenda in my mind.'

There were others, however, who found the place both welcoming and invigorating. Emma Nicholson, the Conservatives' champion of women candidates, first entered the House in 1983 as MP for Devon West and Torridge. 'I felt immediately that I was at home there,' she told us. 'At last, I belonged. I had always known that that was where I ought to be because that's where I function best and where I can achieve most for the people.' Edwina Currie, too, claimed to enjoy dealing with the badinage of Commons' life and the cross-fire of debate.

Yet even women who felt comfortable in that predominantly male environment produced a catalogue of complaints about life in parliament. Why were the hours so absurd? Why did the men behave so boorishly and childishly? Why should MPs in general and women in particular have to put up with poor working conditions? Why were the facilities in parliament so inadequate – no crèche, no shop, no women's hairdresser (only a barber). Conservative MP Teresa Gorman made trenchant demands for a hairdresser, as did Elizabeth Shields, the former Liberal MP for Ryedale, who noted: 'When I requested a hair-dresser's, I was met with roars of male chauvinist laughter.' Parliament had shown little inclination to change.

Many women MPs had to face personal insults and cheap jokes during debates, especially those with a women's angle. Subjects such as pornography and rape incited male MPs to particularly vicious attacks on their female colleagues. Jo Richardson, until 1989 the sole woman member of Labour's shadow cabinet, told us:

> Among the Tories there is a nasty, despicable group who strike a very moralistic stance about what they consider women should be like and what women should do. They rubbish any serious debate about women. I sometimes have to grit my teeth when I get up to make a speech from the front bench. They know it's going to be on women. Half a dozen of them will go 'Oh God no, not again'.

There was more to this behaviour than mere intimidation. It signified both a refusal to allow women their own parliamentary 'space' and a deep-seated discomfort with the presence of women in parliament.

In proportion to their numbers, women MPs tended to have a higher profile than their male colleagues. They had to be better to get there in the first place, and they were inevitably more conspicuous. Over time, they participated in all aspects of the workings of the House and claimed at least some of the rewards and promotions: they become Whips and permanent parliamentary secretaries; they had chaired committees and had sat in the speaker's chair and on the front bench. They had been in the cabinet (the first woman in the cabinet was Labour's Margaret Bondfield in 1929) and, of course, one had become prime minister.

266

However, by 1990, no woman had ever been Chancellor of the Exchequer, Defence Secretary or Foreign Secretary. Only once, between 1974 and 1976, were there two women – Barbara Castle and Shirley Williams – in the cabinet together.[12] No woman had yet followed Mrs Thatcher into her cabinet, although she had promoted women on to her front bench. Traditionally, power resided with those 'male' gods of money and war. High status was conferred on those who worked for them. Areas identified by women as specifically relevant to their own lives were considered less important. As Harriet Harman told us:

> You certainly don't get swept into the shadow cabinet on the basis of your devotion to the under fives or school holiday play schemes. They are not the 'hairy' issues. If you look at what people list in the parliamentary year book as their interests, it's clearly reflected there what the status issues are and what the peer group sees as important areas of politics.

This hierarchy of political values presented women MPs with a dilemma. Most of them were well aware that issues like health, welfare, child care and equal rights were vitally important to women in general; yet these were precisely the areas where their male colleagues would *wish* them to specialize; so long as they were safely packed into a ghetto of 'marginal' concerns, they wouldn't compete with men for the prestige jobs that led up the ladder to power. And if only men climbed the ladder, men would continue to dictate which issues were important and which were not.

In her characteristically robust way, Edwina Currie believed there was always a way of turning a situation to one's own advantage. As Minister for Health, she had seen herself very much at the centre of the stage. 'How many other ministers do you know who have a budget as big as mine?' she demanded. Surely, she said, it was a better bet to concentrate on an area where you weren't in competition with countless other experts all angling for promotion to an over-subscribed ministry. Why compete, for example, with all those chaps who knew about defence when you could more profitably concentrate on a less-favoured corner?

On the other hand, many clever and ambitious women MPs deliberately turned their backs on what was seen to be their 'natural' areas of competence, in order to make their own way in politics. Barbara Castle, for example, refused during her long political career to take on the 'soft' issues, but demanded – and got – the 'hairy' posts, including Minister of Transport and First Secretary of State for Employment and Productivity. But, as Elizabeth Vallance has pointed out, her and other such women's strategy involved a certain sacrifice.

> They took over the largely male definition of what was weighty and what was domestic or trivial and in view of their educational and professional experience, refused to indulge in the trivial which they saw as a distinct, if not conscious, limitation of their potential. They wanted to be equals of their male counterparts and that involved playing the men's game by the rules which were already in existence.[13]

By thus reinforcing the status of 'hard' issues and further undermining the 'soft' ones, they did no service – and arguably a considerable disservice – to the cause of women in general.

A woman would learn, as she entered the Commons, that the successful politician – whatever the party – was the one who spent as much time as possible breathing the Westminster air. As Harriet Harman pointed out:

> For the average MP there is a definite kudos in explaining how little you see your family and how much work you do. Values are turned upside down – the more you abandon your spouse and ignore your children, the more that's regarded as an asset rather than a disqualification for being a good MP. Parliament should not be filled with bog-eyed workaholics who are so overstretched that they don't know where their next meeting is.

The conditions of work and the masculine culture of the Commons made it virtually impossible for anyone with dependent children to be a good parent *and* a powerful politician. Those living in constituencies outside London with children still at school were worst hit – they were bound to be separated for most of the week. If they brought their families to London, then they would be apart at weekends, unless they took their families to visit their constituencies with them. A man with a wife who worked full-time at home was most comfortably cushioned from the difficulties of this desperate life-style; a woman whose husband worked full-time outside the home and who had the main responsibility for parenting (i.e. the *typical* woman) was likely to find the going toughest of all. The procedures and conventions of the Commons were designed to meet the idiosyncratic needs of the male barrister. They continued to do that very well. For more ordinary human beings no concessions were made.

The best hope of changing all this would seem to lie in women MPs getting together and becoming a force to be reckoned with – a strong, cross-party women's lobby – within parliament. Few though they were, they were surely capable of exerting a considerable amount of pressure, behind the scenes and in public. Yet even by 1990 no such lobby had emerged.

The dominant ethos of parliamentary work remained incorrigibly individualistic. One might expect this among Tories and Liberals, but it was no less apparent in the Parliamentary Labour Party. Harriet Harman explained:

> The Labour Party is supposed to reflect collectivism, and yet the PLP operates in a wholly individualistic way. There are built-in disincentives to working collectively and built-in incentives to working on your own, ploughing your own furrow and making sure everybody realizes it's your furrow and not anyone else's. It's a market place rather than a commune.

Women who had acquired some experience of a co-operative, non-confrontational political style outside parliament – and our evidence suggests this was quite common – would find little opportunity to build on it once they got inside. So they were doubly disadvantaged. First, their own experience didn't help them to survive in parliament, let alone to be successful – unlike the experience of men trained up for the competitive, hierarchical world of business, the professions or traditional trade unionism. And secondly, they found themselves caught up in a culture which actively discouraged the one thing that might help them improve their position as women – the practice of sisterhood.

The adversarial nature of party politics in a winner-takes-all electoral system made it especially hard for women to seek alliances across party lines. There were many important issues concerning women where political opinion need not be rigidly divided between Left and Right. Yet too much was invested in party loyalty to enable women to line up with each other. Before the 1987 election, two Labour MPs, Jo Richardson and Clare Short, put forward an early-day motion to counter Tory demands for retribution in the wake of controversial sentencing in a rape case. Their motion advocated more women judges, a review of judicial procedures and support for rape crisis centres. They couldn't get any of the Conservative women MPs to sign the motion. 'If they can't come in with us on rape,' said Clare Short, 'then I don't know what else they can join us on.'[14] Another Labour MP, Diane Abbott, commented: 'I'm sceptical about the possibility of cross-party initiative. I don't think the Tory women would deliver. They are not used to working collectively with other women. Tory women get there by competing with other women, not by working alongside them.'[15] There has usually been a stronger feminist consciousness among Labour than among Tory women MPs, and so it has more often been the Labour women who have invited – and the Tories who have rejected – such cross-party alliances. That said, we found no evidence that the Labour women would be any more inclined than the Tories to break party ranks, should they be invited to do so by women on the other side of the House.

After the 1987 election, however, there were some indications of a change in the atmosphere, as women emerged with a stronger presence in parliament than ever before. On one occasion, Edwina Currie, then Minister for Health, and Harriet Harman, her opposite number on the shadow front bench, debated under the eye of deputy speaker Betty Boothroyd. (So sparse have women been, that these female front-bench confrontations have been rare occurrences. In 1974, following a debate between Barbara Castle and Margaret Thatcher, Terence Lancaster of the *Daily Mirror* felt moved to comment: 'Redhead took on honey blonde yesterday. . . .')[16]

There were no signs of anything approaching a cross-party caucus after 1987, but the increase in numbers suggested a new confidence – a new awareness that women could, if the right issue arose, begin to flex their muscles as a group. The opportunity came with David Alton's Private Member's Bill to limit the period for abortion to eighteen weeks. This key issue drew the women MPs into the chamber as a visible force. The cross-party solidarity was expressed not in the vote itself – for not all women MPs opposed the Bill – but behind the scenes, as women organized and worked together to make it clear that this was one subject on which men would not be allowed to dictate the terms of debate.

The 1987 election also changed things for women within the Parliamentary Labour Party. Many of the new Labour intake had experience of the women's movement – as well as the campaign to democratize and feminize the Labour Party. For the first time, there were enough of them (twenty-one elected in 1987) to buck the individualist trend and put their feminist experience to use, edging towards an agenda for women. A Women's Committee was formed, on the initiative of Jo Richardson, for all women members of the Parliamentary Labour Party. It discussed forthcoming parliamentary business; it tried to ensure that plenty of women sat on parliamentary committees and would speak in key debates on the floor of the House; it took up issues outside the House; it discussed women's involvement in local election campaigns. And, in the two years before the Party changed its rules to help more women get elected to the shadow cabinet, it was partly responsible for ensuring that one woman – Jo Richardson – was voted in.

This new committee provided quite a different environment from the bars and smoking rooms of mainstream parliamentary life. And like women's groups we have encountered elsewhere, it offered a sense of solidarity. 'I was able to go along and express my concerns about the incompatibility between parliamentary and family life,' Harriet Harman told us. 'I could count on people supporting me. It's a sympathetic place to raise that sort of thing.'

The Conservative Party, which was the only other with a female contingent in the House of Commons (seventeen Tory women by 1989, compared with Labour's twenty-two, and one each from the SLD, the Scottish Nationalists and the SDP), developed no group comparable to the Labour Women's Committee. It would have been surprising if they had, since it would have gone deeply against the grain of Tory philosophy. Conservative women had no history of organizing *as women* for the advancement of women. Mrs Thatcher was adept at using her femininity to enhance her own position; the Iron Lady deployed her rarity value at international summits to claim pride of place at photocalls, and was known to mix authority and sternness with the habit of moistening her lips at the dispatch box – a detail that did not pass unnoticed in that temple of masculinity. Other women, on both sides of the House, put their femininity to use, but any advantage would accrue to the individual rather than to the group. Traditionally, the weaponry of sex appeal has done much to divide women and little to unite them.

Mrs Thatcher's lack of commitment to promoting the power of woman had become legendary by the 1990s. But it had also begun to look old-fashioned, even within her own party. Edwina Currie, for example, acknowledged the importance of women's participation in politics at all levels. She told us that as Minister for Health she was presented with lists of nominations for appointees to public bodies. The lists – even those intended for bodies specializing in women's issues – consisted almost entirely of white men aged between fifty-five and sixty. 'To me this feels odd. And the reason it feels odd is that I'm not a white, middle-aged male. I'm not a feminist about it but the representation doesn't fit – it feels unbalanced – and the reason it feels OK to my colleagues is because they are white, middle-aged and male.'

Straws in the wind, perhaps; signs of a very slow but not entirely unsteady shift away from the overpoweringly masculine culture of the House of Commons. For those who wanted women and men to be equally powerful in the mainstream of electoral politics, there was still a formidable distance to travel.

CHAPTER 17

Equal Citizens

'Women are asking why so much political behaviour is so nasty, brutish and long-winded,' Maria Fyfe, Labour MP for Glasgow Maryhill, told the Scottish Constitutional Convention on 7 July 1989. 'Why are too many MPs better at talking than listening?' The newly-established Convention offered an unparalleled opportunity to break the deadlock of male supremacy in that 'ancient and cobwebby construction' which passed for a political system in Britain. Maria Fyfe went on:

> We note that women are often the initiators and dedicated pursuers of single-issue campaigns and movements, such as Tenants' Associations and Community Councils, so how can the political process be changed to welcome these talents and no longer keep women on the margins of the political process, expected to be passive receivers of decisions, and not the makers of decisions?

The case for some form of political independence for Scotland was steadily gathering force. For ten years, Scotland had endured Margaret Thatcher's distant and unrepresentative rule from London, as Scottish support for the Conservative Party ebbed steadily away. Constitutional reform was at last firmly on the agenda of the Labour Party, which had committed itself to a directly-elected Scottish parliament with 'substantial legislative powers'.[1] The Convention was to hammer out the details of a plan for self-government and build around it as broad a consensus as possible. The old model was to be set aside, a new one designed.

The organizers hoped that the Convention's authority as a representative body would be beyond reproach – that is, as far as was possible without the Tories or the Scottish Nationalists, who had refused to take part. Of its 210 members, who included all of Scotland's Labour and SLD MPs, plus two Greens, representatives of other parties, trade unions, churches, local authorities and the Federation of Small Businesses in Scotland, only ten were women. It was designed to be 'a very sober body ... of solid citizens, fitted to be the fathers of a new national body'.[2]

The Convention's claim to be representative was, of course, crucial to its purpose, since its whole case rested on Westminster's failure in that respect. Yet it could hardly appear to be so if women were barely present. There was a built-in problem, in that the church hierarchy was all-male, the Scottish contingent of the Parliamentary Labour Party had but one woman out of forty-nine, and most of the other groupings from which members were drawn were dominated by men. The subordination of women was a recurring feature in movements for independent citizenship, as Sarah Benton pointed out in the *New Statesman* on the eve of the July meeting: 'Whether it is the Broederbond of South Africa or the Irish Republican Brotherhood of the 19th-century Fenianism, or even the Fraternity of the French Revolution, the citizenship of brotherhoods, so implacably proprietorial of women, has been the traditional vehicle for the creation of nations.'[3]

But there was a built-in advantage, too: Scotland had a well-established, broad-based, confident and vocal women's movement, which seemed determined to ensure that the birth of this new Scottish citizenry would not be the birth of a new brotherhood. A working party formed at the Convention's first meeting in March 1989 had the job of finding out how to encourage fuller representation. Chaired by Maria Fyfe, it was supported by the Scottish Convention of Women, the Scottish Women's Forum and a new mass campaign called Woman's Claim of Right in Scotland, which had been launched (in its own words) 'because 52 per cent of this country's population provide just 4 per cent of its MPs.' The working party consulted widely, seeking views on 'almost every aspect of political workings, from the hours an assembly sits, through the need for childare, to voting systems'. Sarah Benton commented: 'In grappling with why political institutions are so alien to women, it tried to get to the heart of what is wrong with the way political institutions in general work. It will give heart to all those who have despaired at making politics work for the people.'[4]

'Women don't just want constitutional reform,' declared Maria Fyfe, reporting back to the Convention in July, 'we want to reform the political process, to challenge those unspoken, indefensible assumptions that politics is a man's world, that parliament is a playground for ex-public school boys where they can display their class antagonisms and their dislike of women.' The key to reform, she said, was making Scotland's new parliament 'user-friendly' for women as well as men. That meant a normal working day, with time built in for constituency activities, time off to match school holidays and take account of family needs, adequate salaries with additional allowances for carers, proper child-care and working facilities for members and their staff, procedures that could be *seen* to be fair, democratic, open and easily understood by newcomers, and a minimum of ritual. 'While fully accepting the need to conduct our affairs with dignity, women express deep dislike of excessive formality – such as the Speaker's Procession – with wigs, buckled shoes and knee breeches. There is no female equivalent of such get-ups, precisely because they are part and parcel of a male power structure.'

What the Scottish women were trying to do, in effect, was to import into the mainstream of representative democracy the political culture of the margins – those campaigns, social movements and community actions where women were already strong. But it wasn't anything lightweight or whacky, or even 'alternative' that they were after (as the word 'margins' might suggest); it was a way of exercising power and interacting with it that was far more in tune with ordinary, everyday experience than anything we have come to associate with 'Politics'. They wanted to make the process more normal, make the unreal real, and thereby render it accessible and workable for women. They had (perhaps) some hope of at least partial success – a prospect which could only highlight the antiquated and intractable nature of the Westminster system.

In choosing a voting system for the new parliament, an important criterion, suggested Ms Fyfe, should be how far it encouraged the election of women. There was no evidence that the public were less likely to vote for women than for men; the blame lay with the selectorate and Scottish women weren't going to stand for it, she said. 'Why, in Norway, are 34 per cent of its parliament women, while in Scotland only four per cent are women? The answer is that Norwegian women made it clear they would put up with it no longer, and that is what is happening here now. We give fair warning to all the political parties!' As for what the new parliament should do, women wanted a Scottish Equal Opportunities Commission; a 'built-in system for protecting women's rights' through a women's committee or Ministry for Women; gender balance in appointments to public bodies; and 'equality audits', published by political parties before each election, 'spelling out exactly what they have done and propose to do, to promote women's rights and bring forward women candidates'.

As we explained at the start of this book, our aim was to find out how to make more women more powerful. Power could be exercised, we acknowledged, in all manner of ways, in private and public spheres, but our main focus was on 'Politics with a capital P'. It was clearly no panacea to have a House of Commons filled with the likes of Margaret Thatcher, any more than it was sufficient for women to 'specialize' in extra-parliamentary activity – however good they might be at it. It was important for women to exercise more power at *all* levels. In our view it was desirable for all kinds of women to exercise more power; what mattered most, though, was getting those who were poorest, most disadvantaged and least powerful to a point where they could enter the political world and scale its heights with as much chance of success as any clean-cut young gent from Balliol and the Bar.

The demands of the Scottish women, if met, could help to achieve that goal, in the event of a new Scottish parliament or assembly. The role of the women's movement in Scotland would be crucial in building the kind of mass campaign that the male establishment couldn't afford to ignore. The prospect of devolved government throughout the UK, with elected assemblies in Wales and the English regions (as proposed in the Labour Party's policy review) did suggest the possibility of breaking the masculine tradition of British politics. Provided the new assemblies, like the Scottish one, became the focus of a strong women's campaign, rules and procedures might be devised that departed from precedents set by Westminster and positively encouraged the participation of women. In a general move to make government more representative, women had a strong card to play. It seemed, moreover, that the narrower the gap between major political decision-making and community-level activities, the easier it was for women to participate and to exercise power – as their experience of the Greater London Council and other metropolitan authorities suggested. If the new assemblies could provide a model of what a legislature should look like in a modern representative democracy, one could imagine pressure mounting to bring the national parliament at Westminster into line.

There were a great many 'ifs' in that scenario. It depended on a change of government, a strong women's campaign, a sequence of cause and effect that might or might not occur, and a minimum of resistance from men. As we pointed out earlier, those who had power seldom surrendered it willingly. Over the centuries, men have found a variety of ways of defending their political advantage. They argued, in the name of philosophy, that it was women's 'natural' function to keep out of the public sphere and devote themselves to domestic duties. They argued, in the name of religion, that it was God's will that women should occupy a subordinate role. They argued, in the name of science, that women had smaller brains and weaker frames and were thus incapable of sharing power with men. They argued, in the name of class struggle, that women must wait to be liberated until 'after the Revolution'. ... More recently, they seemed to have developed a strategy of passive resistance: they would no longer oppose women's demands for change – indeed, they often voiced enthusiastic support – but at the same time they did little or nothing to meet them. Since they already controlled the institutions of power, they could preserve the status quo simply through their own inactivity.

In the face of such resistance, how could the process of change be stimulated? What women experienced, by and large, was a cycle of disadvantage and powerlessness. Their hope lay in halting the cycle and then reversing it, in order to shake off its negative effects and begin to acquire opportunity and power. There were two kinds of development that could help: 'top-down' and 'bottom-up' – and these could interact with each other.

From the bottom up, there needed to be changes in attitudes, in the way women and men perceived themselves and each other, and organized their lives in relation to each other, particularly in the division of domestic responsibilities. These changes might be aided and abetted in various ways by women's movements, which waxed and waned and grouped and re-grouped over time, reflecting as well as provoking change. Attitudes might also be affected by such 'top-down' reforms as laws to promote equal opportunities in education and employment, the provision of child care, and a shorter working day for men and women. There were other measures which could contribute to the process of change by strengthening women's sense of themselves as equal citizens – for example, by deterring violence against women at home and in the streets, by discouraging sexism throughout the communications industry, or by establishing the financial independence of women in tax and benefits. These were all ways of helping to transform the social and political climate – a vital stage in the process of empowering women.

Top-down developments might include the kind of constitutional reforms we have already discussed. They might also include 'positive action' strategies adopted by political parties with the aim of increasing female participation – some already in operation, others yet to be tested. These are measures designed to give special help to women to overcome ingrained patterns of discrimination and prejudice, so that they can compete on equal terms with men. Though not acknowledged as such, the Conservative Party's 'high-fliers' programme was a piece of positive action, designed to give special help to aspiring women parliamentary candidates. So too was the revamping of women's sections by feminists entering the Labour Party in the

1970s, the Labour Party's decision that there should be one woman on every parliamentary shortlist, and similar initiatives by the centre parties.

Measures like these had been introduced for a variety of reasons – out of a principled commitment to equality, as a result of pressure from women, out of political expediency – or a combination of these. The Conservative Party was least philosophically inclined to give anything that seemed like special privileges to women, but that had not deterred it from coaching parliamentary hopefuls. The Liberals (before merging with the Social Democrats) were decidely lukewarm about positive action, because they considered it in conflict with individual freedom, but they had shown interest in making the *style* of politics less alienating to women. The Social Democrats embraced positive action wholeheartedly and this was carried over into the merged Social and Liberal Democrats. The Greens disapproved of special treatment for women, perhaps because they had no need of it, but they, along with the SLD and the Labour Party, tried to expunge sexist language from their proceedings.

In the Labour Party, there was plenty of pressure from women demanding a greater voice, but this had raised fears about the impact of increased female participation on the balance of political forces within the Party. It was argued in some quarters, for instance, that women would be 'used' by the hard Left, while others claimed that, since women activists tended to be middle-class, they threatened to 'dilute' Labour's working-class base. At the time of writing, Labour had no formal strategy for encouraging women to put themselves forward as candidates, but had decided to open up three extra places for women on the Shadow Cabinet. A Fabian pamphlet, *Women's Votes: the Key to Winning* by Patricia Hewitt and Deborah Mattinson, published in 1989, urged the Labour Party to look for ways of increasing the numbers of women on the 'A List' of union-sponsored candidates 'substantially and rapidly'. It also suggested that a new 'List W' be created, with names of women prepared to stand for parliament nominated by unions, party branches or women's sections: 'The initial aim should be to get 300 women on List W (with each region and union being set an appropriate target).

Each year the target should be revised upwards . . . .'[5] The authors had originally floated the idea of three additional places for women on the Shadow Cabinet, and had also proposed a second Deputy Leader post, reserved for a woman (the latter idea had not yet been taken up by the Party).

Hewitt and Mattinson based their case on evidence that female politicians were likely to appeal to female voters. In detailed, qualititative research, groups of women had been shown key words signalling different qualities and asked to decide which were *essential* for a politician, which were *ideal* and which were completely undesirable. The groups took the view that the words which signalled essential qualities were 'management, intelligent, strong, energetic'; ideal qualities were 'charismatic, common sense, trustworthy, caring, inspirational, effective, understanding, independent, witty, courageous, compassionate, fair, practical, generous'; and undesirable qualities were 'ambitious, condescending, insincere, greedy, dogmatic, selfish, expedient, pompous'. In discussions that followed, the groups were asked which qualities they associated with men and which with women: 'the groups generally described the essential qualities as belonging equally to men and women. By contrast, they saw the negative words as male qualities and the positive, ideal qualities as generally female.'[6]

On the basis of this and other research data, the authors went on to argue that positive action to increase women's representation in the Labour Party was not a case of special pleading, but an essential part of making Labour the winning party.

> It is clear that a large number of women voters are more likely to trust women politicians. A majority of men seem to share the view that, at least, women should be more equally represented, and many share the preference for women politicians. A political party which visibly has more women politicians at every level is, therefore, likely to win more support than one perceived as a more male party.[7]

The question of political will was clearly crucial to the introduction of positive action. It was not unreasonable to speculate, on the approach of Margaret Thatcher's fourth general election campaign, that there would be an increasing scramble for the women's vote, and that this would give all parties a greater determination to display a female presence.

Another useful source of pressure could be the European Community, where the presence of women both in domestic legislatures and in the European parliament was significantly higher than in Britain. In the 1989 European elections, Britain returned eighty-one MEPs, of whom twelve were women. So women accounted for more than 14 per cent of the British contingent in Europe, compared with just over 6 per cent of MPs at Westminster. One reason why women had more seats in Europe was that – until the 1990s, at least – British parties had, in their characteristically insular fashion, attached little importance to the European Community. It was not seen as a place where power resided; fewer men felt moved to compete for the Euro-constituencies, and women moved into the space. No doubt the closer integration of Europe, which seemed likely to follow the introduction of a single market in 1992, would alter these perceptions. It remained to be seen whether women would hold on to their gains. In other member countries women were already better represented than in Britain. Altogether, women held 96 out of the 518 seats in the European parliament (more than 18 per cent).

We saw in Chapter 1 that most other European countries had a higher proportion of women in their domestic parliaments than Britain; in most major parties, including those of the Centre and Right, there was a greater commitment to equal representation than in the major British parties. As Britain moved closer to the European Community it seemed possible that a kind of peer-group pressure would come into play, encouraging British political parties to improve their performance on this front. And nowhere was this more likely than on the Left. In her comparative study, *Women and European Politics*, Joni Lovenduski observed that, while centre parties in Nordic countries had been notably active in encouraging women, and in France there had been a kind of competitive bidding between Left and Right for women's support, 'on the whole, it has been parties of the Left which have been most inclined to promote women.'[8]

By the late 1980s, the main parties of the Left in most Western European countries had either achieved a level of representation of 20 per cent or more, or introduced a *quota* to force the pace of change. For example, the Social Democrats Party in West Germany voted at their 1988 conference for a 40 per cent quota of all elected positions in the party, to be achieved by 1992; they joined the Norwegian Labour Party and the Social Democratic Party of Denmark, which had already adopted 40 per cent quotas. In the Swedish Social Democratic Party, women accounted for more than 30 per cent of MPs. The Spanish and Portuguese socialist parties had adopted quotas of 25 per cent, while the French, Italian and Belgian socialists had 20 per cent quotas.

In Labour's Policy Review, published in 1989, there was reference to the party taking: 'a number of initiatives to ensure greater participation and representation of women and black people at all levels.' The initiatives were unspecified and remained mysterious, but the Policy Review went on to express interest 'in examining the action taken by our sister party in West Germany, the SPD, which has adopted a quota system.' Hewitt and Mattinson urged in their Fabian pamphlet that Labour should follow the example of its sister parties in Europe and adopt a 'target of 40 per cent women MPs by the end of the century'.[9] There was a significant difference between a 'target' and a 'quota', the first being something you aspire to, the second something you must achieve. 'Although the target would not, and could not, force any individual constituency party to select a woman in preference to a man,' they explained, 'it would help to concentrate the minds of Labour Party members on the need to select more women candidates, particularly in safe and winnable seats.'[10]

One reason why the British Left continued to lag behind was that quotas were hard to introduce in the British system of single-member constituencies and simple majority elections. Most other Western European countries (France and Britain being the only exceptions) had adopted proportional representation (PR). Under this system, the number of votes cast for each party determined how many representatives each had in the legislature. The system varied from country to country, but most commonly, parties would draw up lists of candidates to stand in large, multi-member constituencies; how many got in from each list would depend on how many votes were cast for that party. In some PR systems (such as the Italian one) voters were able to rank individual candidates in order of preference.

Women generally fared better as parliamentary candidates under PR. One plausible explanation was that a list system put decision-making into the hands of national or regional party centres, and that national party élites were more likely to promote women than were local selectorates, if only because national élites were more responsive to new intellectual currents. The point is not that party centres would override the voters' natural preferences for men, but that local selection committees may be more susceptible to tradition and prejudice, especially when forced to put (as it were) all their eggs in one basket. Joni Lovenduski reported that parties 'have less to lose and appear more willing to risk standing women as candidates in winnable positions on multi-member constituency lists'.[11] She also suggested that preference voting could have a positive effect: 'it allows the electorate to inform the parties of support for women candidates, assuming, of course, that such support exists.'[12] Judging by the findings of Hewitt and Mattinson, there might well be some preference for women candidates, if such a system were introduced in Britain.

The most common arguments against PR have been that it leads to weak and unstable governments, and that it makes it hard for one party to achieve a big enough majority to carry out a radical programme. The Greens and the centre parties came out in favour of PR not surprisingly, since it would win them a presence in parliament that reflected their share of the vote. The Labour Party remained officially opposed, but growing numbers of Labour Party members supported PR; there was even a majority of Labour MPs who favoured it for electing a new Scottish assembly.[13] It seemed likely that support for PR would grow, in line with a trend, common in other European countries, towards a fragmentation of party-political allegiances. It was a feature of a post-industrial society that voters were less likely to identify themselves first and foremost as members of a class, and so were less likely to line up automatically behind class-based parties. Instead they might identify with one or more of the new social and political movements that had been changing the face of European politics since the late 1960s: women's movements, student movements, anti-racist, gay and lesbian, and environmental movements. This new diversity of political identities fuelled the case for an electoral system that enabled voters to choose and be represented by a wider range of parties. It was possible that working-class women stood to gain from the decline of the class-based party. It offered them a chance of asserting themselves, and being acknowledged as a distinct and powerful constituency, whose interests overlapped with those of other groups – rather than being submerged in a working-class party whose agenda continued to reflect the dominant interests of men.

For women and men to be equally represented in the House of Commons would require, in 1990, an extra 283 women, more than six times the current number – and 283 fewer men. The Upper House made no claim to be representative, based as it was (uniquely) on inheritance and patronage. Only 5 per cent of those eligible to sit in the House of Lords were women. It was a relic of feudalism, long overdue for thorough reform. A modern second chamber, its members elected by PR, based on regional constituencies, could go a long way towards increasing the presence and power of women in the legislature. The Labour Party promised an elected second chamber in its Policy Review, although it stopped short of opting for PR. The SLD and the Greens wanted similar action taken – and even leading Tories were regularly heard to advocate curbing the hereditary factor. (Sceptics would point out, however, that on past occasions, when *all* major parties appeared to be united in the cause of reform, the Lords had survived unscathed.)

Constitutional reform on its own would not bring women equal power with men. It needed to be combined with positive action by parties and a general change in attitudes. But suppose such a combination occurred and women did gain a significantly stronger presence in parliament, what would be the effect? We might reasonably assume that if women were represented in greater numbers, they would begin to *reinforce* the cultural changes that had helped to get them there. Within parliament, the atmosphere would perhaps become less pretentious, ritualized, competitive and exclusive, and more accessible, informal and co-operative. Pressure would mount to make working conditions more humane and 'user-friendly', more in tune with the needs of parents and children. Outside parliament, as politics came to be seen as a woman's world no less than a man's, we should expect to see a deeper shift in public perceptions about the meaning and purpose of 'Politics', as well as the role of women and men.

We might see a change in political priorities, with the 'hairy' issues (money, arms, jobs, trade, industry) ceasing to predominate and greater importance being attached to 'bread and butter' issues affecting the fabric of everyday life (health, child care, education, housing, environment, social services). More specifically, we should hope to find a stronger political will to fight sexism and discrimination against women.

By 1990, according to the current policy documents of the Conservatives, the Labour Party and the SLDP, these parties agreed, broadly speaking, about the issues that mattered most to women: equal opportunities in education and employment; the right to choose to combine parenthood and paid work; flexible working hours; better training and re-training; access to child care; social and economic recognition of their responsibility as informal carers; and safe neighbourhoods. The biggest difference, unsurprisingly, was that the Tories claimed they had already achieved, or were in the process of achieving, these objectives, while the opposition parties claimed the Tories had singularly failed to do so, and were in fact making matters worse.

No less predictably, the parties had different priorities and diverged over strategy, in line with the philosophical differences we have already discussed. The Tories stressed the importance of initiatives in the private and voluntary sectors (on training and child care, for instance); they were evidently concerned that women's paid work should not interfere with their domestic responsibilities, stressing 'flexibility' rather than equal opportunity, and giving tax incentives to married couples where wives stayed at home. They favoured 'targeting' of benefits to help only the neediest, and sought heavier punishments to deter crime. They were opposed to positive action (i.e. special measures designed to help women overcome entrenched patterns of discrimination); they were opposed to redistributive measures, to increased public spending and to any extension of the powers of local government.[14]

The Labour Party favoured public provision of child care, encouraged fathers to take more responsibility at home, and proposed a national minimum wage to increase women's earnings, as well as a 'generous increase' in the non-means-tested Child Benefit. It promised detailed 'positive action programmes', to be pursued by local and regional authorities, and the use of 'contract compliance' (i.e. organizations contracted to provide goods or services would have to comply with equal opportunity policies). The cornerstone of Labour's agenda for women was a new cabinet-level Minister for Women with her own department, dealing 'specifically with policies directed towards ending women's inequality and eliminating discrimination against women'. The new ministry would oversee enforcement of equal rights laws and the work of the Equal Opportunities Commission, and make sure other government departments pursued effective strategies for improving the position of women. Its 'key priorities' would be 'the implementation of child-care policy and the creation of a safer environment for women'. It was also supposed to 'open up new channels of communication with and between women, listening to and articulating their concerns and ideas'.[15] Certainly, Labour's approach had improved since the early 1980s, when women still appeared as an afterthought in the policy documents of the time. The proof of the pudding would of course be in the eating, and it remained to be seen whether the meal would be served.

The Greens, as we've said, had not developed their policies on women to a point where they could be evaluated. The Social and Liberal Democrats, like Labour, favoured positive action and contract compliance to enforce equal opportunities. Unlike Labour, they stressed the importance of 'ensuring equal representation of women on all appointed bodies,' including the judicial bench and police authorities.[16] They did not want a Min-

istry for Women, in common with the Tories, who poured scorn
on the idea: 'It is not for politicians and bureacrats to decide
how women should find fulfilment. It is certainly not for Labour's
patronising and bullying Ministry for Women.'[17]

The question of whether special or separate treatment for
women would help or hinder their cause would no doubt continue to be hotly debated. It seemed to us to be less a matter
of principle (as some would argue) than a matter of strategy.
For example, a Ministry for Women could be used to contain
and defuse women's demands, by absorbing protest, doing little
of material consequence and employing those who might otherwise do more valuable work for women in other government
departments. It could, on the other hand, stimulate and focus
women's energies and make sure that other government departments introduced the changes women were demanding. Much
would depend on how closely it kept in touch with ordinary
women. More important still, the success of this and other
strategies aimed at improving the lot of women would depend
on the strength of political will among those who wielded power
– and that, in turn, would be affected by the strength of women's
presence in parliament and government.

As Maria Fyfe pointed out to the Scottish Constitutional Convention, what counted was not just changing the rules, but
changing the political process – to break the cycle of disadvantage
and powerlessness and reconnect politics with the people.
Britain had to make a leap from the nineteenth to the twenty-first
century, to develop a poltical culture in which women felt as
much at ease as men, and where power stemmed not from accident of birth or privilege, but from rights enshrined in a modern
constitution, enjoyed by all as equal citizens.

Notes

Chapter 1: Can Any Woman Make It?

1 'Review and Appraisal: Part 1 – General Development', presented to the World Conference to Review and Appraise the Achievements of the United Nations Decade for Women: Equality, Development and Peace, Nairobi, July 1985, quoted in 'Women: a World Report', *New Internationalist*, Methuen, 1985.

2 'Women: a World Report', ibid.

3 Ibid.

4 Hansard Parliamentary Debates, Vol. 187, Col. 825–6, 1987.

5 *Labour Leader*, 14 March 1903.

Chapter 2: From Plato to the Primrose League

1 A. Clark, *The Working Life of Women in the Seventeenth Century*, George Routledge & Sons, 1919.

2 S. Moller Okin, *Women in Western Political Thought*, Virago, 1980.

3 Plato, *The Republic*, Penguin, 1955.

4 Ibid.

5 S. Moller Okin, op cit.

6 Ibid.

7 Ibid.

8 Ibid.

9 Ibid.

10 M. Wollstonecraft, *A Vindication of the Rights of Women*, 1st edn, 1792.

11 Ibid.

12 B. Taylor, *Eve and the New Jerusalem*, Virago, 1983.

13 Ibid.

14 D. Thompson, in *The Rights and Wrongs of Women*, edited and introduced by J. Mitchell and A. Oakley, Pelican, 1976.

15 S. Rowbotham, *Hidden from History*, Pluto Press, 1973.

16 D. Thompson, op cit.

17 *Northern Star*, 1841. Quoted in B. Taylor, *Eve and the New Jerusalem*, Virago, 1983.

18 B. Taylor, op cit.

19 Ibid.

20 Ibid.

NOTES

21 Ibid.

22 Ibid.

23 A. Sachs and J. Hoff Wilson, *Sexism and the Law*, Martin Robertson, 1978.

24 Ibid.

25 Justice, 1896. Quoted in J. Evans et al., *Feminism and Political Theory*, Sage, 1986.

26 Justice, 1894. Quoted in J. Evans, et al., op cit.

27 J. Liddington, *The Life and Times of a Respectable Rebel*, Virago, 1984.

28 H. Mitchell, *The Hard Way Up*, Virago, 1977.

29 Ibid.

30 Justice, 1902. Quoted in J. Evans et al., op cit.

31 *The Clarion*, 1896. Quoted in J. Evans et al., op cit.

32 H. Mitchell, op cit.

33 J. Liddington, op cit.

34 B. Campbell, *The Iron Ladies*, Virago, 1987.

35 Ibid.

36 Ibid.

37 Ibid.

38 Ibid.

39 H. G. Wells, *Anne Veronica*, Virago, 1980.

40 S. Rowbotham, op cit.

41 D. Spender, *Time and Tide Wait for No Man*, Pandora, 1984.

42 B. Campbell, *Wigan Pier Revisited*, Virago, 1984.

43 C. Cockburn, *Women, Trade Unions and Political Parties*, Fabian Research Series, No. 349.

44 Ibid.

45 M. Goot and E. Reid, *Women and Voting Studies: Mindless Matrons or Sexist Scientism*, Sage, 1975.

46 J. Blondel, *Voters, Parties and Leaders*, Pelican, 1963.

47 Ibid.

48 P. R. Lazarsfeld et al., *The People's Choice*, Columbia University Press, 1986.

49 C. Cockburn, op cit.

50 Ibid.

51 Ibid.

52 *Everywoman*, June 1987.

Chapter 3: Lessons from the Coalfields

1 N. Dolby, *Norma Dolby's Diary: An Account of the Great Miners' Strike*, Verso, 1987.

2 V. Allen, *Militant Trade Unionism: a re-analysis of industrial action in an inflationary situation*, Merlin Press, 1966.

3 L. Beaton, *Shifting Horizons*, Canary Press, 1985.

4 V. Seddon (ed.), *The Cutting Edge: Women and the Pit Strike*, Lawrence and Wishart, 1986.

5 Ibid.

6 North Yorkshire Women Against Pit Closures, 'Strike 84–85'. Quoted in J. Stead, *Never The Same Again: Women and the Miners' Strike*, The Women's Press, 1987.

7 V. Seddon, op cit.

8 Ibid.

Chapter 4: Making Connections

1 B. Campbell, *Wigan Pier Revisited*, Virago, 1984.

Chapter 5: The Impact of Feminism

1 Quoted in A. Coote and B. Campbell, *Sweet Freedom*, Basil Blackwell, 1987.

2 *Shrew*, October 1989.

3 S. Rowbotham, in Rowbotham et al., *Beyond the Fragments*, Merlin Press, 1979.

4 J. (Joreen) Freeman, 'Tyranny of Structurelessness', in *The Second Wave*, Vol. 2 (1).

5 Quoted in L. Segal, in Rowbotham et al., op cit.

6 Ibid.

7 Ibid.

Chapter 6: Black Women Organize

1 B. Bryan et al., *The Heart of the Race: Black Women's Lives in Britain*, Virago, 1985.

2 Ibid.

3 Ibid.

4 Ibid.

5 Ibid.

6 Ibid.

7 Ibid.

8 *Race Today*, September 1974.

9 P. Trivedi, *Feminist Review*, Autumn 1984.

10 Ibid.

11 Ibid.

12 A. Wilson, *Finding a Voice*, Virago, 1978, 1985.

13 B. Bryan et al., op cit.

14 Ibid.

15 Ibid.

16 Ibid.

17 Ibid.

NOTES

18 Ibid.
19 Ibid.
20 Ibid.
21 Ibid.

Chapter 7: The Spirit of Greenham

1 B. Harford and S. Hopkins (eds), *Greenham Common: Women at the Wire*, The Women's Press, 1984.
2 Ibid.
3 Ibid.
4 Ibid.
5 *The Leveller*, 11–14 June 1982.
6 B. Harford and S. Hopkins, op cit.
7 B. Norden, in *Spare Rib*, September 1985.

Chapter 8: Up the Organization

1 S. Goodenough, *Jam and Jerusalem*, Collins, 1977.
2 Ibid.
3 Ibid.
4 M. Stott, *Organization Woman*, Heinemann, 1978.

Chapter 9: Workplace Politics

1 B. Drake, *Women in Trade Unions*, Virago, 1984.
2 Ibid.
3 Ibid.
4 Ibid.
5 Ibid.
6 Ibid.
7 Ibid.
8 Ibid.
9 Ibid.
10 C. Cockburn, *Women, Trade Unions and Political Parties*, Fabian Research Series, No. 349.
11 Association of Scientific, Technical and Managerial Staff, 'Women in Insurance: A Study of Female Representation in ASTMS', report to the Insurance National Advisory Committee, Research Department, February 1984.
12 K. Holman, *Organising Women in Trade Unions*, Central London Community Law Centre.
13 'Working in Britain', MORI, 1985.
14 C. Cockburn, op cit.

NOTES

15 *Guardian*, 2 September 1985.

16 C. Brown, *Black and White Britain*, Policy Studies Institute, 1984.

17 TUC, 'Black and Ethnic Minority Women in Employment and Trade Unions', a TUC Report, February 1987.

18 C. Cockburn, op cit.

19 Inland Revenue Staff Federation, 'Best Practice and Realistic Expectations: The Role of Women in the IRSF', 1986.

20 Quoted in K. Holman, op cit.

21 A. Coote and B. Campbell, *Sweet Freedom*, Basil Blackwell, 1987.

22 Quoted in K. Holman, op cit.

Chapter 10: The Women's Party

1 Women's Party manifesto, quoted from *Britannia*, 1918.

2 D. Mitchell, *Queen Christabel*, Macdonald & Jane's, 1977.

3 B. Castle, *Sylvia and Christabel Pankhurst*, Virago, 1987.

4 A. Marwick, *Women at War, 1914–1918*, Fontana, 1977.

5 J. Liddington, *The Life and Times of a Respectable Rebel*, Virago, 1984.

6 B. Castle, op cit.

7 D. Mitchell, op cit.

8 Women's Party manifesto, op cit.

9 B. Castle, op cit.

10 S. Pankhurst, *The Suffragette Movement*, Virago, 1977.

11 Ibid.

Chapter 11: Labour and Equality

1 E. Hobsbawm, *The Age of Empire, 1875–1914*, Weidenfeld & Nicolson, 1987.

2 L. Segal, *Is the Future Female?*, Virago, 1987.

3 *Feminist Review*, No. 23, 1986.

4 Ibid.

5 H. Wainwright, *Labour: A Tale of Two Parties*, Hogarth Press, 1987.

6 Labour Party, survey by the South-West Region.

7 J. Liddington, *The Life and Times of a Respectable Rebel*, Virago, 1984.

8 *Feminist Review*, No. 12, 1984.

9 H. Wainwright, op cit.

10 *Politics and Power 3: Sexual Politics, Feminism and Socialism*, Routledge & Kegan Paul, 1981.

11 L. Loach, in *Spare Rib*, October 1985.

12 *Feminist Review*, No. 24, 1986.

NOTES

Chapter 12: At Home with the Tories

1 I. Gilmour, *Inside Right*, Quartet, 1978.

2 *Going Places. Women in the Conservative Party*, Conservative Political Centre, 1980.

3 B. Campbell, *The Iron Ladies*, Virago, 1987.

4 M. Phillips, *Observer Magazine*, 2 May 1982.

5 *Going Places. Women in the Conservative Party*, Conservative Political Centre, 1980.

6 *Seizing Our Opportunities*, European Union for Women, 1982.

7 B. Campbell, *The Iron Ladies*, Virago, 1987.

Chapter 13: The Centre and the Greens

1 *Freedom and Choice for Women: A Liberal-SDP Alliance Policy Proposal*, Hebden Royd Publications Ltd., 1986.

2 *A Liberal Handbook for Women*, Women's Liberal Federation, 1982.

3 *Women's Link, Liberal Information Network Bulletin*, No. 2, 1985.

4 Ibid.

5 *Spare Rib*, May 1987.

6 Ibid.

7 Letter in *Guardian*, 23 January 1988.

8 'Social and Liberal Democrats, Partners for Freedom and Justice', Federal White Paper No. 2.

Chapter 14: Standing for the Council

1 Survey by West Midlands County Council Women's Sub-Committee, 1985.

2 L. Hunt, 'The GLC Women's Committee, 1982–6', GLC Public Information Branch, 1986.

3 'Representation of Women at County Council Level in Local Government, 1981–1985 and 1985–1989', Survey by the 300 Group.

4 'Royal Commission on Local Government in England, 1966–69', Redcliffe-Maud Report (HMSO), 1969.

5 P. Hollis, *Ladies Elect*, Oxford University Press, 1987 (Source, Municipal Year Books).

6 Ibid.

7 Ibid.

8 J. Hills, 'Women Local Councillors – A Reply to Bristow', Local Government Studies, January/February 1982. Analysis of the Robinson Report on Committee on the Remuneration of Local Councillors, HMSO, 1977.

9 J. Barron et al., 'Married to the Council? The Private Costs of Public Service', Report to the Leverhulme Trust, Department of Economics and Social Science, Bristol Polytechnic, 1988.

NOTES

10 Ibid.
11 Ibid.
12 J. Hills, op cit.
13 R. Brown, *Going Places: Women in the Conservative Party*, Conservative Political Centre, 1980.
14 M. Benn, 'The truth will out', *Guardian*, 11 November 1987.

Chapter 15: Town-Hall Feminism

1 L. Hunt, 'The GLC Women's Committee, 1982–6', GLC Publication Information Branch, 1986.
2 Ibid.
3 H. Wainwright, *Labour: A Tale of Two Parties*, Hogarth Press, 1987.
4 L. Hunt, op cit.
5 Ibid.
6 Ibid.
7 Ibid.
8 'Local Authority Equal Opportunities Policies: Report of a Survey by the Equal Opportunities Commission', EOC, 1988.
9 'Women and Housing. A report based on the results of women's views as users of the housing service', Greenwich Council, 1985.
10 B. Campbell, 'The chauvinist chop?', *Guardian*, 18 August 1986.
11 I. Stone, 'Equal Opportunities in Local Authorities', HMSO, 1988.
12 L. Hunt, op cit.
13 Round-table discussion in *Marxism Today*, July 1986.
14 *Spare Rib*, July 1986.
15 *A Taste of Power*, edited by M. Mackintosh and H. Wainwright, Verso, 1987.
16 'Media Coverage of Local Government in London', Goldsmiths' Media Research Group, Department of Communications, Goldsmiths' College, 1987.
17 Ibid.
18 Ibid.
19 'Seizing our Opportunities: A Woman's Guide to Public Life', European Union of Women, 1982.
20 J. Barron et al., 'Married to the Council? The Private Costs of Public Service', Report to the Leverhulme Trust, Department of Economics and Social Science, Bristol Polytechnic, 1988.

Chapter 16: 'I Spy Strangers!'

1 A. Trollope, *Can You Forgive Her?*, Panther, 1973. First published in 1864.
2 A. Sampson, *Anatomy of Britain*, Hodder and Stoughton, 1962.
3 Ibid.
4 P. Hewitt and D. Mattinson, *Women's Votes: The Key to Winning*, Fabian Research Series No. 353.

5 A. Coote and B. Campbell, *Sweet Freedom*, Basil Blackwell, 1987.

6 J. Hills, *Candidates: the Impact of Gender*, Parliamentary Affairs, vol. 34. No. 2.

7 The 300 Group.

8 E. Vallance, *Putting Women in the House*, Equal Opportunities International, vol. 1, No. 4.

9 E. Vallance, *Women in the House*, Athlone Press, 1979.

10 V. Brittain, *Lady into Woman*, Dakers, 1953.

11 J. Ruddock, *The House Magazine*, 8 May 1989.

12 E. Vallance, op cit.

13 Ibid.

14 B. Campbell, 'House call from the class of '87', *Guardian*, 21 July 1987.

15 L. Jobey, 'Is gender a parliamentary issue?', *Independent*, 26 June 1987.

16 A. Coote and B. Campbell, op cit.

Chapter 17 : Equal Citizens

1 Labour Party, 'Meet the Challenge, Make the Change', Final report of Labour's Policy Review for the 1990s.

2 S. Benton, 'New Caledonia' in *New Statesman and Society*, 7 July 1989.

3 Ibid.

4 Ibid.

5 P. Hewitt and D. Mattinson, *Women's Votes: the Key to Winning*, Fabian Research Series No. 353.

6 Ibid.

7 Ibid.

8 J. Lovenduski, *Women and European Politics*, Wheatsheaf Books, 1986.

9 P. Hewitt and D. Mattinson, op cit.

10 Ibid.

11 J. Lovenduski, op cit.

12 Ibid.

13 S. Benton, op cit.

14 Conservative Party, *Opening Doors for Women*, May 1989.

15 Labour Party, op cit.

16 Social and Liberal Democrats, *Partners for Freedom and Justice*, Federal White Paper No. 2.

17 Conservative Party, op cit.

Index

INDEX

Gorman, Teresa, 266
Granada Television, 107
Grand General Union of the
  United Kingdom, 145
Grantham, 3, 5–6
Great Yarmouth Labour Club, 61
Greater London Council (GLC),
  250, 277; bill to abolish, 255;
  Equal Opportunities Unit, 234;
  outreach work 247–8; women's
  committee, 231–5, 240, 242, 243,
  244; Women's Support Unit,
  234
Greater London Development
  Plan, 233
Greece, 22
Green Party, 209–11, 213–14, 274,
  279, 283, 284; National Council,
  209, 209–10, 210; policy
  document, 286
Greenham Common women's
  peace camp, 56, 74–5, 119–27,
  169, 181
Greenpeace, 75
Greenwich, London, Council,
  236–7, 243, 246; Equality Unit,
  236; Women and Housing
  group, 237; women's unit, 240
Greer, Germaine, 89
Grender, Ollie, 201
Grunwick strike, 94, 106
Guardian, The, 207
Gutteridge, Sue, 28, 43

Hackney Empire, 142
Hackney, London, Council,
  women's and race units, 248
Hackney North and Stoke
  Newington (constituency), 178
Hackney Peace Groups, 124
Halewood, Ford factory, 97
Hard Way Up, The (Mitchell), 37
Hardie, James Keir, 24, 37
Harford, Barbara, 121
Haringey, London, 109–10
Harlow, Essex, 249
Harman, Harriet, 52–3, 255–6,

259–60, 263–4, 265, 267, 268,
  269, 270, 271
Hartley, Eve, 43
Hastings, Fred, 7–8
Hastings, Jean, 7–8
Hawkinds, Andy, 230, 231, 248
Hayes, Jil, 204–5
health, 85; *see also* National Health
  Service
health screening, 156, 157
Heart of the Race, The (Bryan et al.),
  102, 103, 110, 111
Heath, Edward, 97, 188, 198
Heathrow Airport, 110
Henderson, Arthur, 179
Henshall, Miss, 146
Hewitt, Patricia, 279, 280, 282, 283
Hillon, Bernadette, 155
Hobbes, Thomas, 30–1
Hobsbawm, Eric, 168
Hodge, Margaret, 218, 223, 225,
  228, 243–4, 246, 251, 264
Hollis, Patricia, 217–18
Holman, Kate, 149
Home Office, 107
Hoddless, Mrs Adelaide Hunter,
  129
Hopkins, Sarah, 121
House of Commons, 19, 255–61,
  265–72, 276; number of women
  MPs, 20, 21, 50, 175–6, 257–8,
  284; Private Members' Bills
  against discrimination, 97
House of Lords, 284; number of
  women members, 21
House Magazine, The, 265
housing, 211, 225–6
Howarth, Rosalind (Countess of
  Carlisle), 40
Huddersfield, 82
Hudson, Janet, 80, 167
Hudson, Paul, 80
Humber, Doreen, 66, 67, 70
Humber, Pip, 66
Hutchinson, Moretta, 189, 197,
  198
Hutton, Sally, 89

301

INDEX

immigration laws, 110

Immigration and Nationality Act, 106

Imperial Typewriters strike, 106

Independent Labour Party (ILF), 36, 38, 161, 179

India, women's liberation movement in, 114–15

Indian Workers' Association of Great Britain, 109

Inland Revenue Staff Federation, 153

Inner London Education Authority, 182

Inside Right (Gilmour), 187

Intermediate-Range Nuclear Forces (INF) Treaty, 125

International Marxist Group, 176

Ireland, 22

Irish Republican Brotherhood, 274

Iron Ladies (Campbell), 189

Islington, North London, Council, 218, 223, 225, 226, 228, 243, 251; Women's Committee, 246

Italy, 22; socialist party, 282

Joachim, Margaret, 47, 260

Johnson, Monica, 185

Joint Council for the Welfare of Immigrants, 138

Jones, Maggie, 47

juries, women on, 132

Justice, 36–7, 38

Kaldor, Mary, 259

Kane, Marie, 238, 240, 246–7

Keep Britain Tidy campaign, 132

Kellner, Peter, 55–6

Kenney, Annie, 162

Kensington Ladies' Discussion Society (later Fawcett Society), 136

Kensington, London, Borough Council, 217

Kent, Duchess of, 133

Kenya, 23

Kesteven and Grantham Girls' School, 5

King, Martin Luther, 121

King's Cross Women's Centre, 243

Kinnock, Glenys, 174–5

Kinnock, Neil, 117, 140

Labour Clubs, 177

labour, division of, 87, 98–9

labour Leader, 24

Labour Party, 28, 67, 80, 107, 124, 140, 154, 188, 205, 212; annual conference, 178; black sections, 178; Christabel Pankhurst and, 24, 163; conferences, 147; Constituency Labour Parties (CLPs), 184; and constitutional reform, 273, 274; councillors, 220, 226; and councils, 234, 236, 238; and equal opportunities, 279, 280; and GLC, 231–2; London, 44, 177; Manchester City constituency, 168–9; meetings, times of, 176; and miners' strike, 74, 75; National Executive Committee (NEC), 178–9, 184–5; number of women members, 166; number of women MPs, 21, 258–9, 272; number of women officials at ward level, 175–6; number of women in shadow team, 21; in parliament, 269, 271; percentage of national vote, 209; policy review, 186, 277, 282, 284, 285, 286; and proportional representation, 283; role of women in, 167–86; and support for black women's groups, 116–17; times of meetings, 43; women councillors, 215–16, 219, 220–2, 224–5; women Parliamentary candidates, 161, 260–3, 265; women supporters, 55; women's committees, 175–6,

302

INDEX

Maudsley Hospital, South
London, 139, 140, 141, 143
Mayall, Heather, 51
meetings, times of, 43, 152, 157,
221
men, involvement with women's
groups, 67, 81–2, 84, 116, 117
Merrin, Mary, 78, 82
Merseyside, 229; County Council,
192, 224, 239
Michie, Ray, 202
Militant Tendency, 185–6
Mill, John Stuart, 24
Miller, Doreen, 50, 262, 262–3
miners' strike (1984–5), 61–76, 88,
104, 126–7, 169, 180, 181
Miners' Welfare, 61
Ministry for Women (projected),
21, 175, 186, 238, 276, 286–7
Mitchell, Hannah, 37, 38
Mitchell, Juliet, 89
Mohamed, Atiha, 249
Molesworth, Cambridgeshire,
peace camp, 122
MORI poll, 150
Morrell, Frances, 182, 186
Mozambique, 104
MSF (Manufacturing Science
Finance), 149
Mulvey, Christ, 123

Namibia, uranium mining in, 125
National Abortion Campaign, 92
National Association of Local
Government Women's
Committees, 249–50
National Childbirth Trust, 136
National Council for Civil
Liberties, 137, 138
National Council for Voluntary
Organizations, 138
National Council of Women, 247
National Federation of Women
Workers, 147–8
National Federation of Women's
Institutes, *see* Women's
Institutes

National Front, 116
National Health Service, 56, 68,
74, 139, 149, 156
National Labour Women's
Committee, 178, 183
National Society for the
Prevention of Cruelty to
Children (NSPCC), 223
National Union of General
Workers, 148
National Union of Journeymen
Felt Hatters, 146
National Union of Mineworkers
(NUM), 63, 64, 65, 71, 73–4
National Union of Public
Employees (NUPE), 157, 158,
184, 185
National Union of Students, 52,
205
National Union of Tailors and
Garment Workers, 157
National Union of Teachers, 151
National Union of
Townswomen's Guilds, 135–6
National Women Liberals'
Association (NWLA), 40
NATO (North Atlantic Treaty
Organization), 126
Nelson, Pat, 46, 79, 80
Nelson, Lancashire, 217
Netherlands, 22
Neuberger, Rabbi Julia, 206, 207,
208
New Cross fire, 112
New Statesman, 56, 274
Newbridge, Gwent, 74
Newbury, Berkshire, magistrates'
court, 122
Nicaragua, 169, 181
Nicholson, Emma, 42, 45, 47,
196–8, 258, 259, 262; and 'high-
flyers' programme, 45, 196,
263
Norden, Barbara, 126
Northern College, Wentworth
Castle, near Barnsley, 13–14
Northern Ireland, 68

INDEX

Northern Star, 32
Norway, 22, 276; Labour Party, 282
Norwich, 216
Nottinghamshire, 63, 69
nuclear disarmament, 74, 75, 84, 209, 211; *see also* Campaign for Nuclear Disarmament; Greenham Common women's peace camps
nuclear weapons, 56
nursery places, 24
nurses' strike (1988), 139–44

Okin, Susan Moller, 29
Oldham, 169
Oliver, Tony, 81
Open University, 10, 11, 81
opinion polls, 56
Organising Women Trade Unionists (Holman), 149
Organization of Women of Asian and African Descent (OWAAD), 109–12
Owen, David, 207
Owenites, 32, 33
Oxford, 5, 14; Ruskin College, 90; Somerville College, 5; Students' Union, 200; University Conservative Association, 6

Pakistan, 106, 107, 115
Pankhurst, Christabel, 24, 161, 162, 163–4
Pankhurst, Emmeline, 37, 162, 163
Pankhurst, Sylvia, 162–3, 164
Pankhurst Centre, Manchester, 250
'Pardner' system, 102–3
parental leave, 157
Paris, demonstrations in (1968), 87–8
parliament, *see* House of Commons; House of Lords
part-time and casual work, 149, 156

'Partnership for Progress', 207
Patel, Pragla, 113–17, 116, 117
Paterson, Emma, 145
peace movement, 68, 209; *see also* Campaign for Nuclear Disarmament (CND); Greenham Common women's peace camps; nuclear disarmament
Peace Pledge Union, 44
Peckham, South London, 259; (constituency), 255
People's Charter, 32
People's Choice, The (Lazarsfeld et al.), 54
Perrigo, Sarah, 171, 183
Pershing missiles, 126
Pettifor, Ann, 182–5
Phillips, Dorothy, 74
Phillips, Marion, 179, 180, 217
Plato, 29–30
Plymouth, Sutton (constituency), 265
police powers, 85, 112
political power: definition, 19
Portugal, 22; socialist party, 282
Potter, Cath, 168–9, 183
Powell, Enoch, 172
Prashar, Usha, 138
Primrose League, 39
proportional representation, 282–4
Prosser, Margaret, 149, 151
Puerta Cabeza, Nicaragua, 169
Punjab, 115

racism, 85, 104, 105, 111, 112, 113, 152, 178, 190, 227, 230, 234, 245, 284
Radford, Pauline, 63, 65–8, 70
Radio Four, 50
Radio Nottingham, 67
rape cases, sentencing in, 270
Raynford, Lancashire, 188
RCG (Revolutionary Communist Group), 140

INDEX

RCP (Revolutionary Communist Party), 140
Reagan, Ronald, 125
Red Wedge, 142
Reform Bill (1867), 24
Reid, Elizabeth, 53
Representation of the People Act (1918), 41
Republic, The (Plato), 29–30
Richardson, Jo, 21, 175, 260, 266, 270, 271
Richmond and Barnes (constituency), Young Wives Group, 193
Riley, Kathryn, 236–7, 243, 246
Roberts, Alfred, 3–5, 16
Roberts, Beatrice, 4, 5
Roberts, Muriel, 4
Roberts family, 44
Robin Redbreast, 245
Rochdale, Great Manchester, 106, 107
Roche, Barbara, 42
Rogers, Barbara, 56
Rose, Janice, 181
Rotary Club, 48
Rotherhithe Community Planning Centre, 47, 228
Rousseau, Jean-Jacques, 31
Rowbotham, Sheila, 91
Royal Arsenal Co-operative Society, 44
Ruddock, Joan, 259, 265
Ruskin College, Oxford, 90
Russell, Dora, 179
Ryedale (constituency), 204, 266

Sachs, Albie, 35
St Helen's, 239
St Helen's North (constituency), women's committee, 192
St Thomas's Hospital, 255
Salford, Greater Manchester, 182
Sampson, Anthony, 257
Saturday Review, 36
Savage, Betty, 67
Scafe, Suzanne, 102

Scanlan, Teresa, 154–6
Scarman, Lord, 111
Scotland, 273–7; assembly for (projected), 283; councils with women's committees, 249; and miners' strike, 74
Scottish Constitutional Convention, 273–5, 275, 287
Scottish Convention of Women, 274
Scottish Nationalist Party, 21, 274; number of women MPs, 272
Scottish Women's Forum, 274
Seear, Baroness (Nancy), 202, 203, 207
Segal Lynne, 94, 95, 170–1
Seizing Our Opportunities, 192, 251
Sex Discrimination Act (1975), 250
sexism, 85, 87, 103–4, 152, 227, 230, 234, 245, 278; in language, 204, 209, 210
sexual harassment, 156, 157
Sheffield, 7, 8, 26, 46, 50, 79, 80, 121, 167, 216
Sheffield Co-ordinating Centre against Unemployment, 14
Shelter, 138, 259
Shields, Elizabeth, 266
Shifting Horizons (Beaton), 66
Short, Clare, 270
Shrew, 88
Slipman, Sue, 205, 207, 208–9
Smethwick, West Midlands, 161, 163, 164
Smith, Cyril, 173
Smyth, Maggie, 191, 194, 195, 219–20
Social Democratic Federation (SDF), 36–7, 38
Social Democratic Party (Denmark), 282
Social Democratic Party (West Germany), 282
Social Democratic Party (SDP), 52, 199, 200, 205–7, 211, 213, 262, 263; Council for Social Democracy, 206; and equal